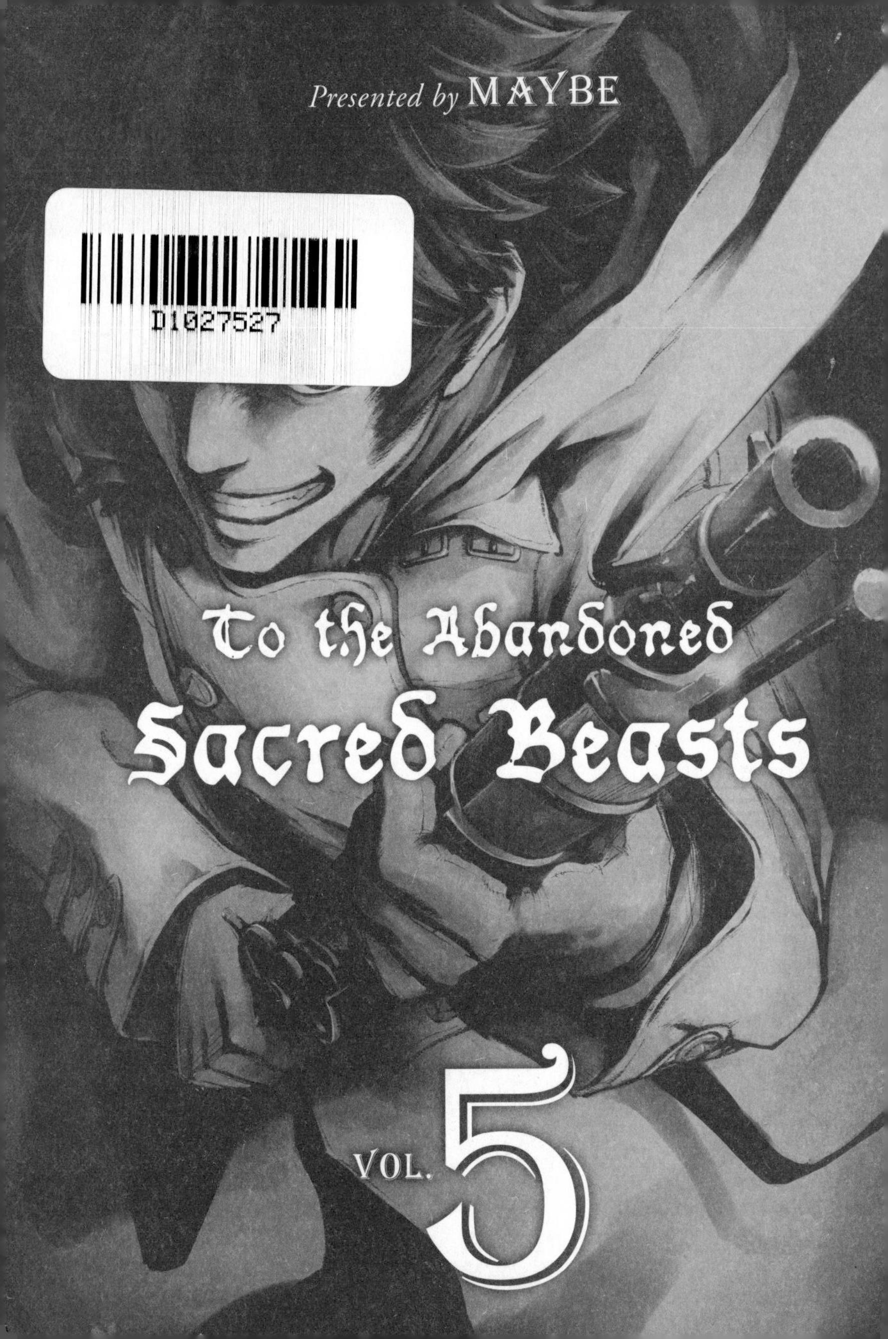
Presented by MAYBE
To the Abandoned
Sacred Beasts
VOL. 5

CONTENTS

Chapter 23: The Beacon of Rebellion

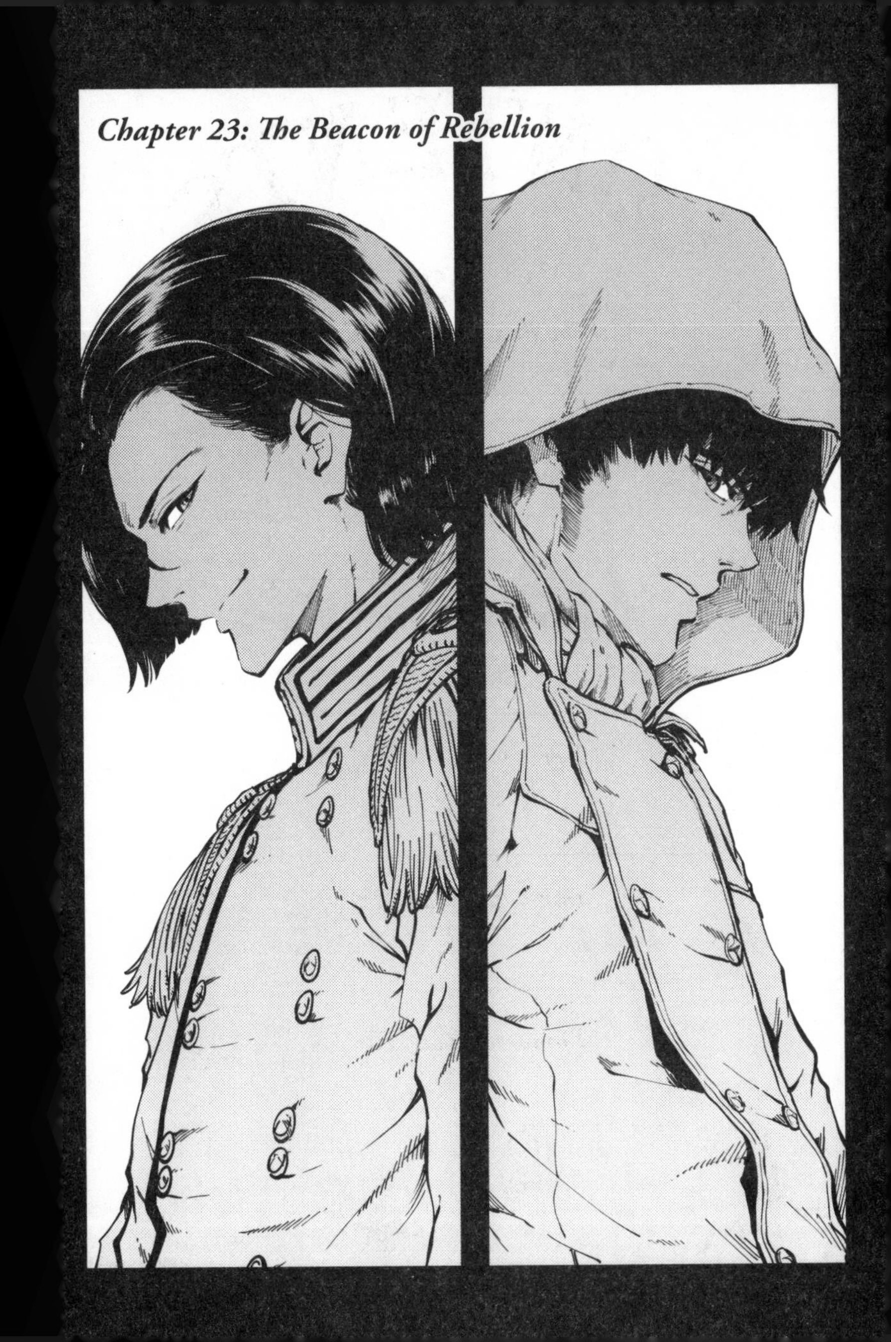

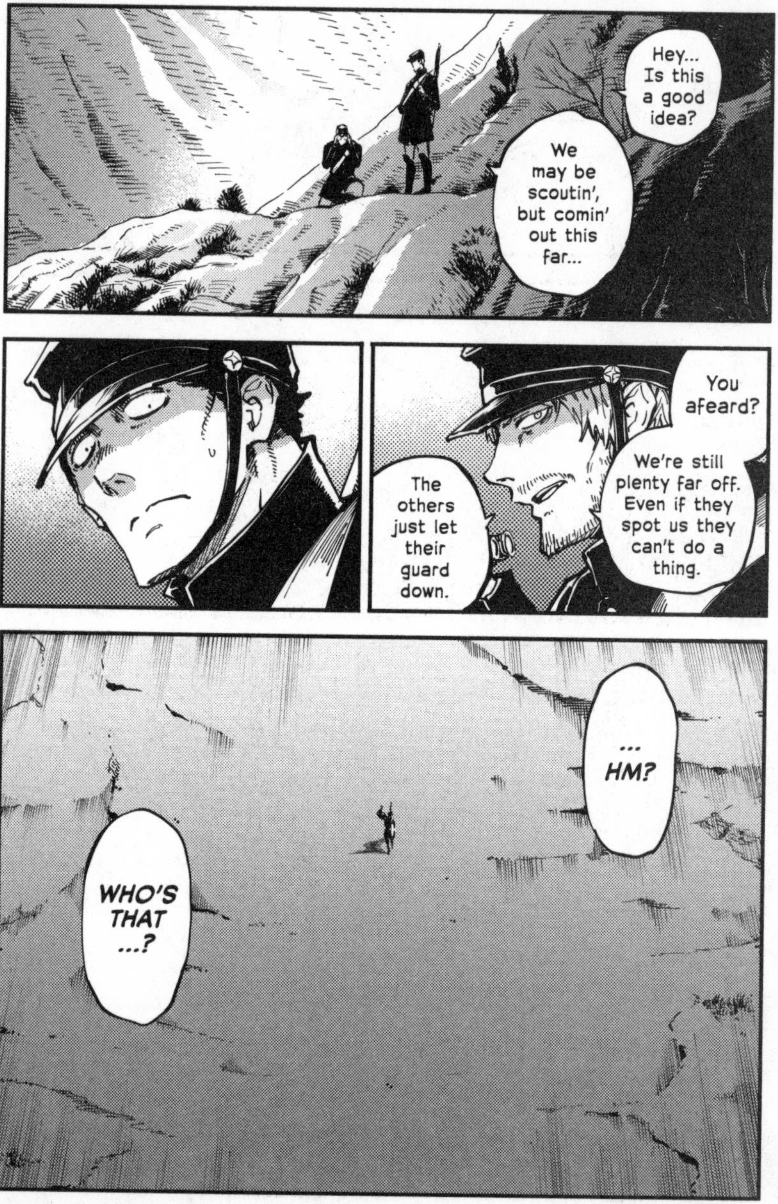
Hey... Is this a good idea?
We may be scoutin', but comin' out this far...
You afeard?
We're still plenty far off. Even if they spot us they can't do a thing.
The others just let their guard down.
...HM?
WHO'S THAT ...?

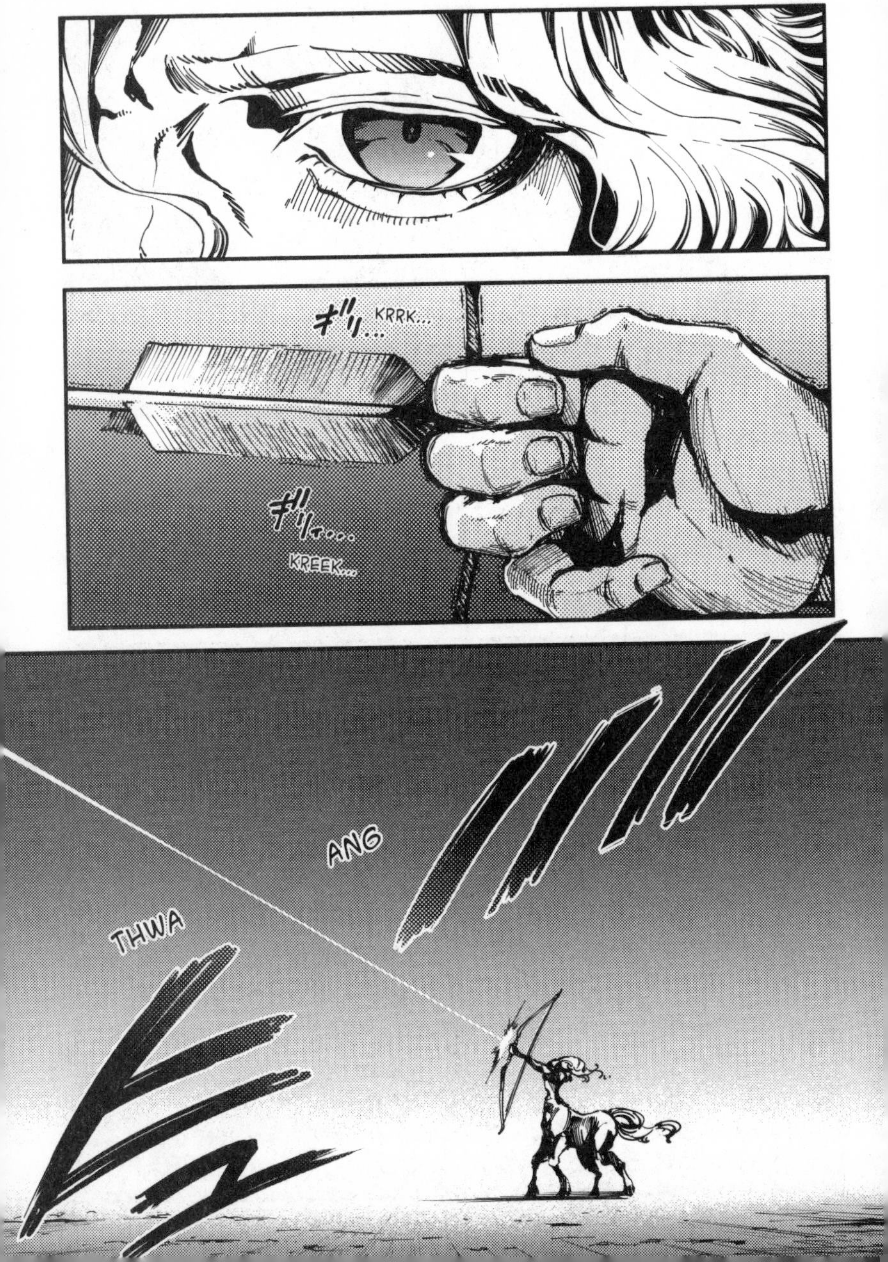
ギリ...
KRRK...
ギリィ...
KREEK...
THWA
ANG

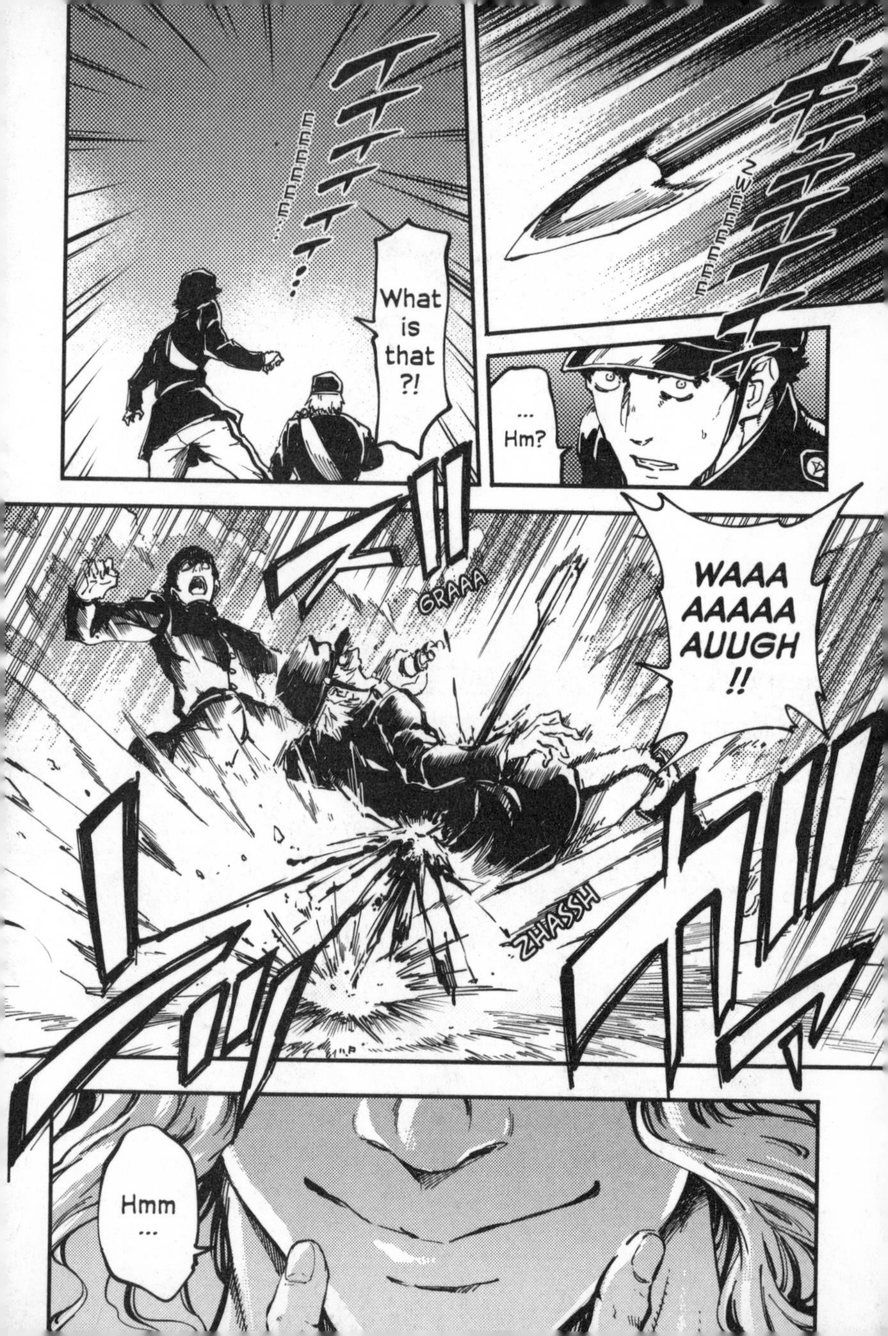
ZWEEEEEEEE
... Hm?
EEEEEEE...
What is that ?!
WAAA AAAAA AUUGH !!
GRAAA
ZHASSH
Hmm ...

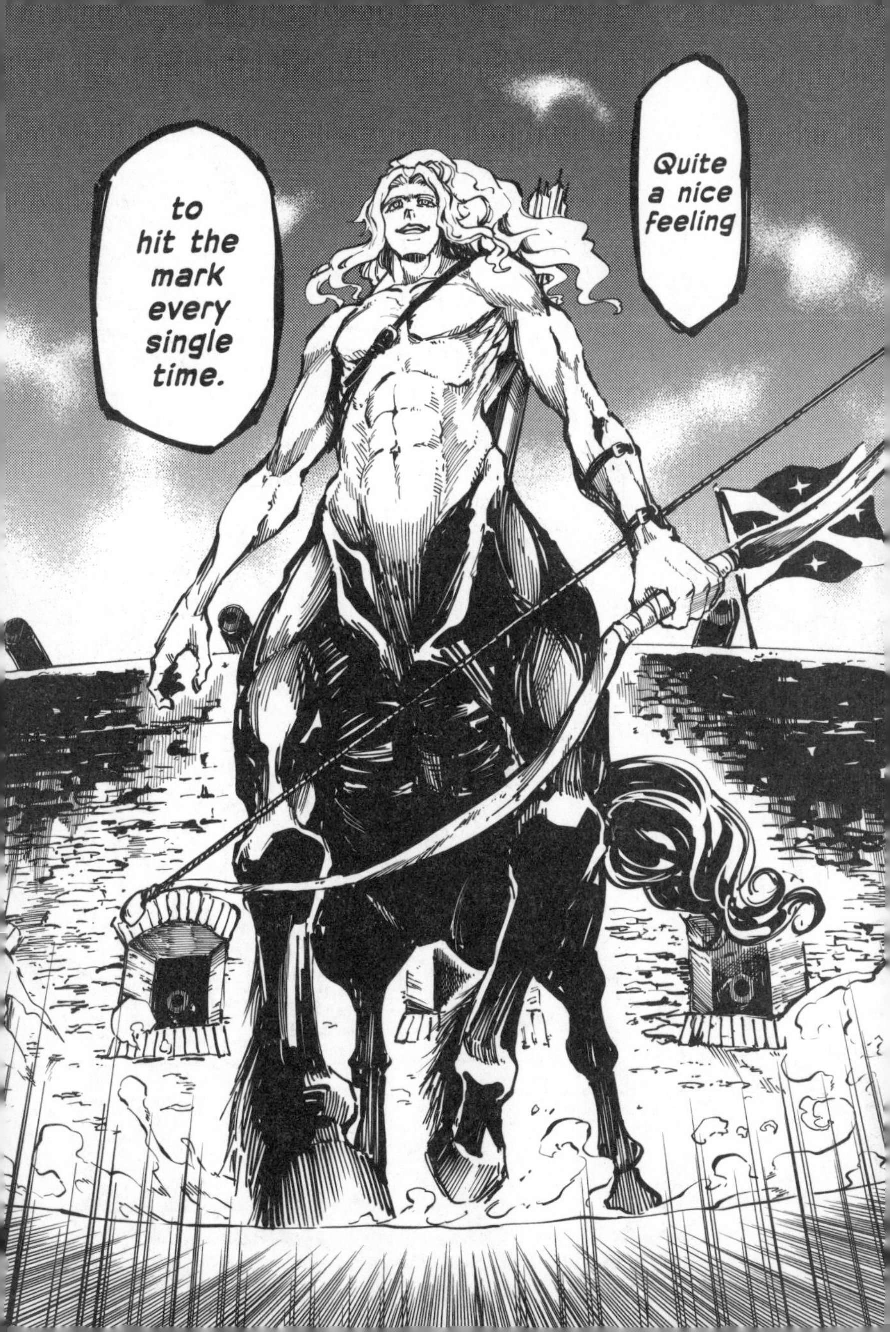
Quite a nice feeling
to hit the mark every single time.

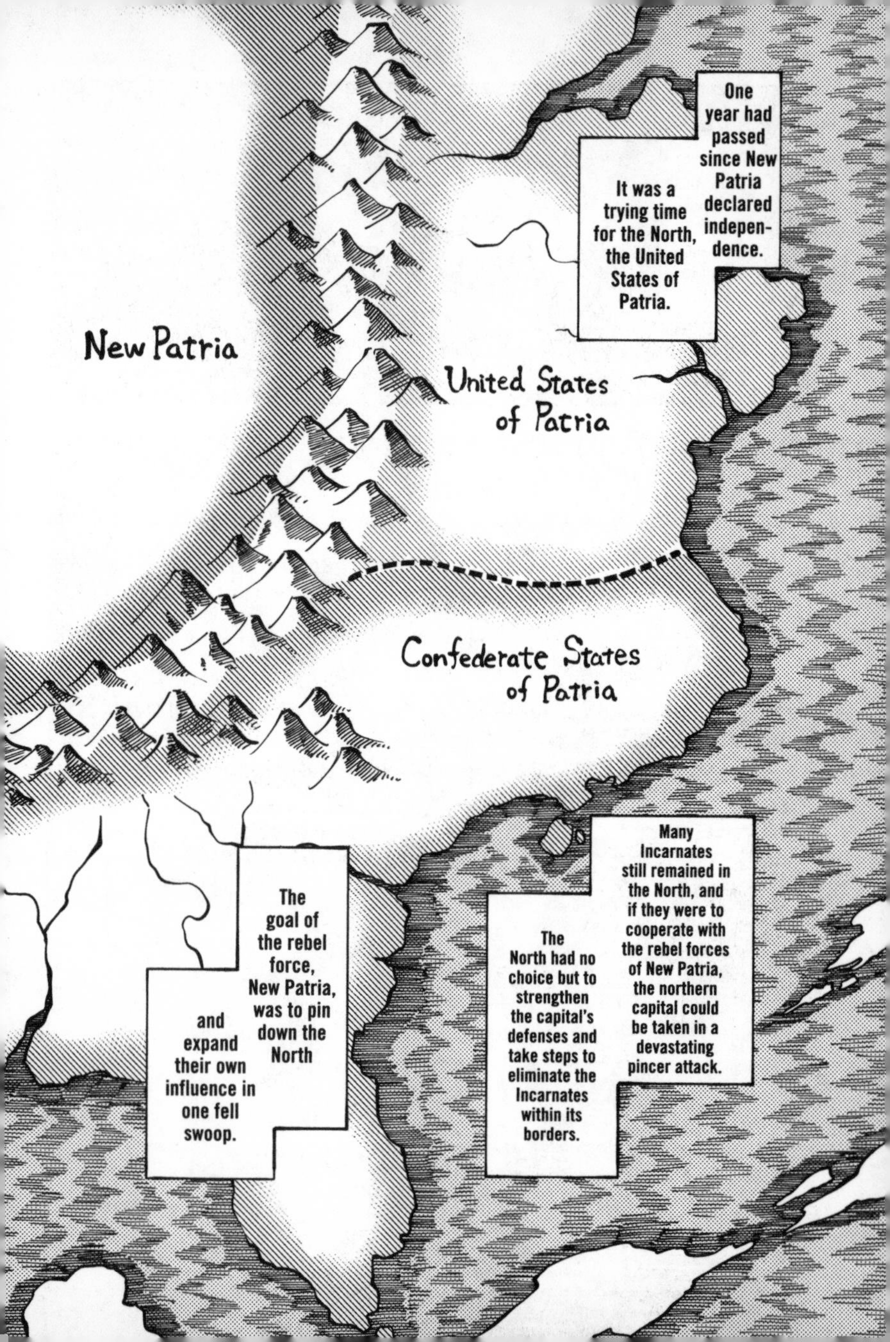
One year had passed since New Patria declared independence.
It was a trying time for the North, the United States of Patria.
New Patria
United States of Patria
Confederate States of Patria
Many Incarnates still remained in the North, and if they were to cooperate with the rebel forces of New Patria, the northern capital could be taken in a devastating pincer attack.
The North had no choice but to strengthen the capital's defenses and take steps to eliminate the Incarnates within its borders.
The goal of the rebel force, New Patria, was to pin down the North
and expand their own influence in one fell swoop.

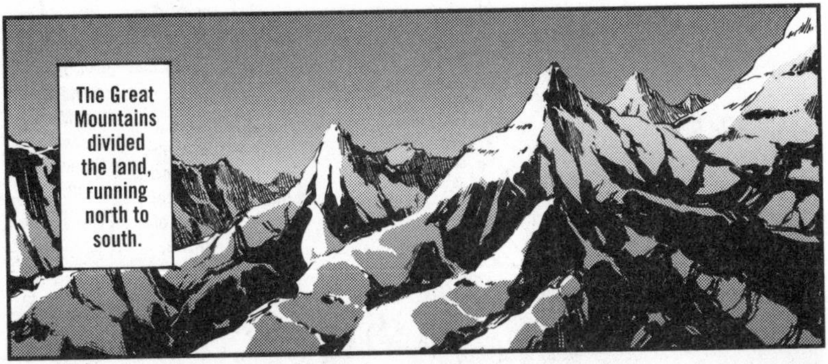
The Great Mountains divided the land, running north to south.

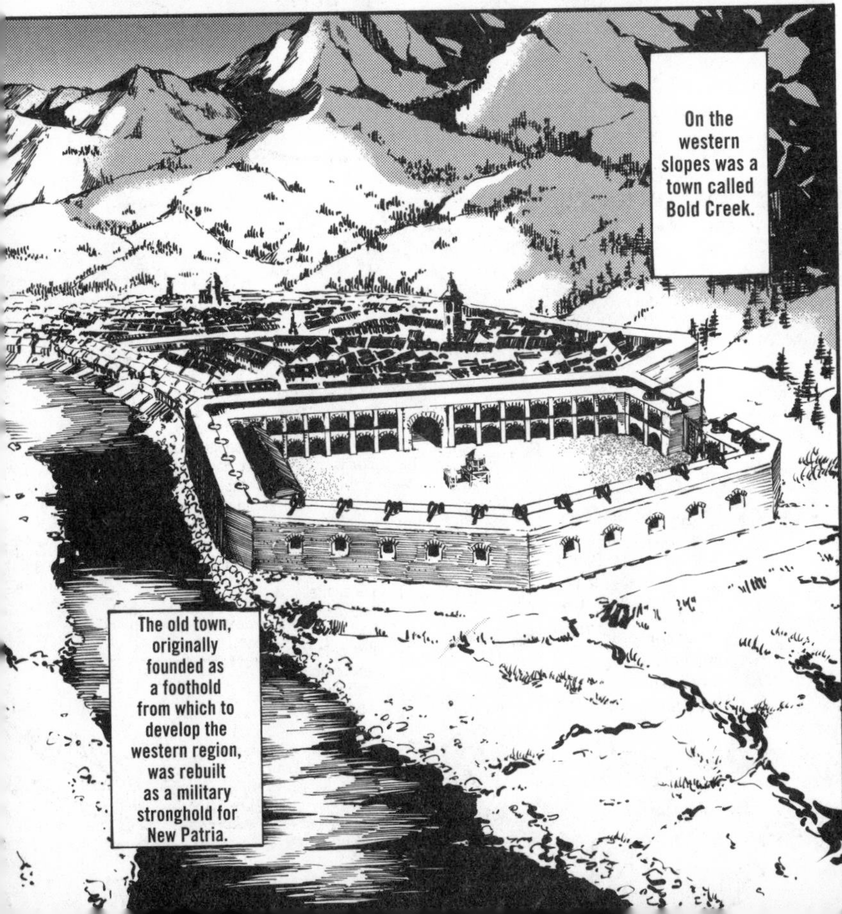
On the western slopes was a town called Bold Creek.
The old town, originally founded as a foothold from which to develop the western region, was rebuilt as a military stronghold for New Patria.

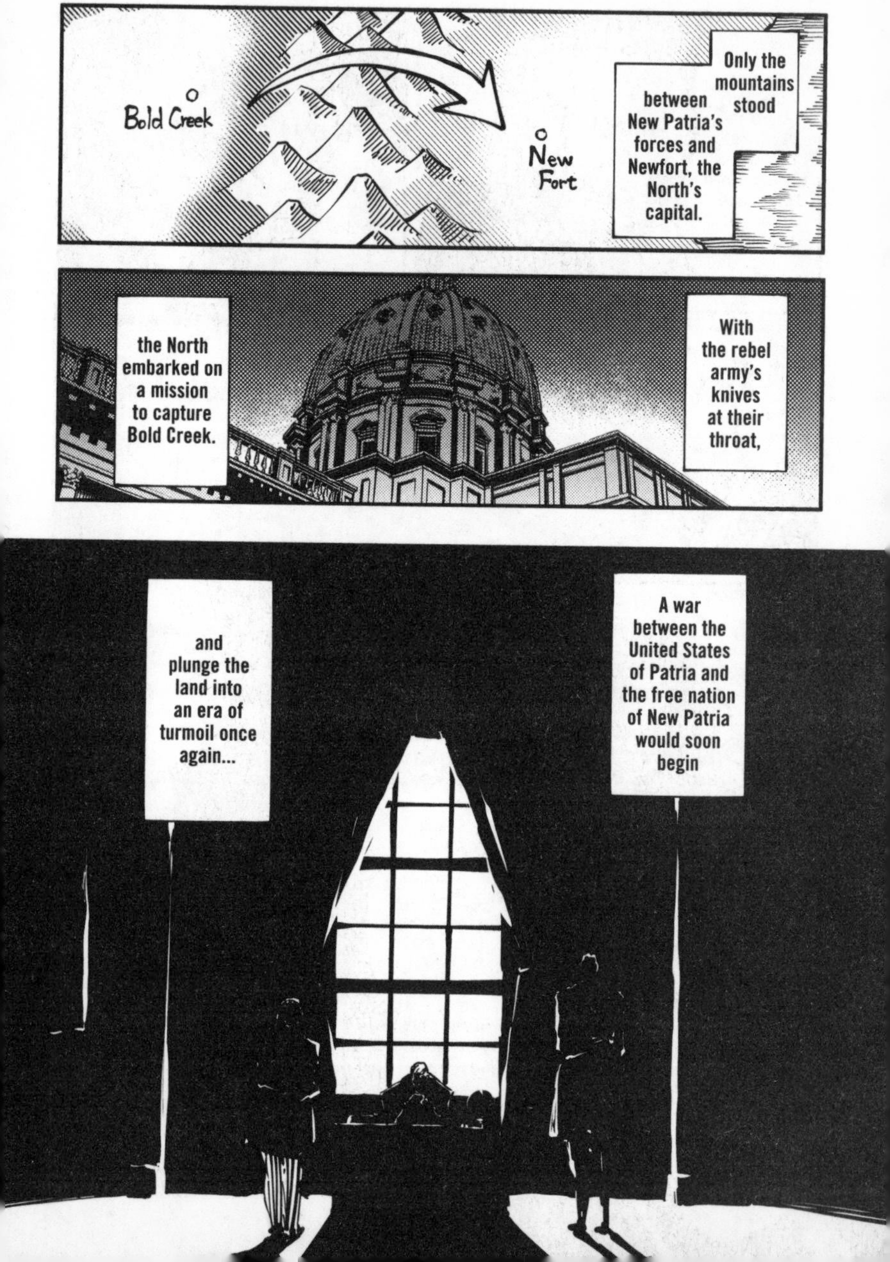
Only the mountains stood between New Patria's forces and Newfort, the North's capital.
New Fort
Bold Creek
With the rebel army's knives at their throat,
the North embarked on a mission to capture Bold Creek.
A war between the United States of Patria and the free nation of New Patria would soon begin
and plunge the land into an era of turmoil once again...

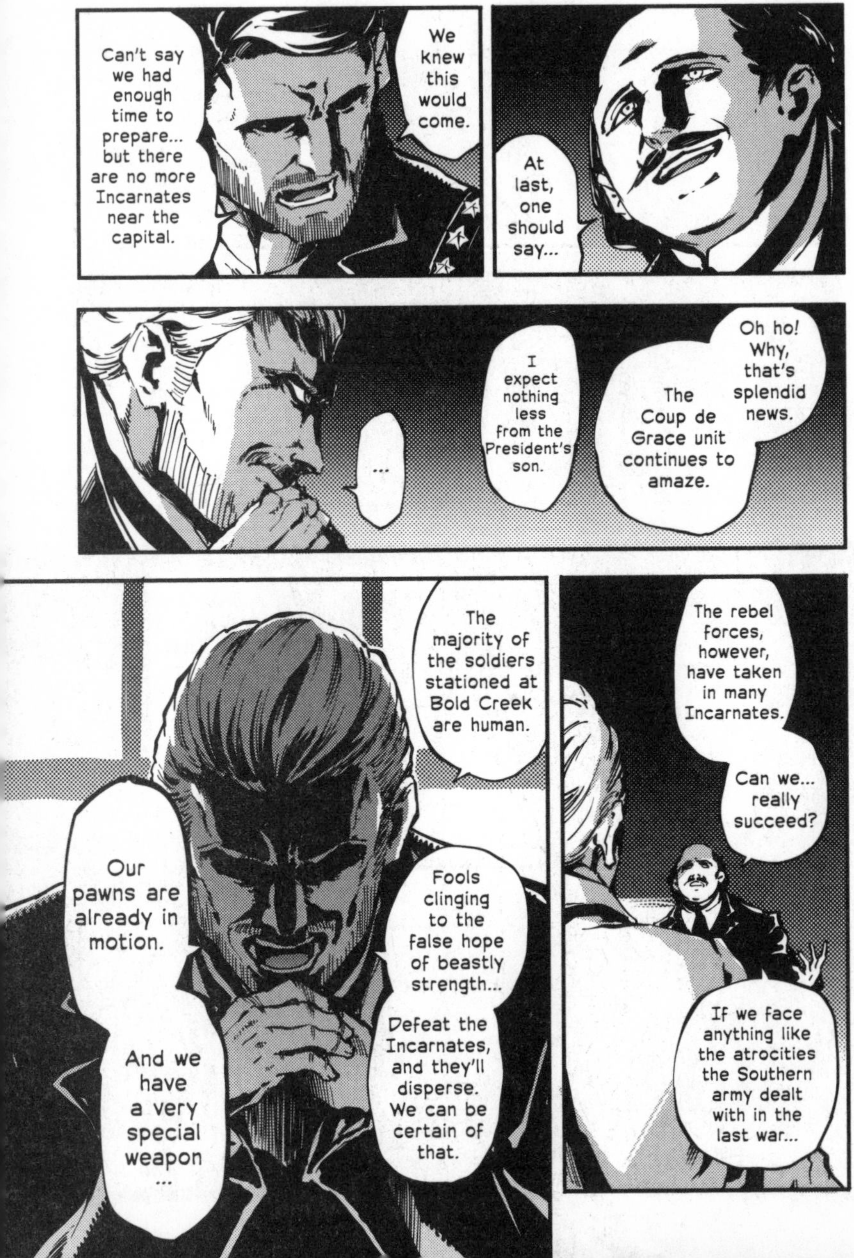
At last, one should say...
We knew this would come.
Can't say we had enough time to prepare... but there are no more Incarnates near the capital.
Oh ho! Why, that's splendid news.
The Coup de Grace unit continues to amaze.
I expect nothing less from the President's son.
...
The rebel forces, however, have taken in many Incarnates.
Can we... really succeed?
If we face anything like the atrocities the Southern army dealt with in the last war...
The majority of the soldiers stationed at Bold Creek are human.
Fools clinging to the false hope of beastly strength...
Defeat the Incarnates, and they'll disperse. We can be certain of that.
Our pawns are already in motion.
And we have a very special weapon ...

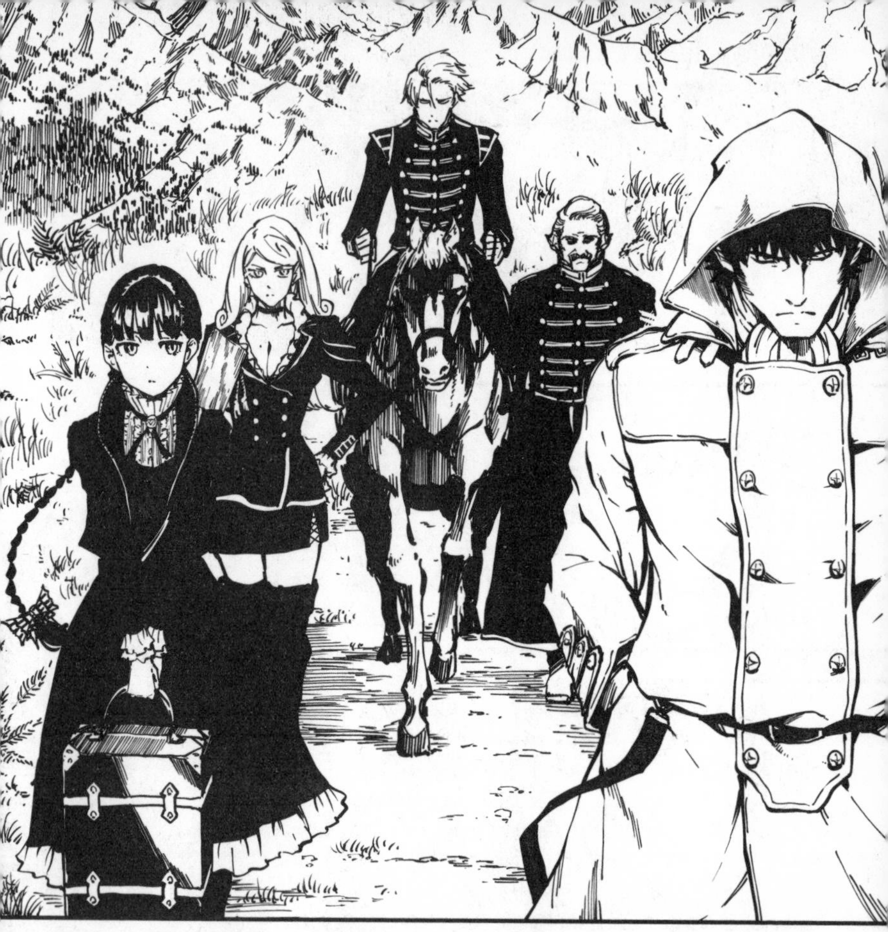
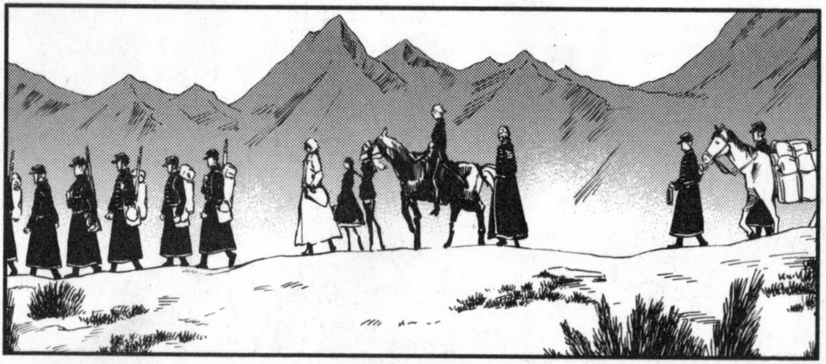

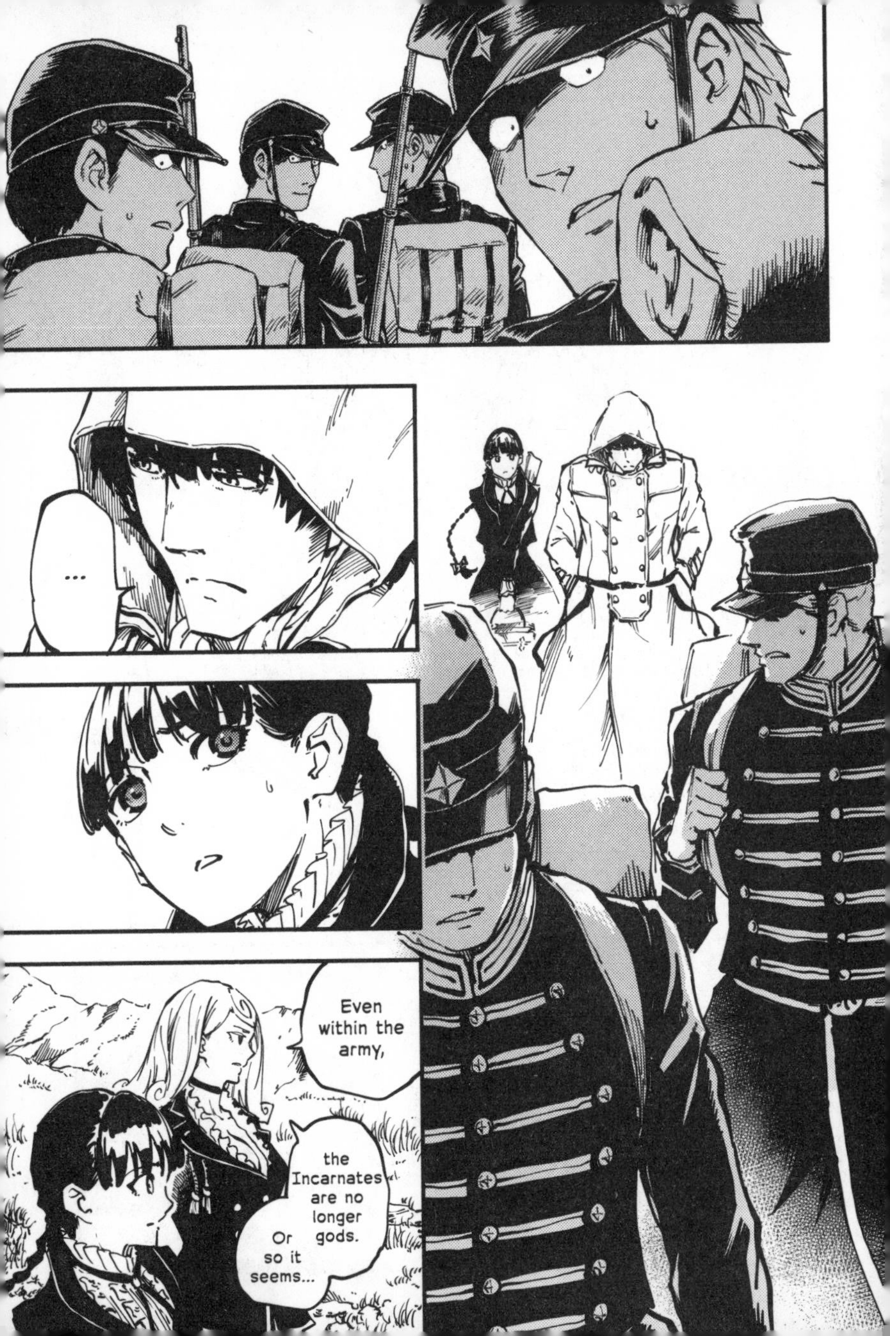
...
Even within the army,
the Incarnates are no longer gods.
Or so it seems...

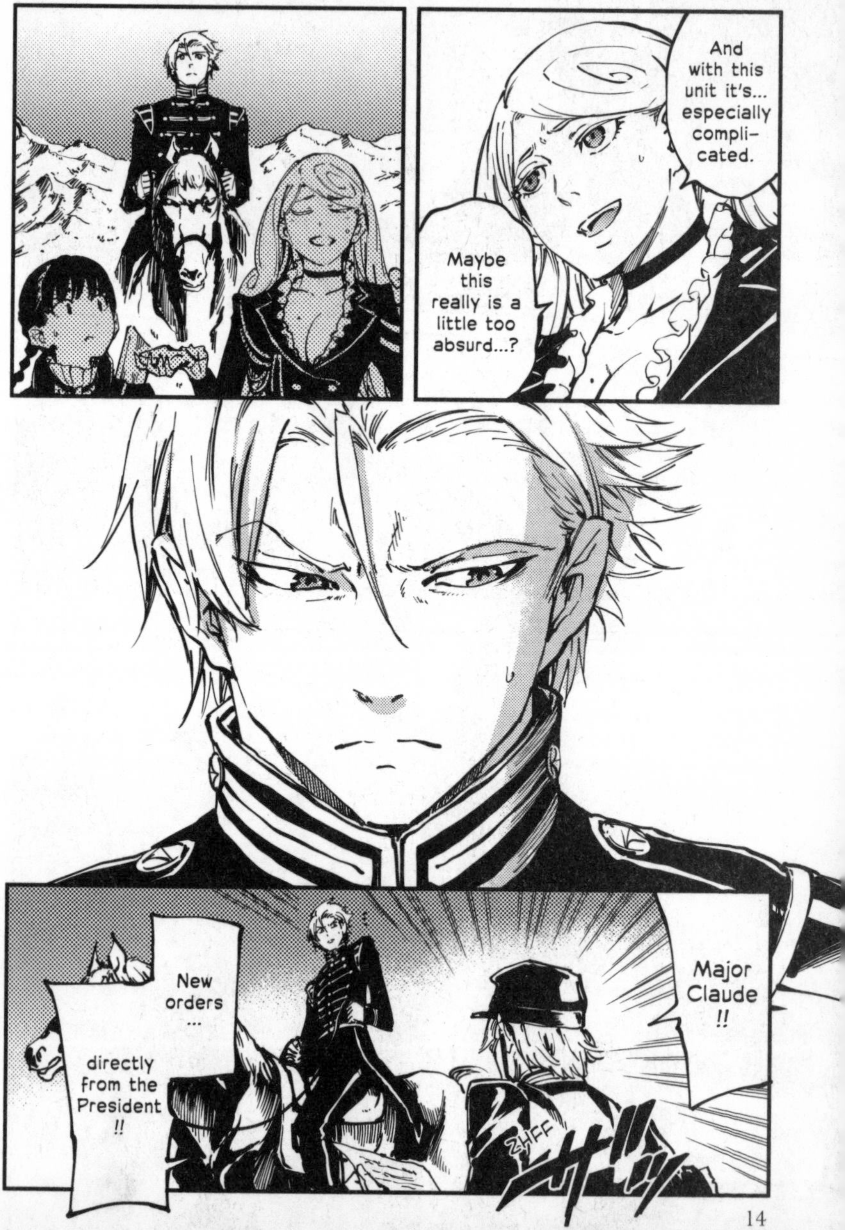
And with this unit it's... especially compli-cated.
Maybe this really is a little too absurd...?
Major Claude !!
ZHFF
New orders ...
directly from the President !!

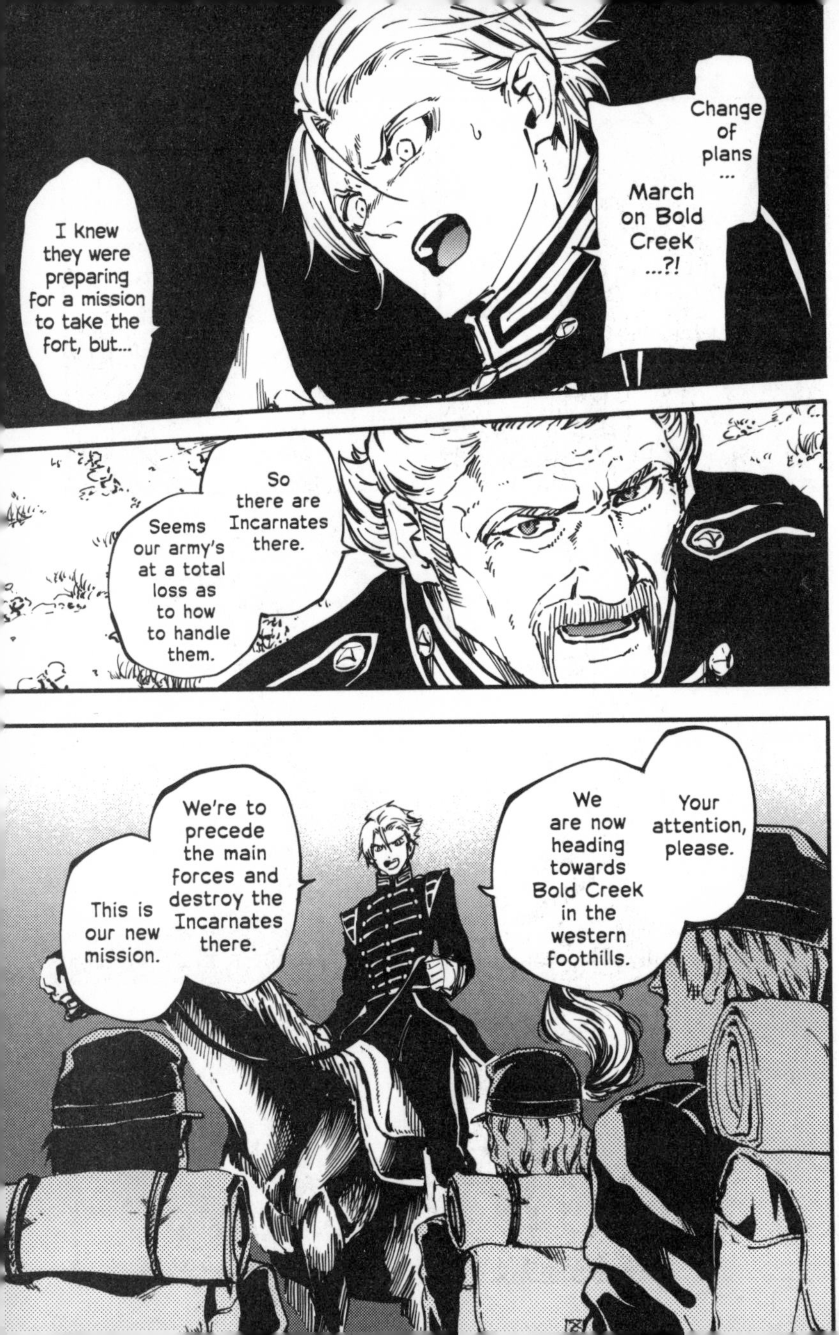
Change of plans ... March on Bold Creek ...?!
I knew they were preparing for a mission to take the fort, but...
So there are Incarnates there.
Seems our army's at a total loss as to how to handle them.
Your attention, please.
We are now heading towards Bold Creek in the western foothills.
We're to precede the main forces and destroy the Incarnates there.
This is our new mission.

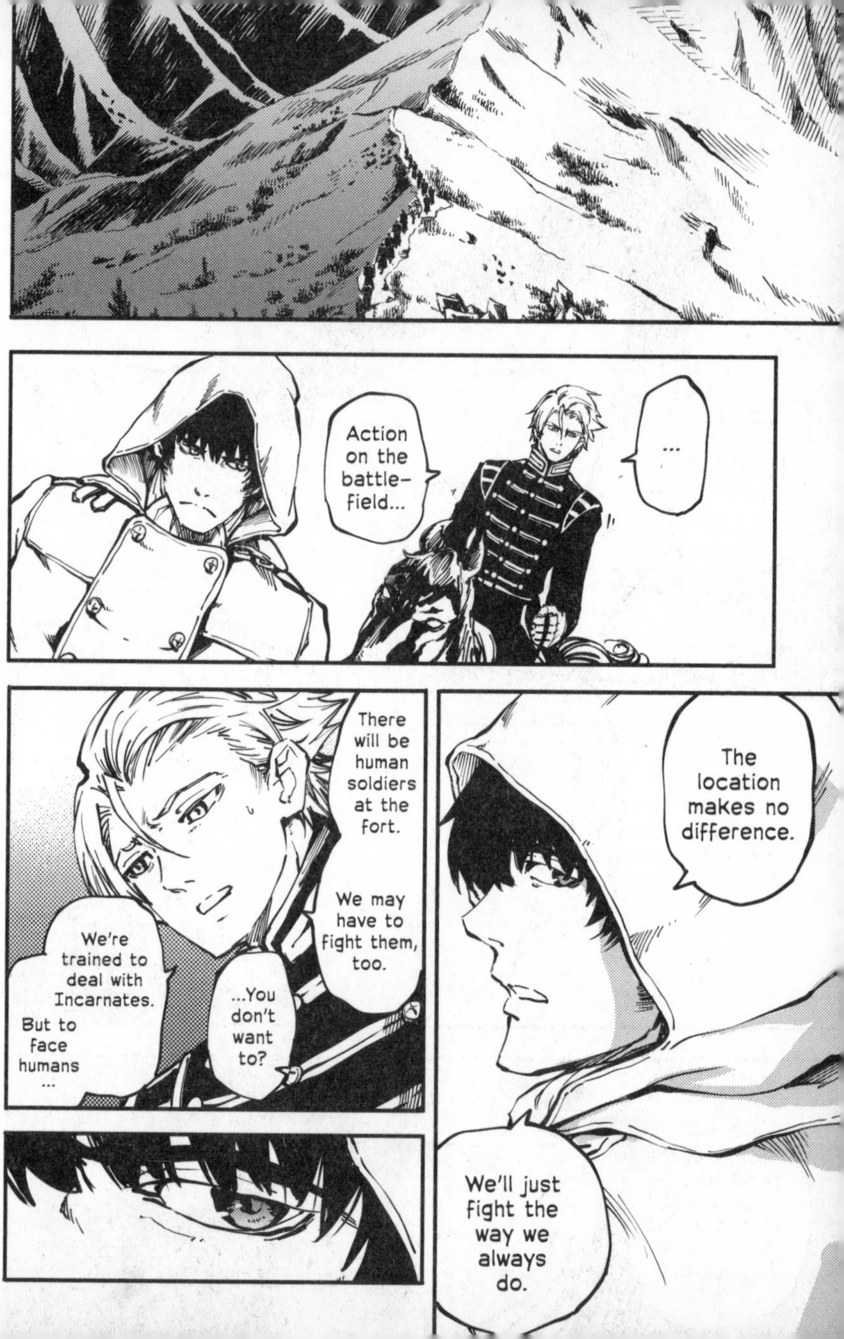
...
Action on the battle-field...
The location makes no difference.
We'll just fight the way we always do.
There will be human soldiers at the fort.
We may have to fight them, too.
We're trained to deal with Incarnates.
But to face humans...
...You don't want to?

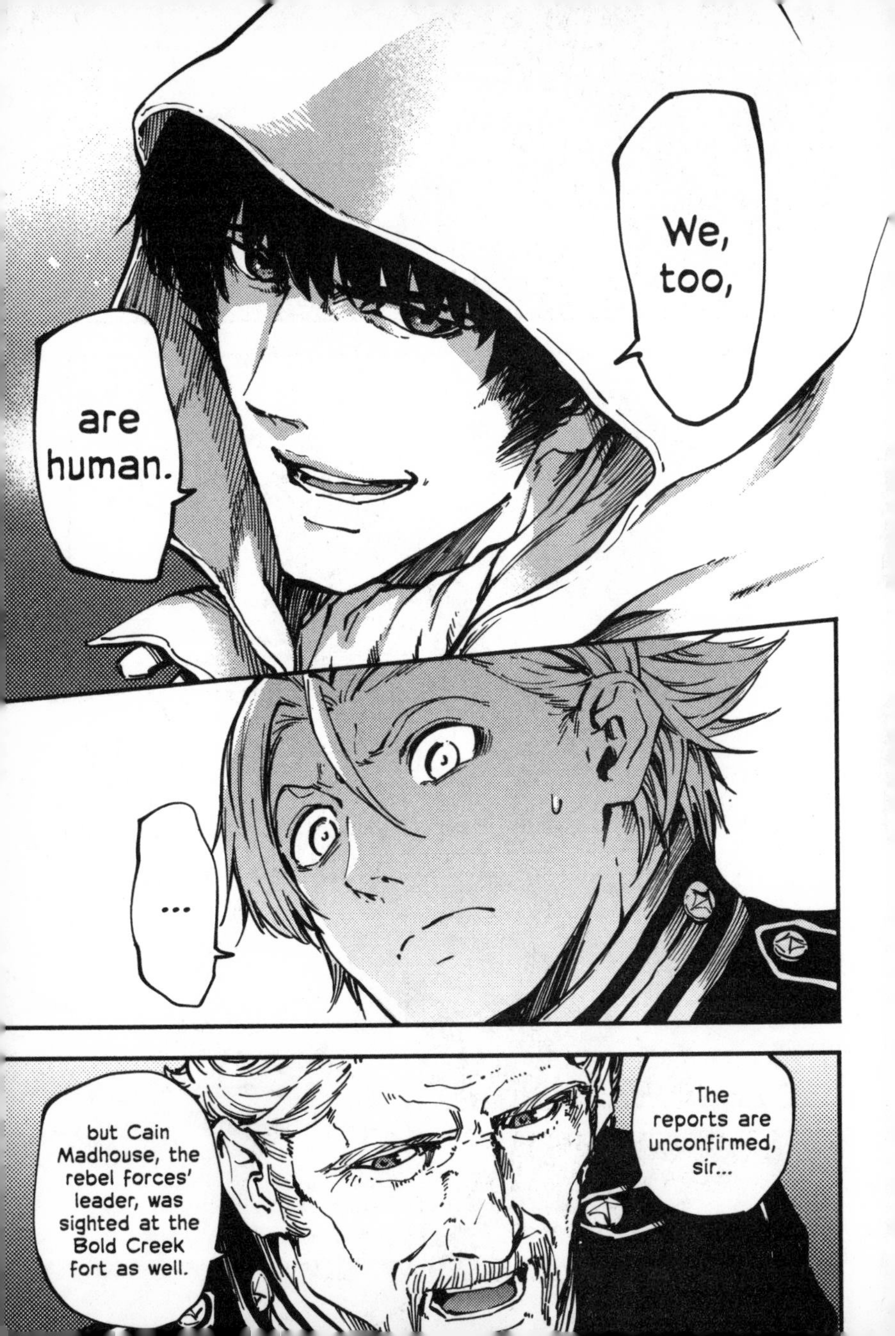
We, too,
are human.
...
The reports are unconfirmed, sir...
but Cain Madhouse, the rebel forces' leader, was sighted at the Bold Creek fort as well.

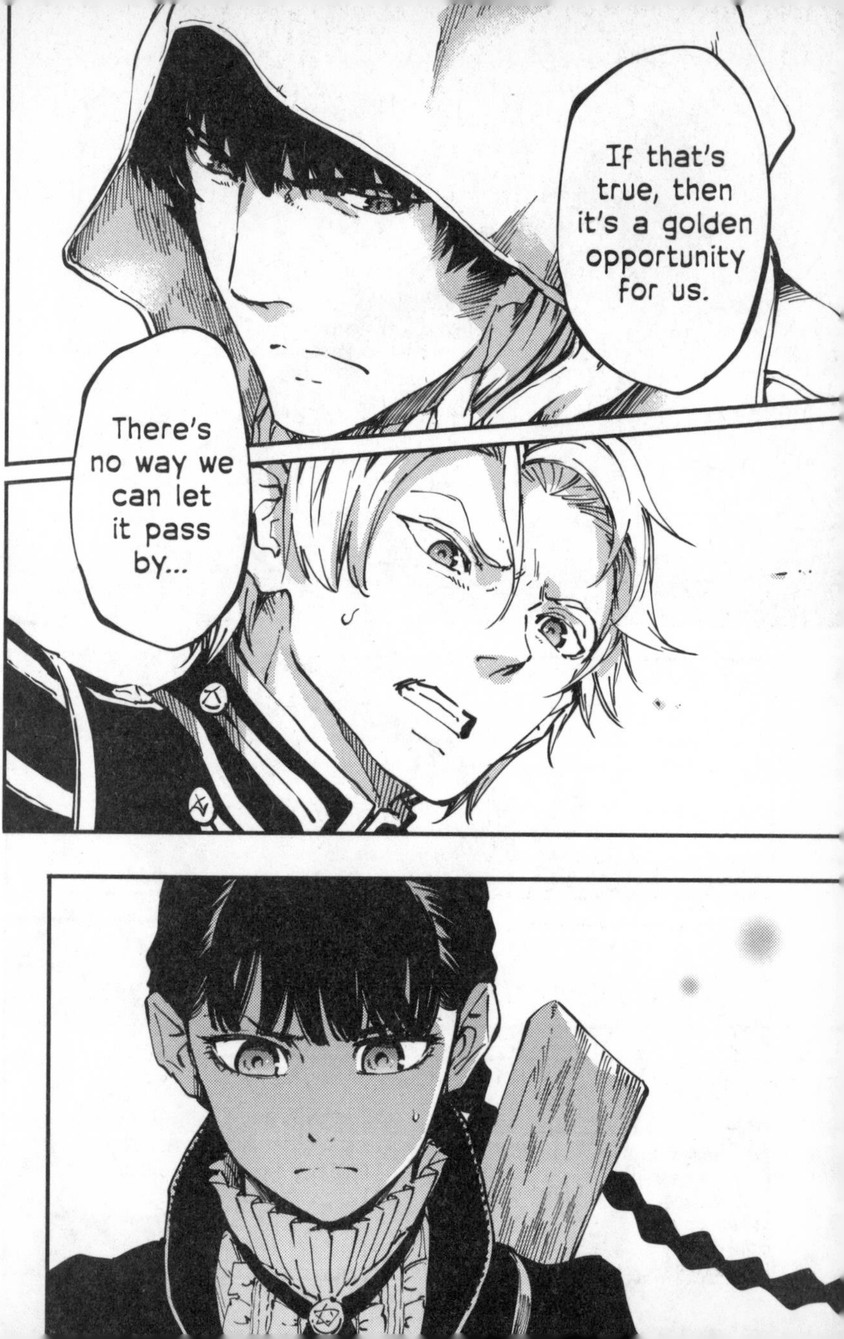
If that's true, then it's a golden opportunity for us.
There's no way we can let it pass by...

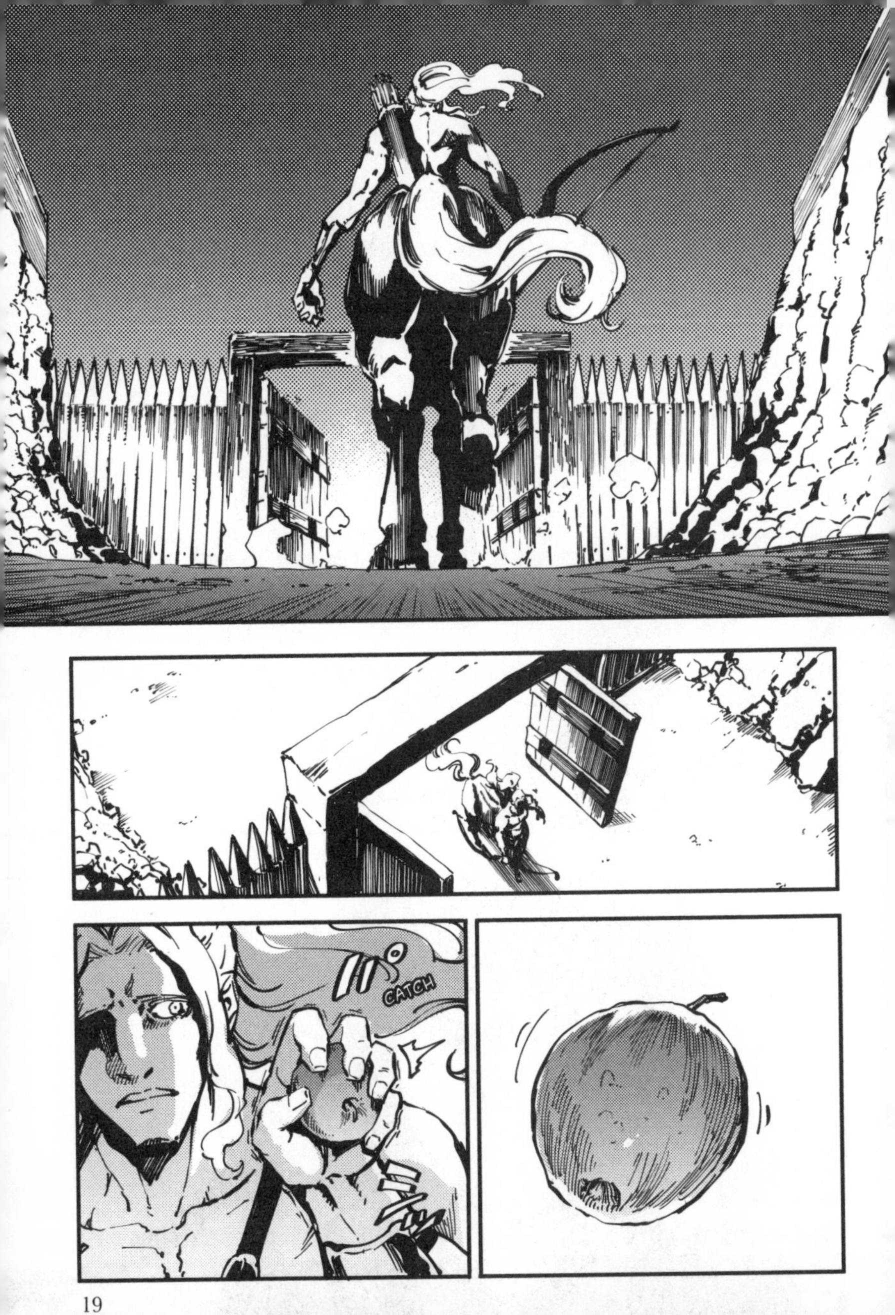
CATCH

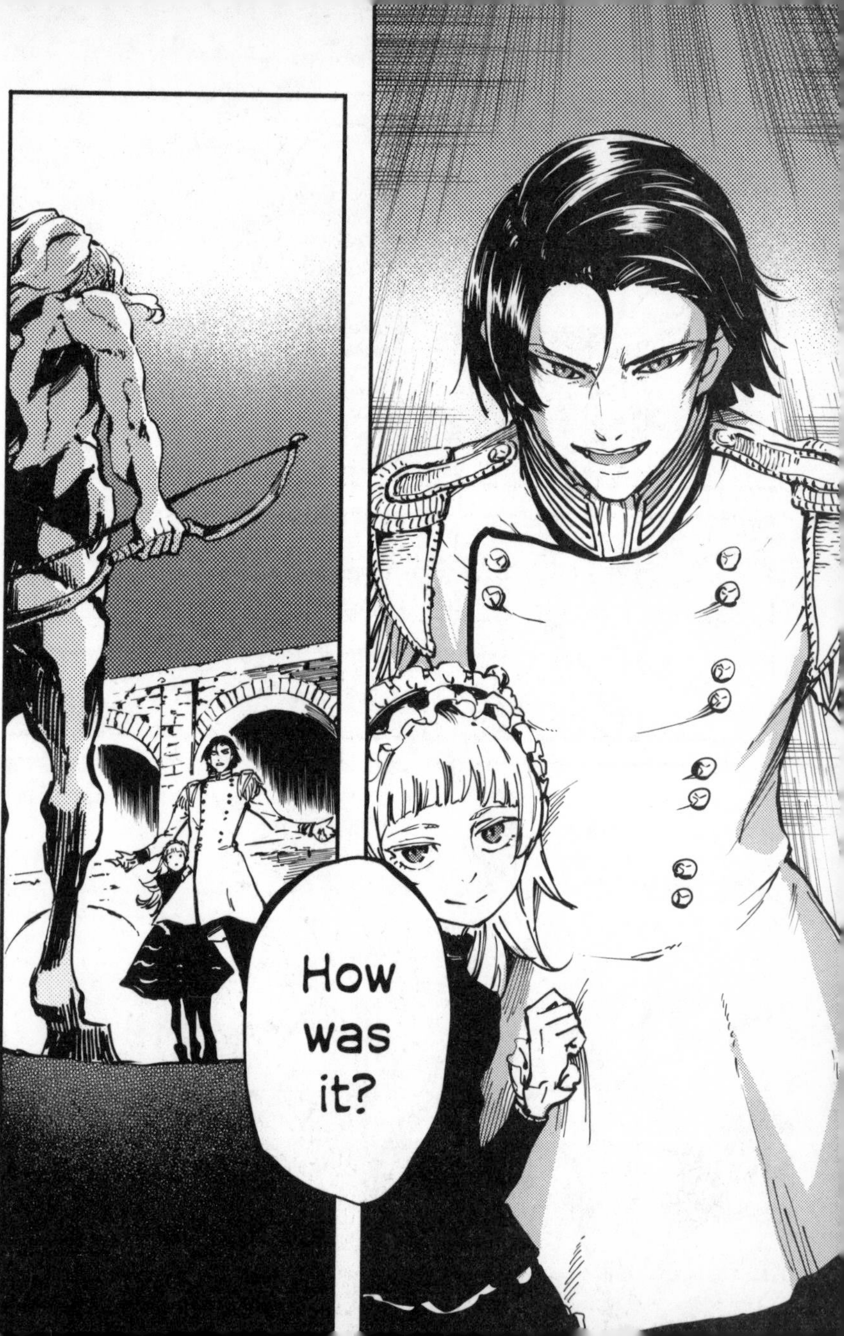
How was it?

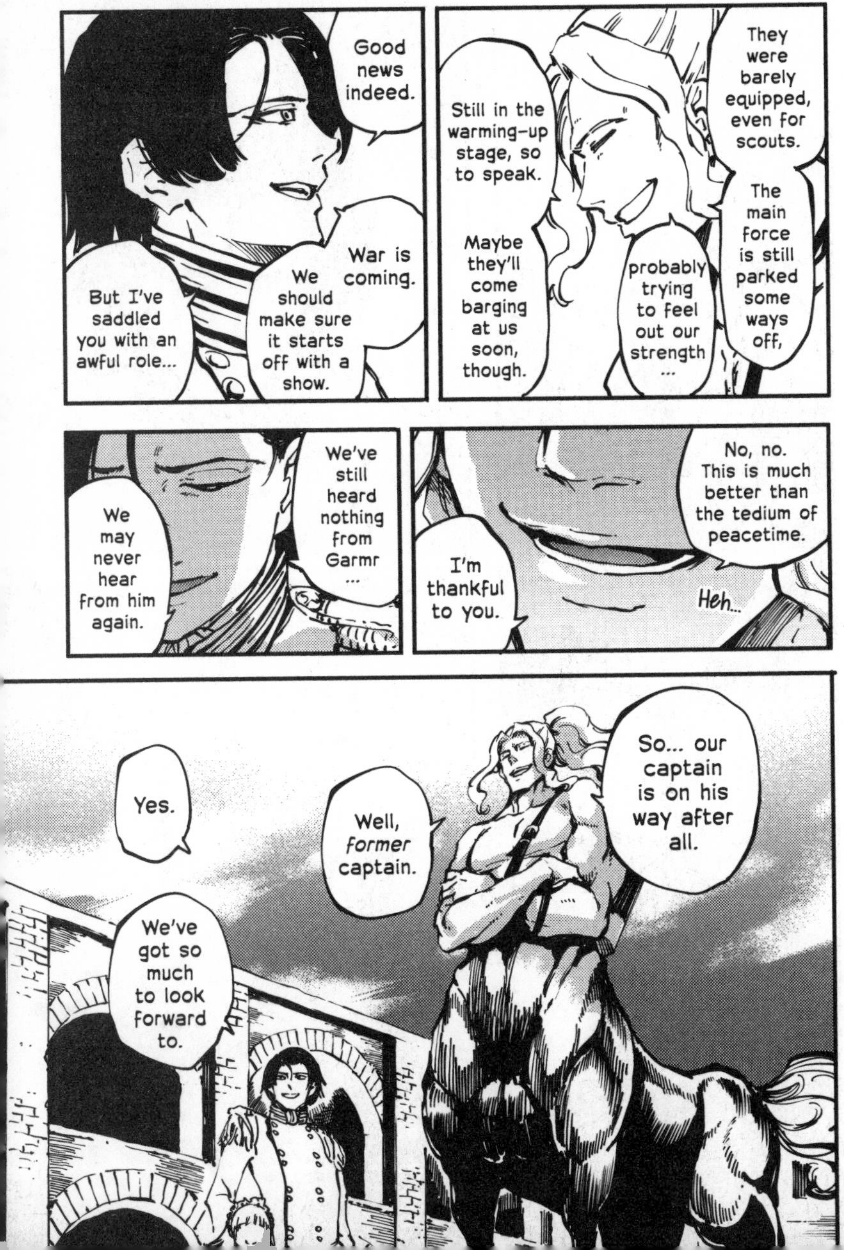
They were barely equipped, even for scouts.
The main force is still parked some ways off,
probably trying to feel out our strength...
Still in the warming-up stage, so to speak.
Maybe they'll come barging at us soon, though.
Good news indeed.
War is coming.
We should make sure it starts off with a show.
But I've saddled you with an awful role...
No, no. This is much better than the tedium of peacetime.
Heh...
I'm thankful to you.
We've still heard nothing from Garmr...
We may never hear from him again.
So... our captain is on his way after all.
Well, *former* captain.
Yes.
We've got so much to look forward to.

To the Abandoned
Sacred Beasts

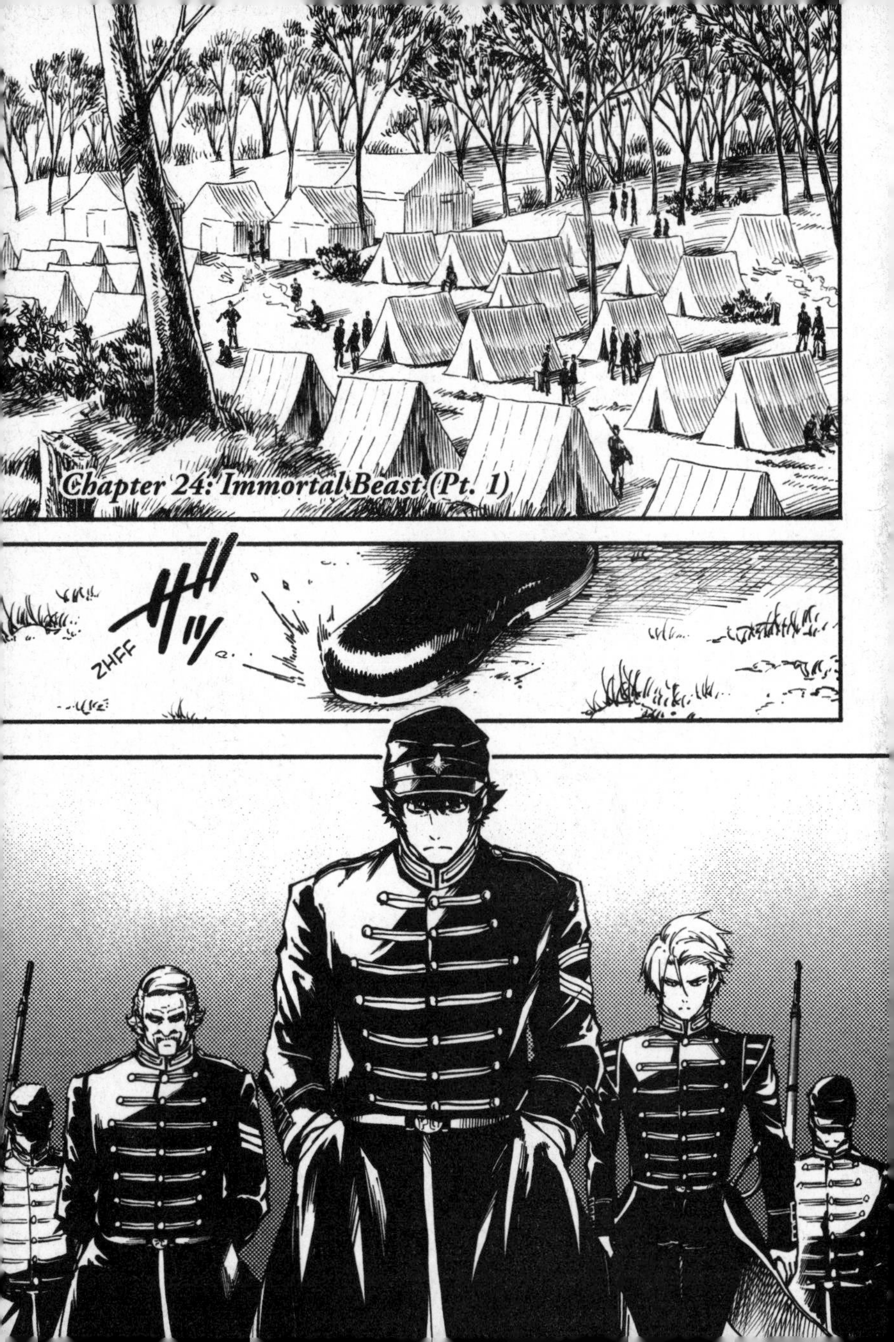
Chapter 24: Immortal Beast (Pt. 1)
ZHFF

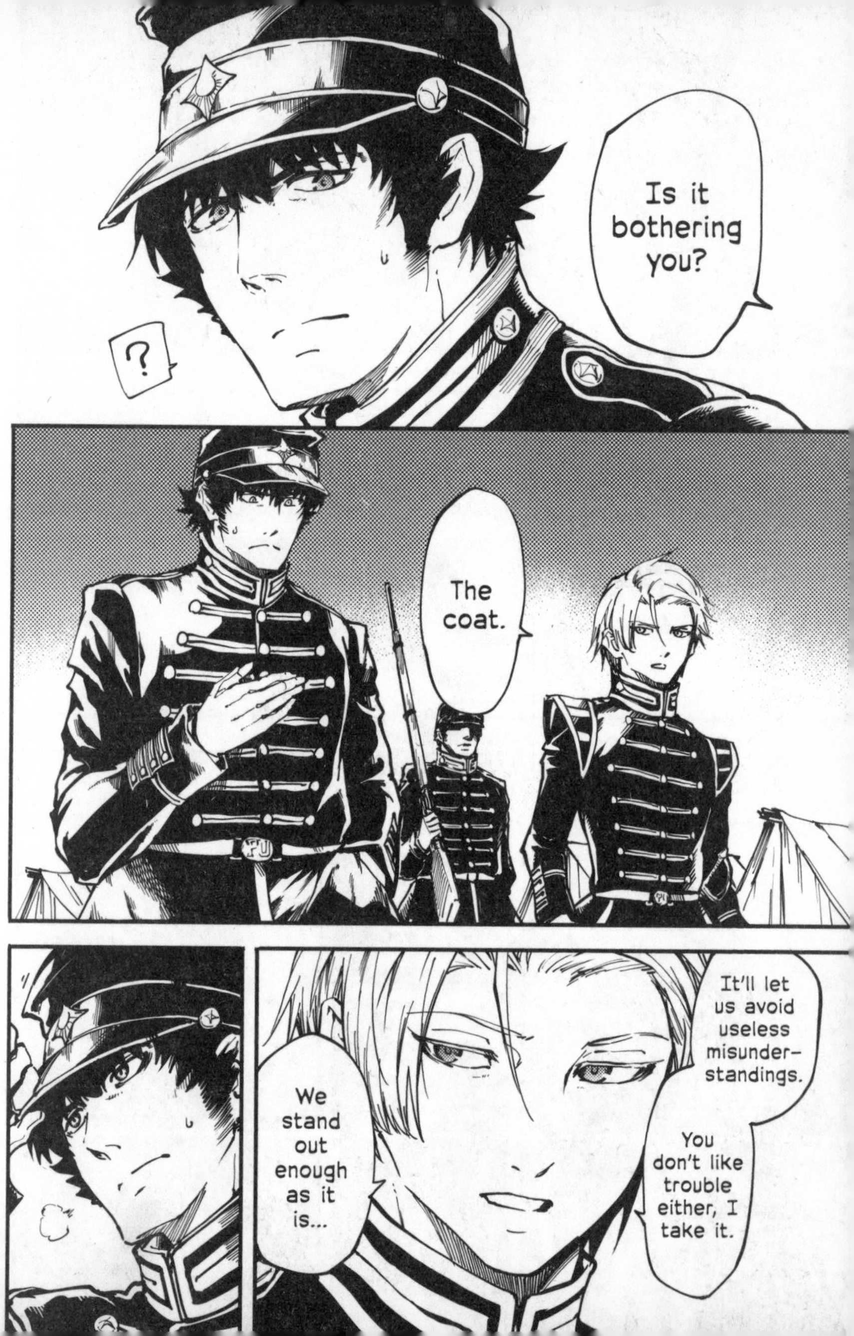
Is it bothering you?
?
The coat.
It'll let us avoid useless misunder-standings.
We stand out enough as it is...
You don't like trouble either, I take it.

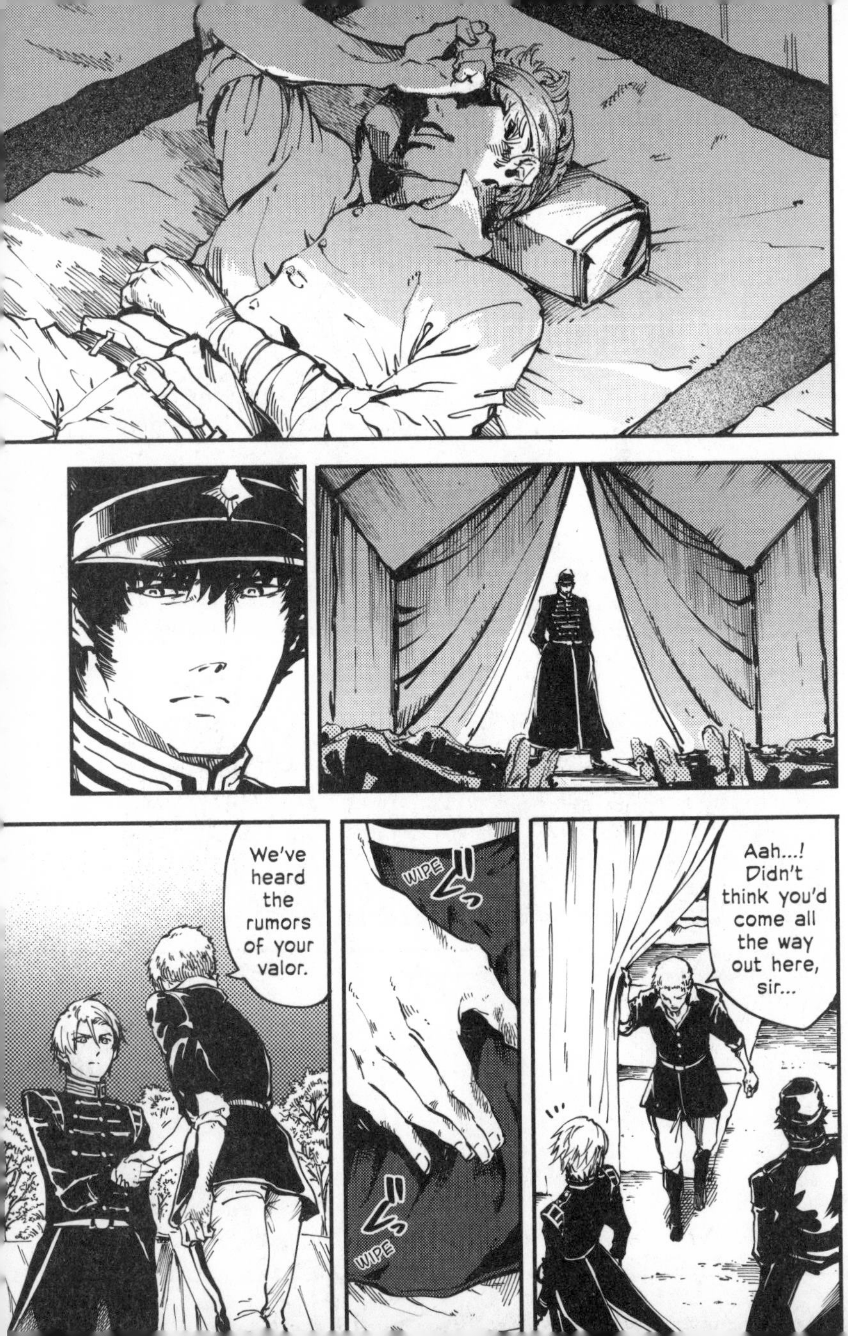
Aah...! Didn't think you'd come all the way out here, sir...
WIPE
WIPE
We've heard the rumors of your valor.

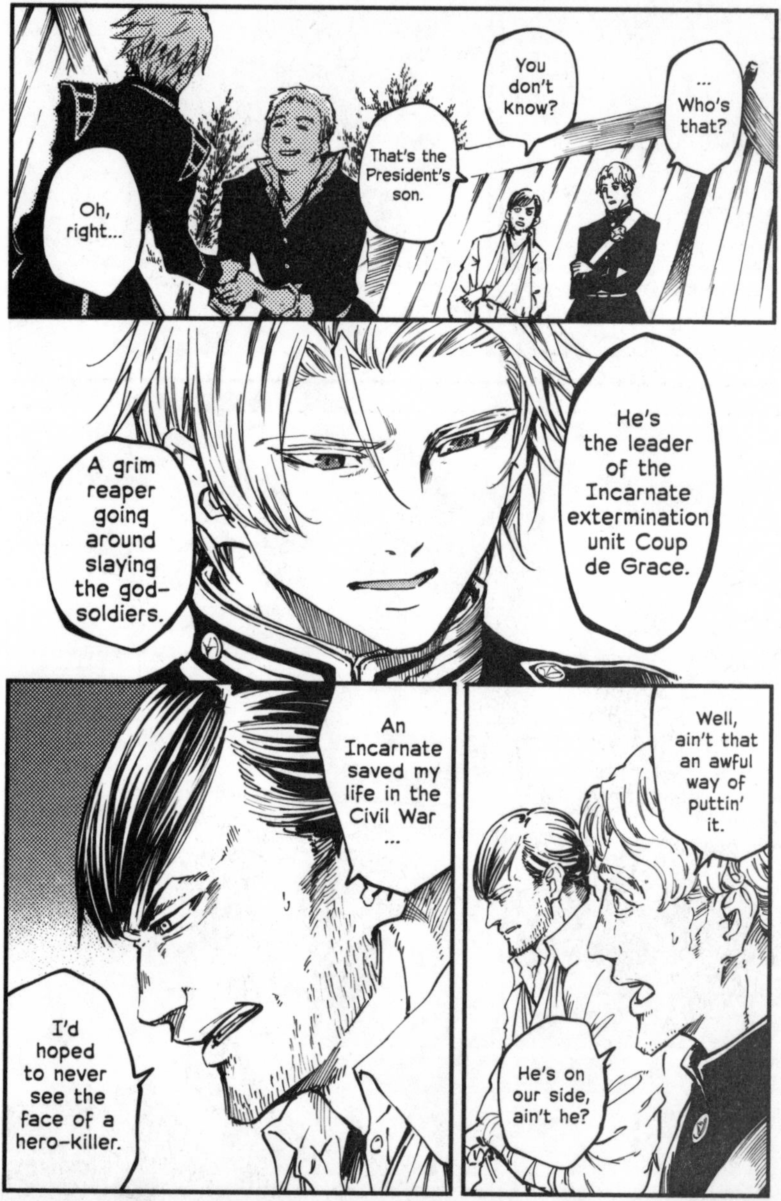
... Who's that?
You don't know?
That's the President's son.
Oh, right...
He's the leader of the Incarnate extermination unit Coup de Grace.
A grim reaper going around slaying the god-soldiers.
Well, ain't that an awful way of puttin' it.
He's on our side, ain't he?
An Incarnate saved my life in the Civil War ...
I'd hoped to never see the face of a hero-killer.

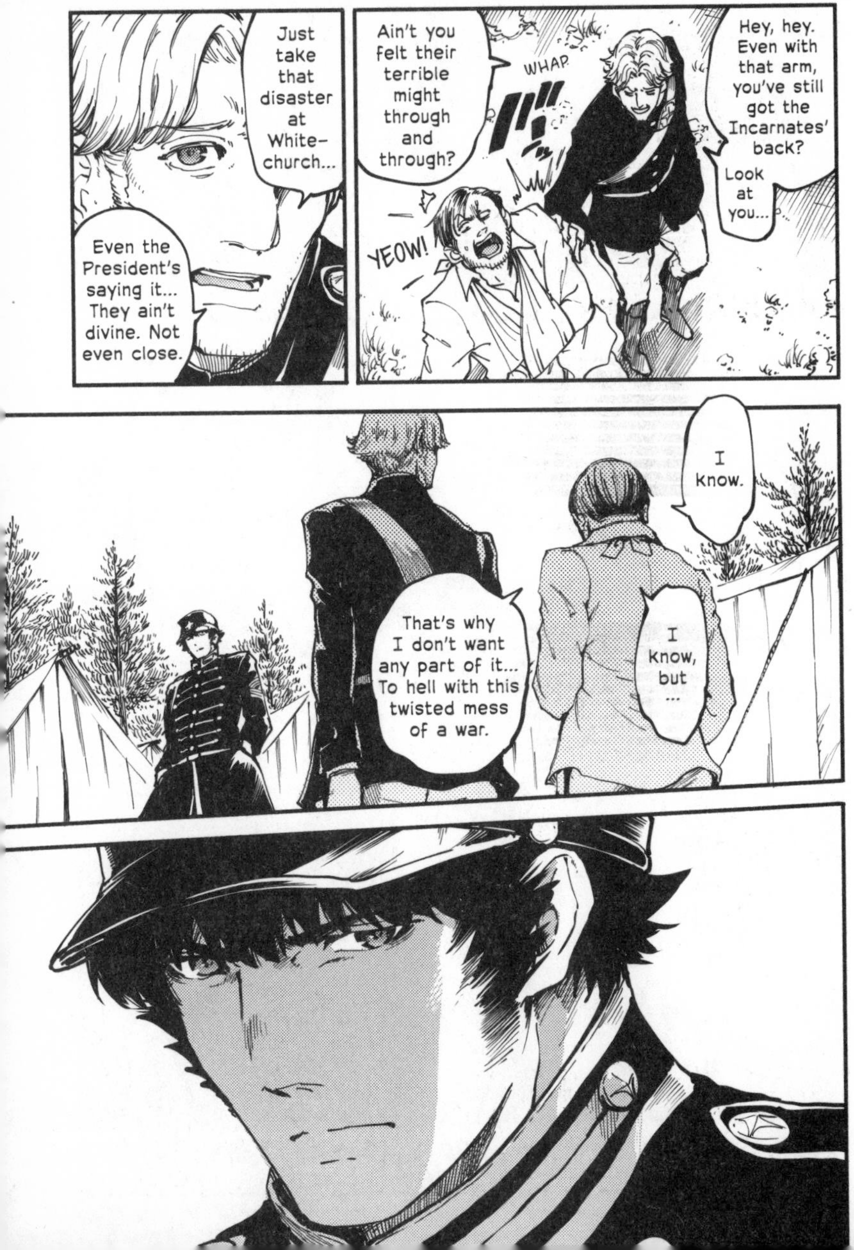
Hey, hey. Even with that arm, you've still got the Incarnates' back?
Look at you...
WHAP
YEOW!
Ain't you felt their terrible might through and through?
Just take that disaster at White-church...
Even the President's saying it... They ain't divine. Not even close.
I know.
I know, but ...
That's why I don't want any part of it... To hell with this twisted mess of a war.

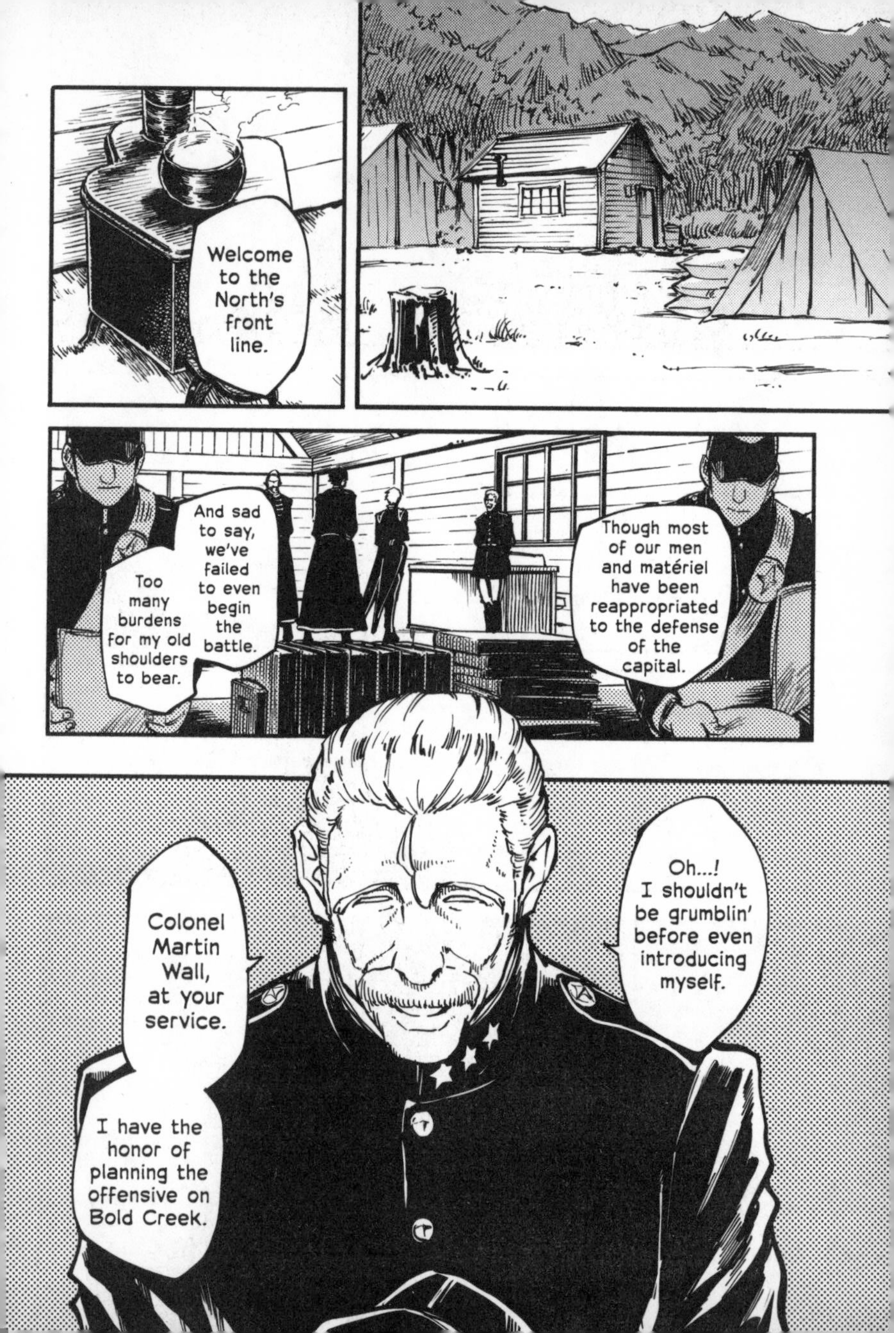

Welcome to the North's front line.
Though most of our men and matériel have been reappropriated to the defense of the capital.
And sad to say, we've failed to even begin the battle.
Too many burdens for my old shoulders to bear.
Oh...! I shouldn't be grumblin' before even introducing myself.
Colonel Martin Wall, at your service.
I have the honor of planning the offensive on Bold Creek.

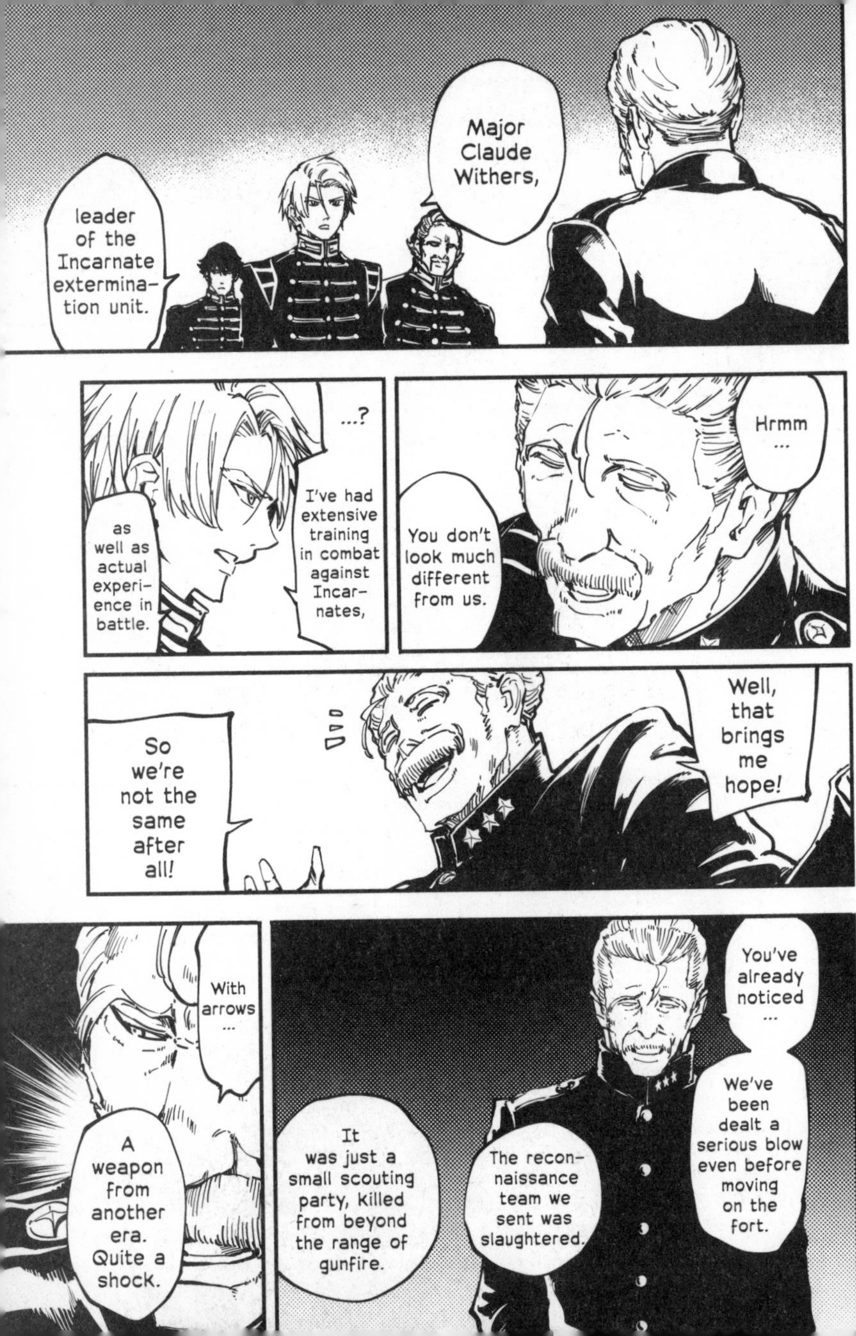
Major Claude Withers,
leader of the Incarnate extermination unit.
Hrmm ...
You don't look much different from us.
...?
I've had extensive training in combat against Incarnates,
as well as actual experience in battle.
Well, that brings me hope!
So we're not the same after all!
You've already noticed ...
We've been dealt a serious blow even before moving on the fort.
The reconnaissance team we sent was slaughtered.
It was just a small scouting party, killed from beyond the range of gunfire.
With arrows ...
A weapon from another era. Quite a shock.

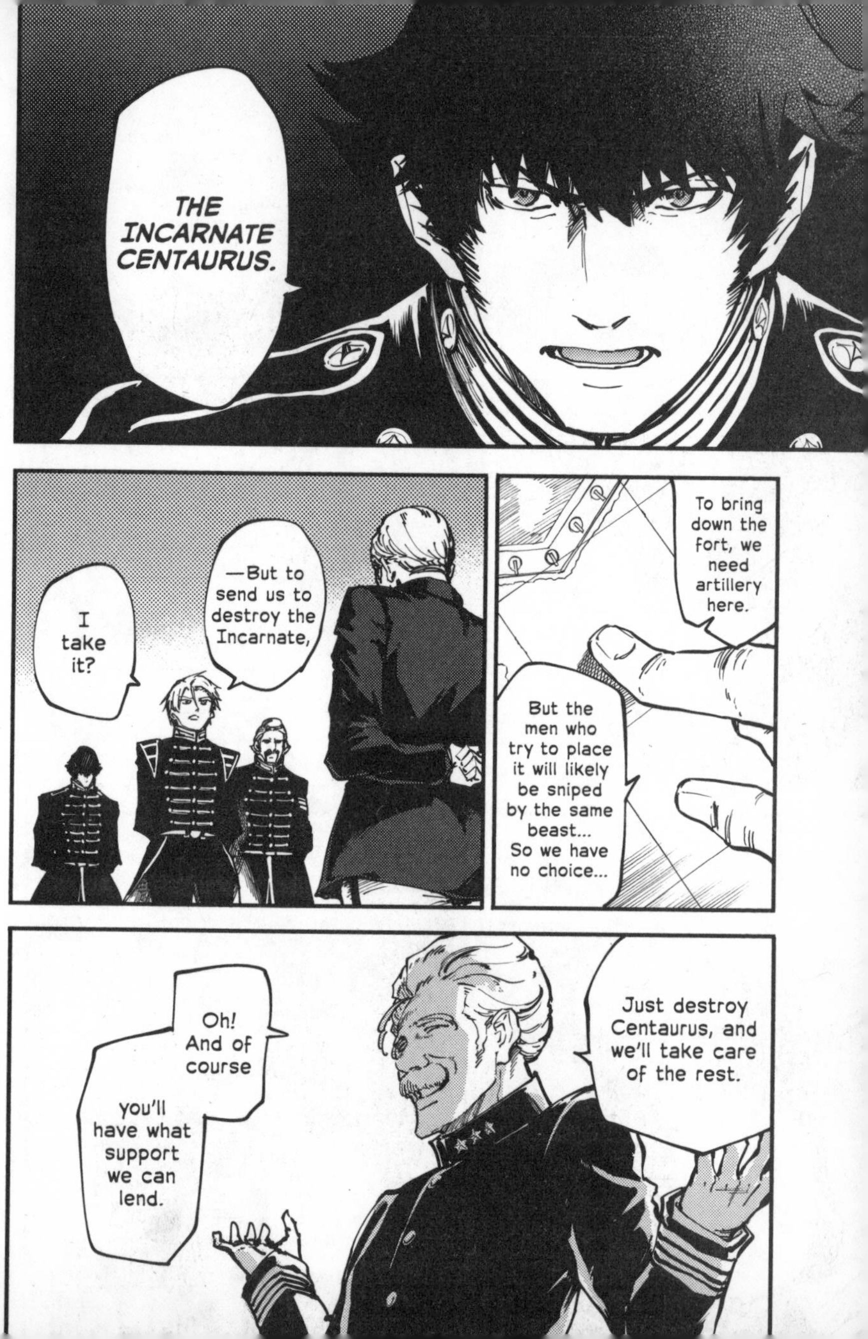
THE INCARNATE CENTAURUS.
To bring down the fort, we need artillery here.
But the men who try to place it will likely be sniped by the same beast... So we have no choice...
—But to send us to destroy the Incarnate,
I take it?
Just destroy Centaurus, and we'll take care of the rest.
Oh! And of course
you'll have what support we can lend.

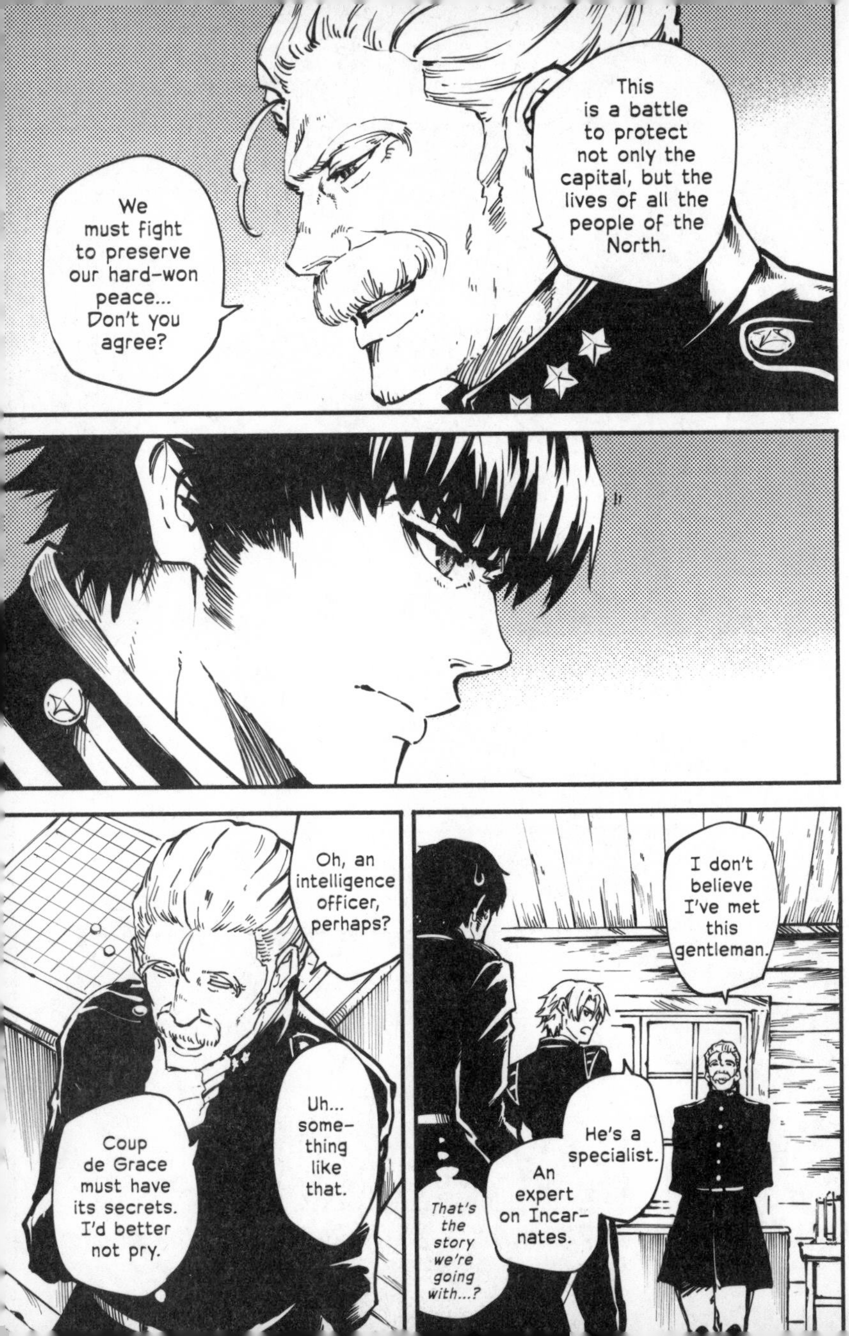
This is a battle to protect not only the capital, but the lives of all the people of the North.
We must fight to preserve our hard-won peace... Don't you agree?
I don't believe I've met this gentleman.
He's a specialist.
An expert on Incarnates.
That's the story we're going with...?
Oh, an intelligence officer, perhaps?
Uh... something like that.
Coup de Grace must have its secrets. I'd better not pry.

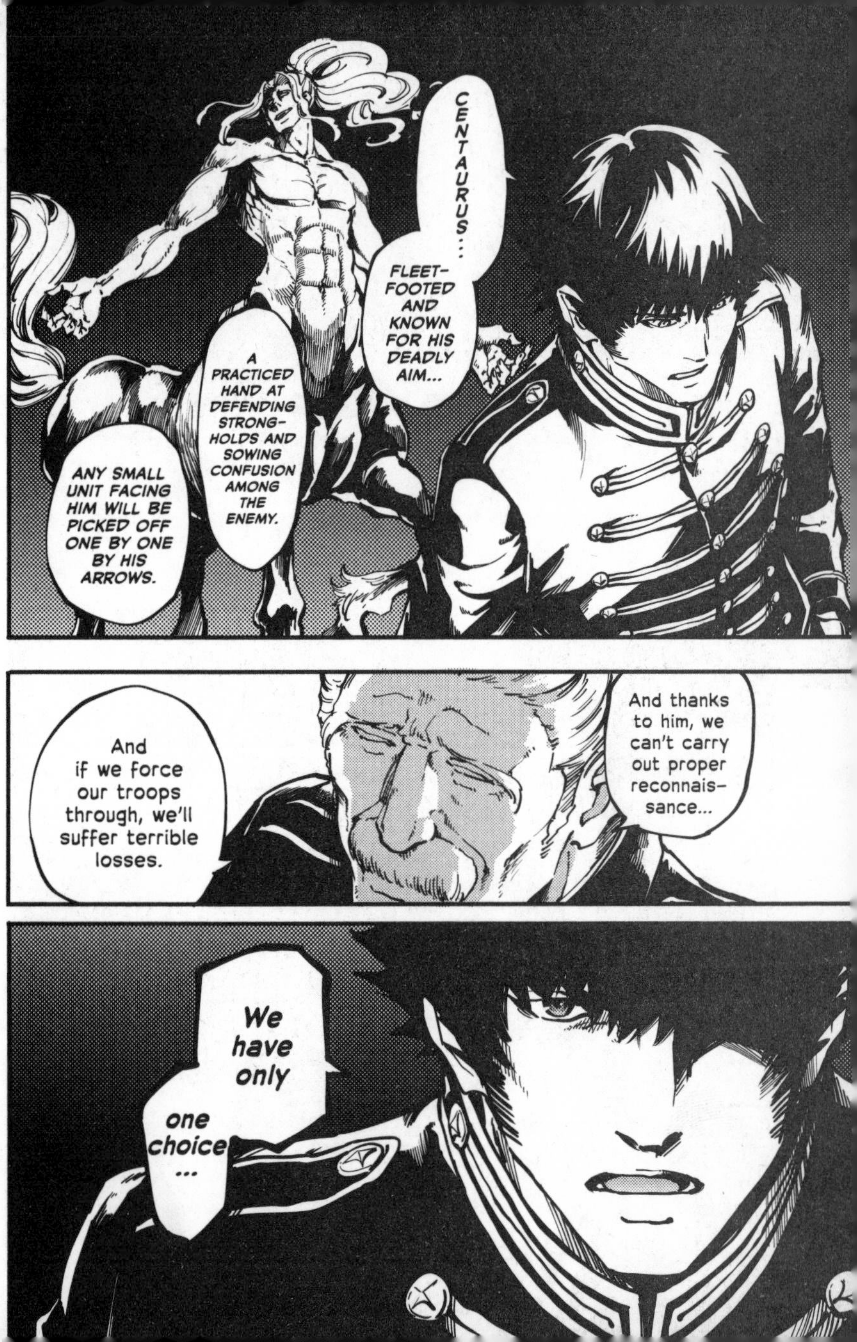
CENTAURUS...
FLEET-FOOTED AND KNOWN FOR HIS DEADLY AIM...
A PRACTICED HAND AT DEFENDING STRONG-HOLDS AND SOWING CONFUSION AMONG THE ENEMY.
ANY SMALL UNIT FACING HIM WILL BE PICKED OFF ONE BY ONE BY HIS ARROWS.
And thanks to him, we can't carry out proper reconnais-sance...
And if we force our troops through, we'll suffer terrible losses.
We have only one choice...

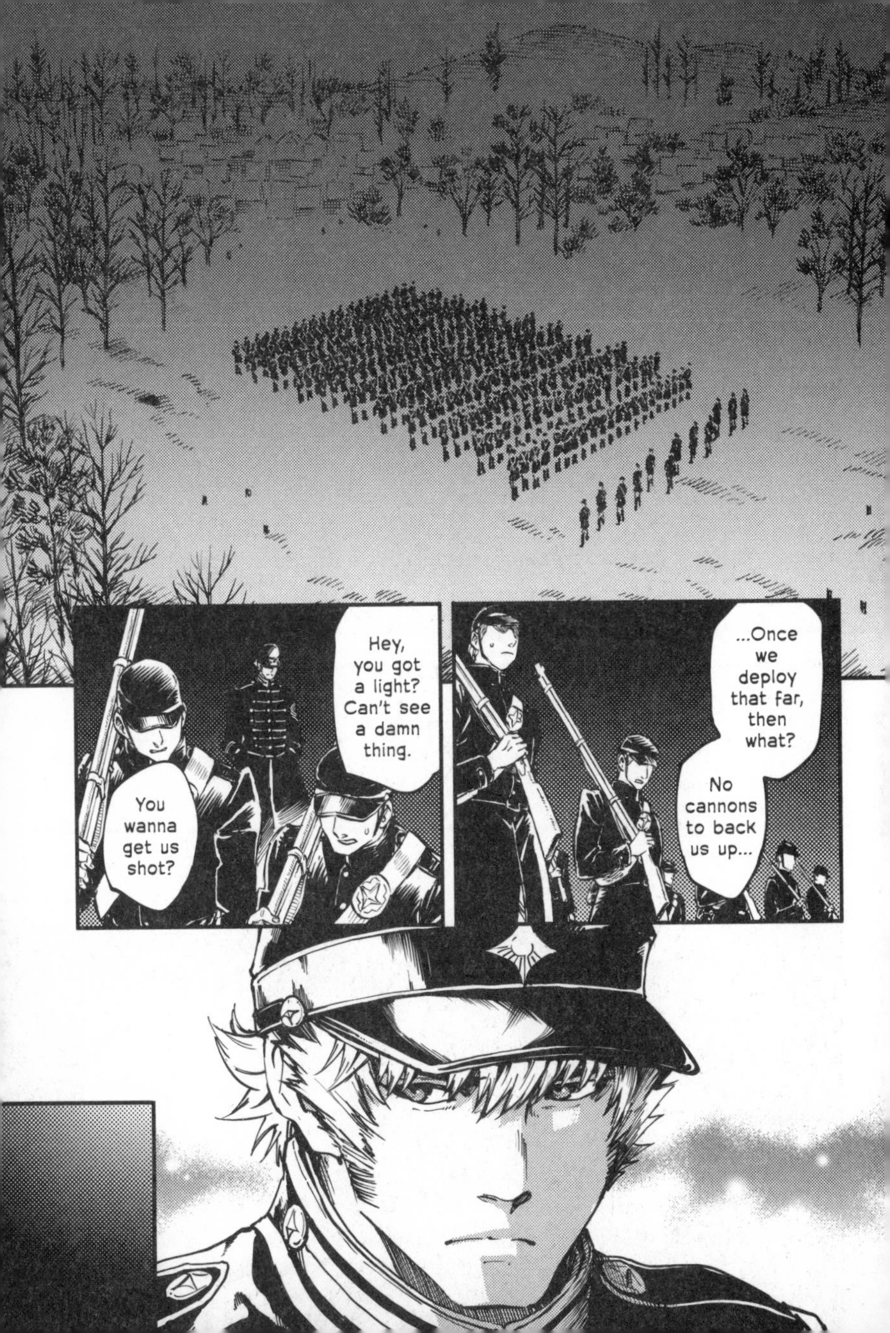
...Once we deploy that far, then what?
No cannons to back us up...
Hey, you got a light? Can't see a damn thing.
You wanna get us shot?

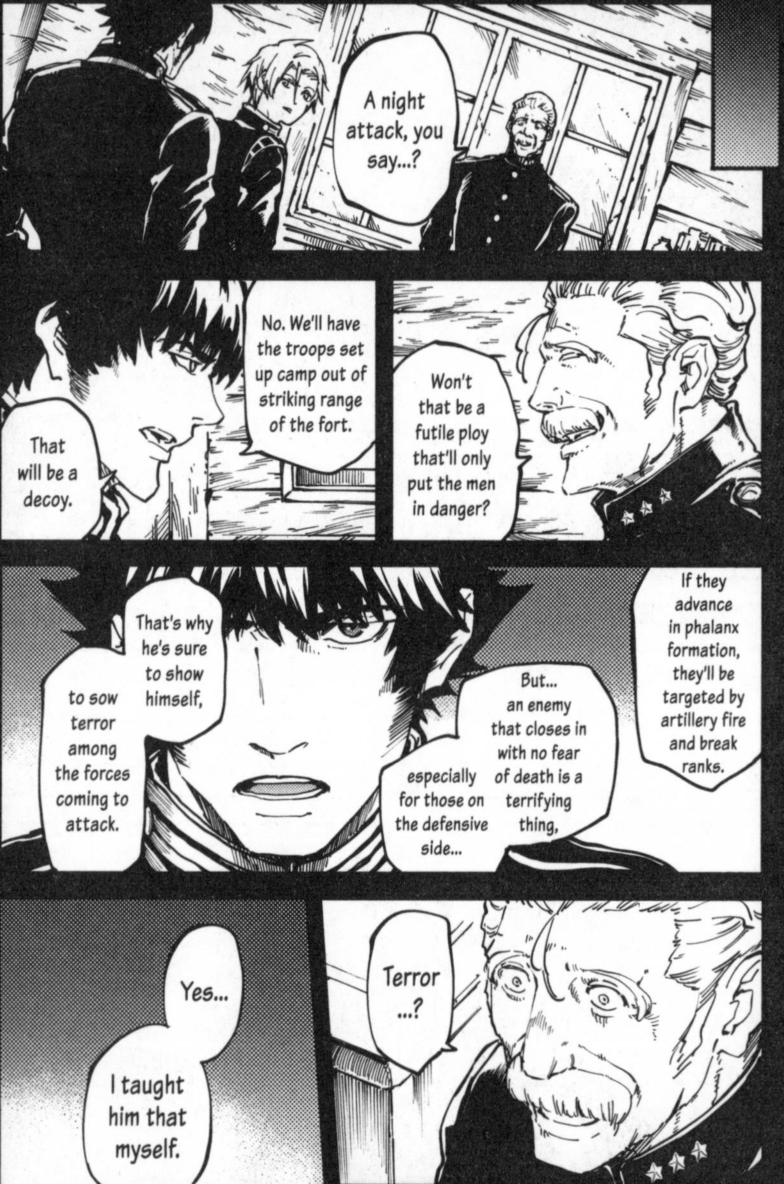
A night attack, you say...?
Won't that be a futile ploy that'll only put the men in danger?
No. We'll have the troops set up camp out of striking range of the fort.
That will be a decoy.
If they advance in phalanx formation, they'll be targeted by artillery fire and break ranks.
But... an enemy that closes in with no fear of death is a terrifying thing,
especially for those on the defensive side...
That's why he's sure to show himself,
to sow terror among the forces coming to attack.
Terror ...?
Yes...
I taught him that myself.

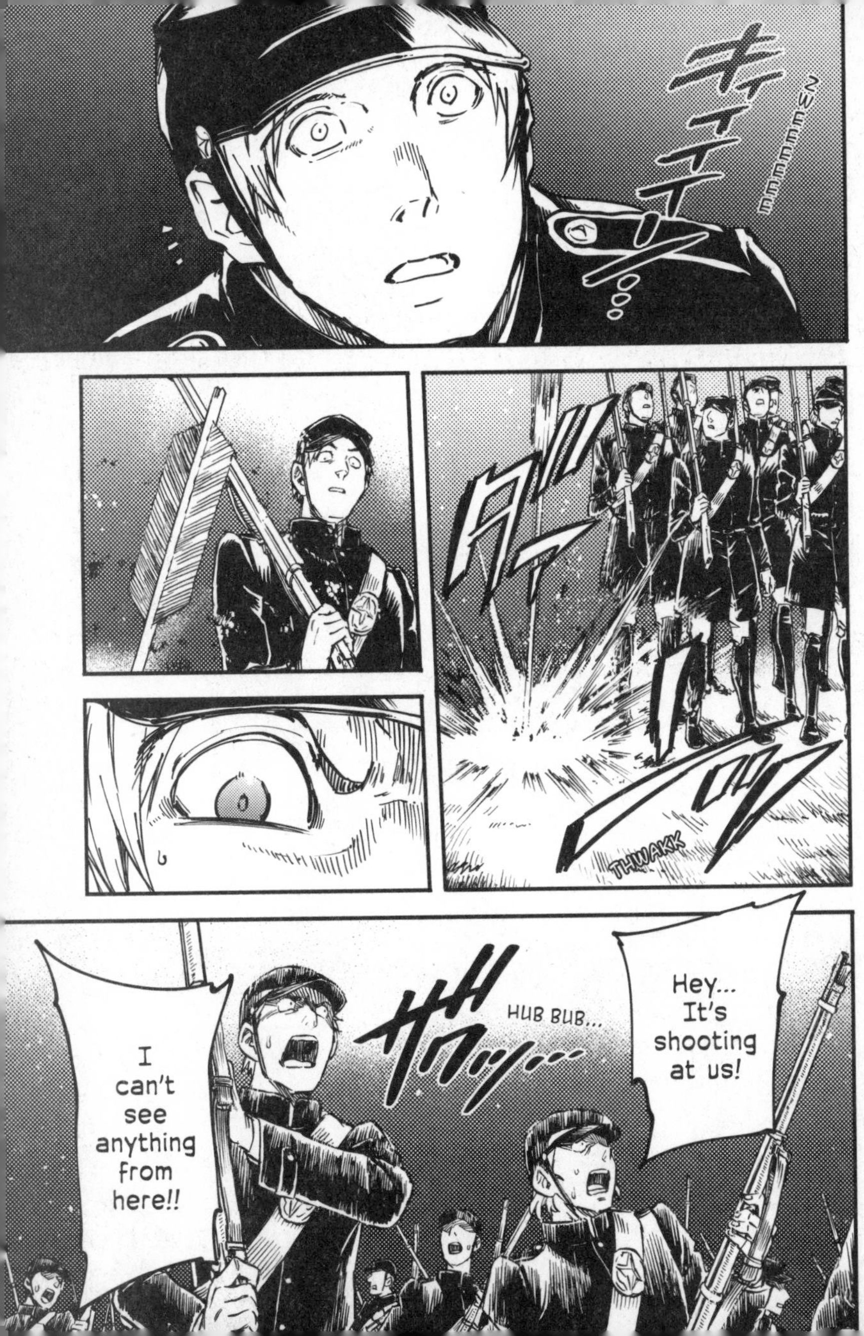
ZWEEEEEE
THWAKK
Hey... It's shooting at us!
HUB BUB...
I can't see anything from here!!

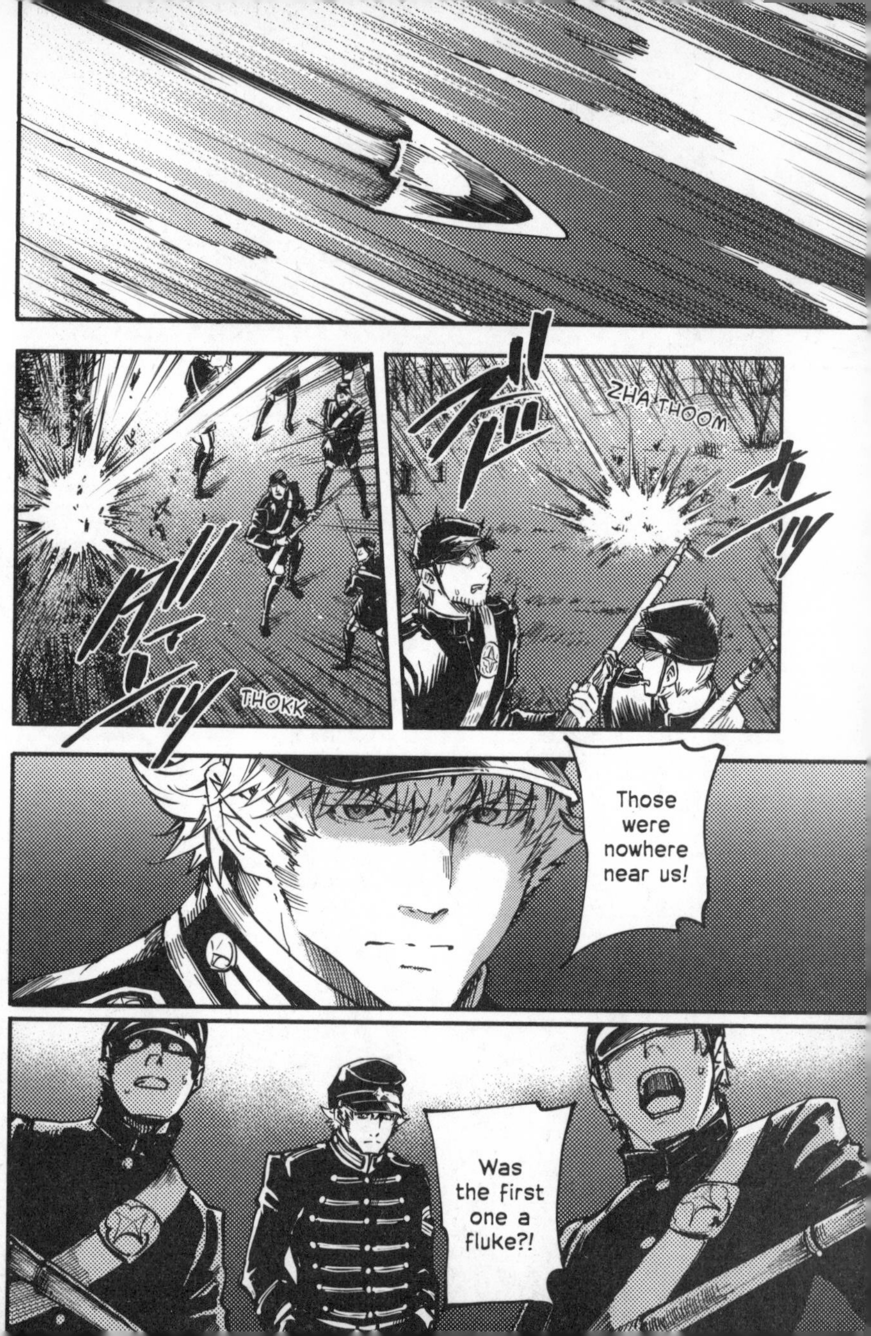
ZHA THOOM
THOKK
Those were nowhere near us!
Was the first one a fluke?!

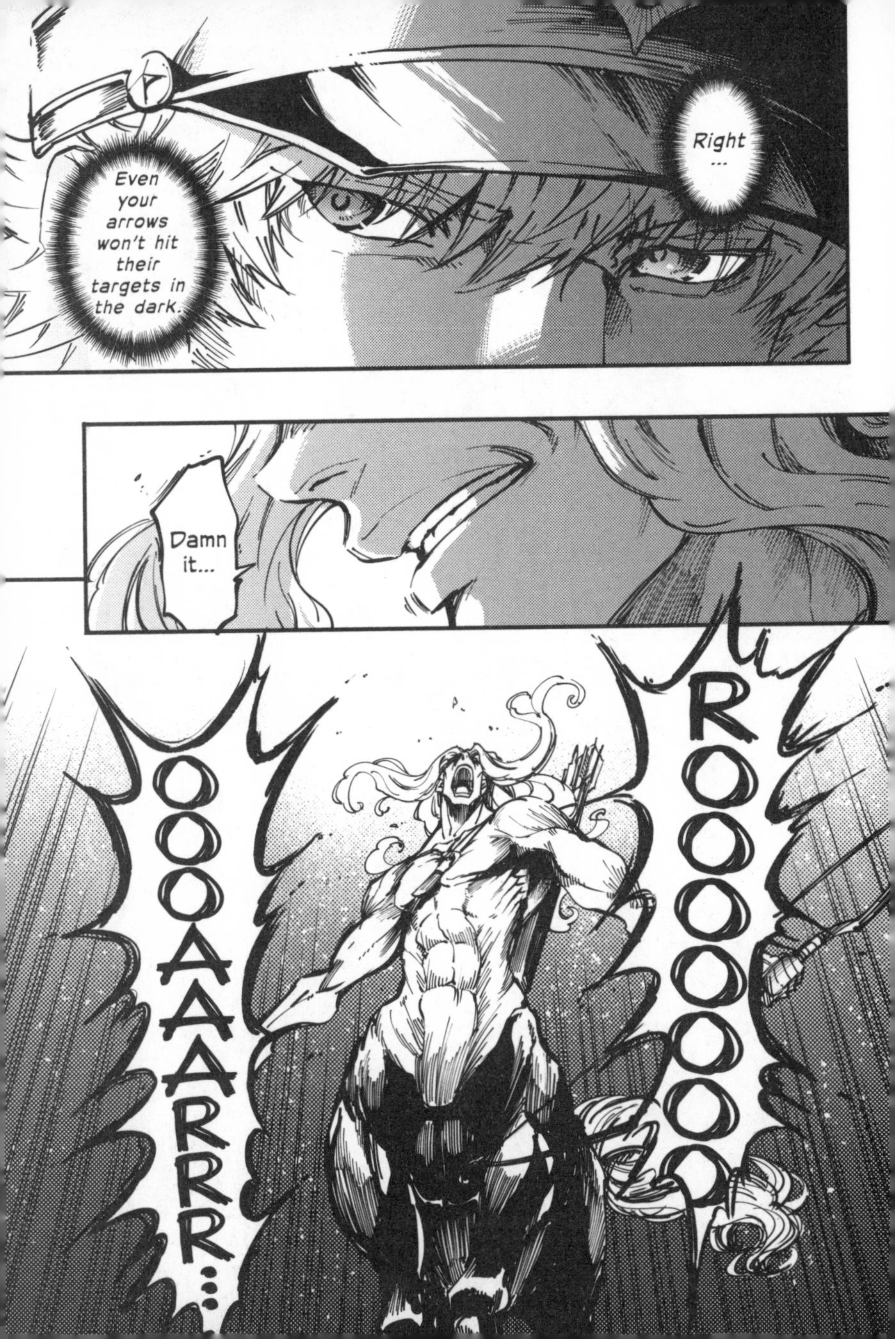
Right ...
Even your arrows won't hit their targets in the dark.
Damn it...
ROOOOOOO
OOOAAARRR...

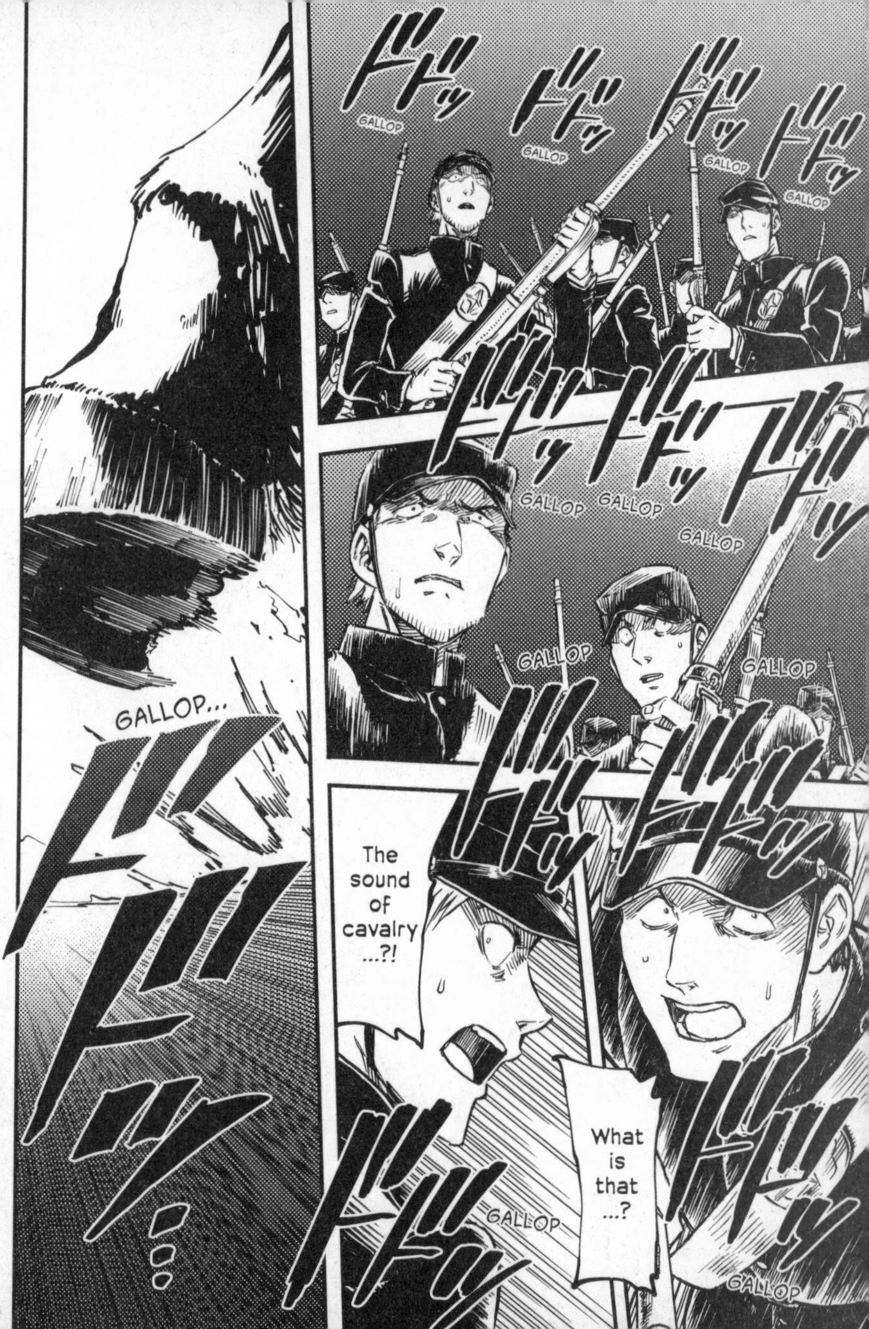
GALLOP
GALLOP
GALLOP
GALLOP
GALLOP
GALLOP
GALLOP
GALLOP
GALLOP
What is that ...?
The sound of cavalry ...?!
GALLOP
GALLOP
GALLOP...

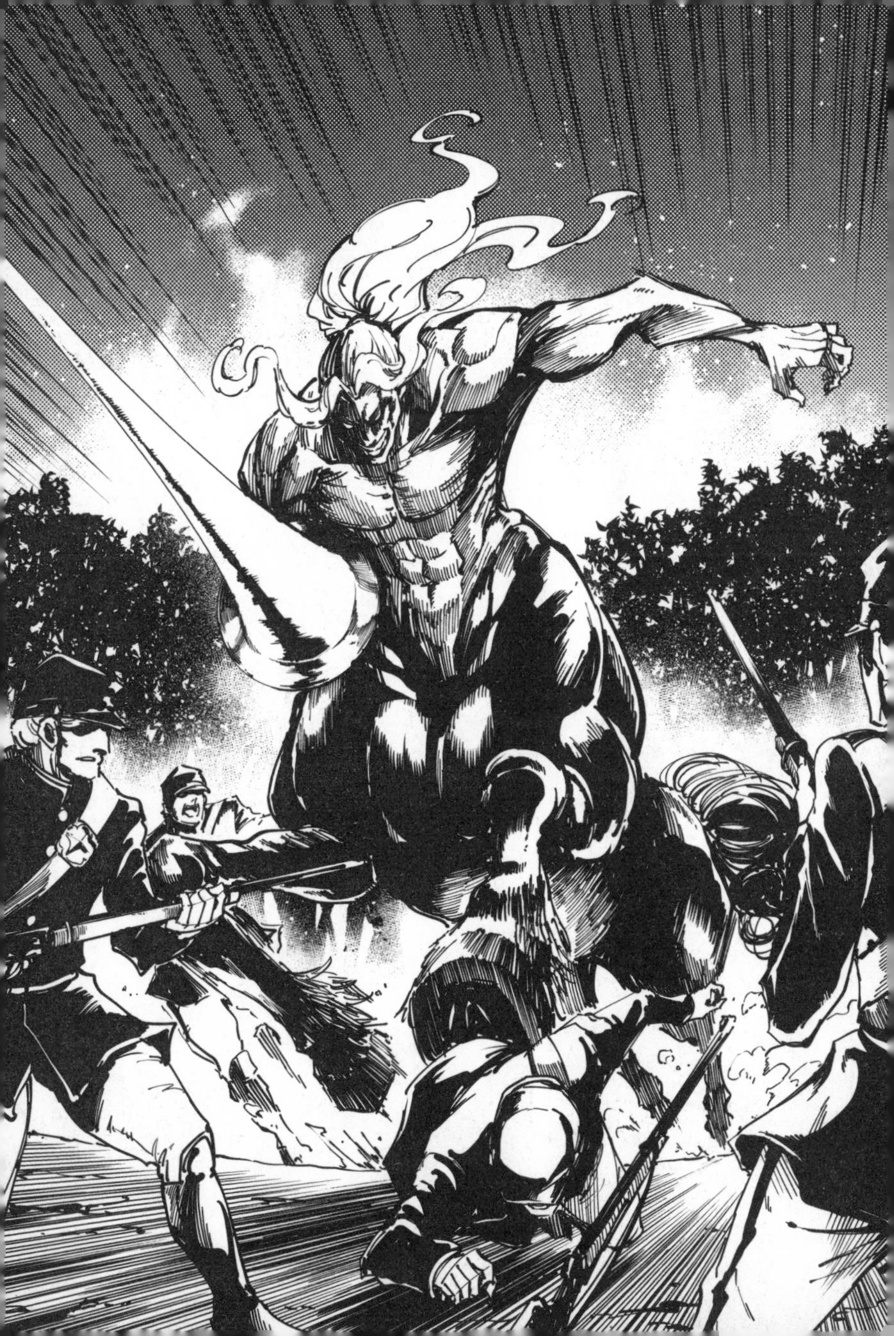

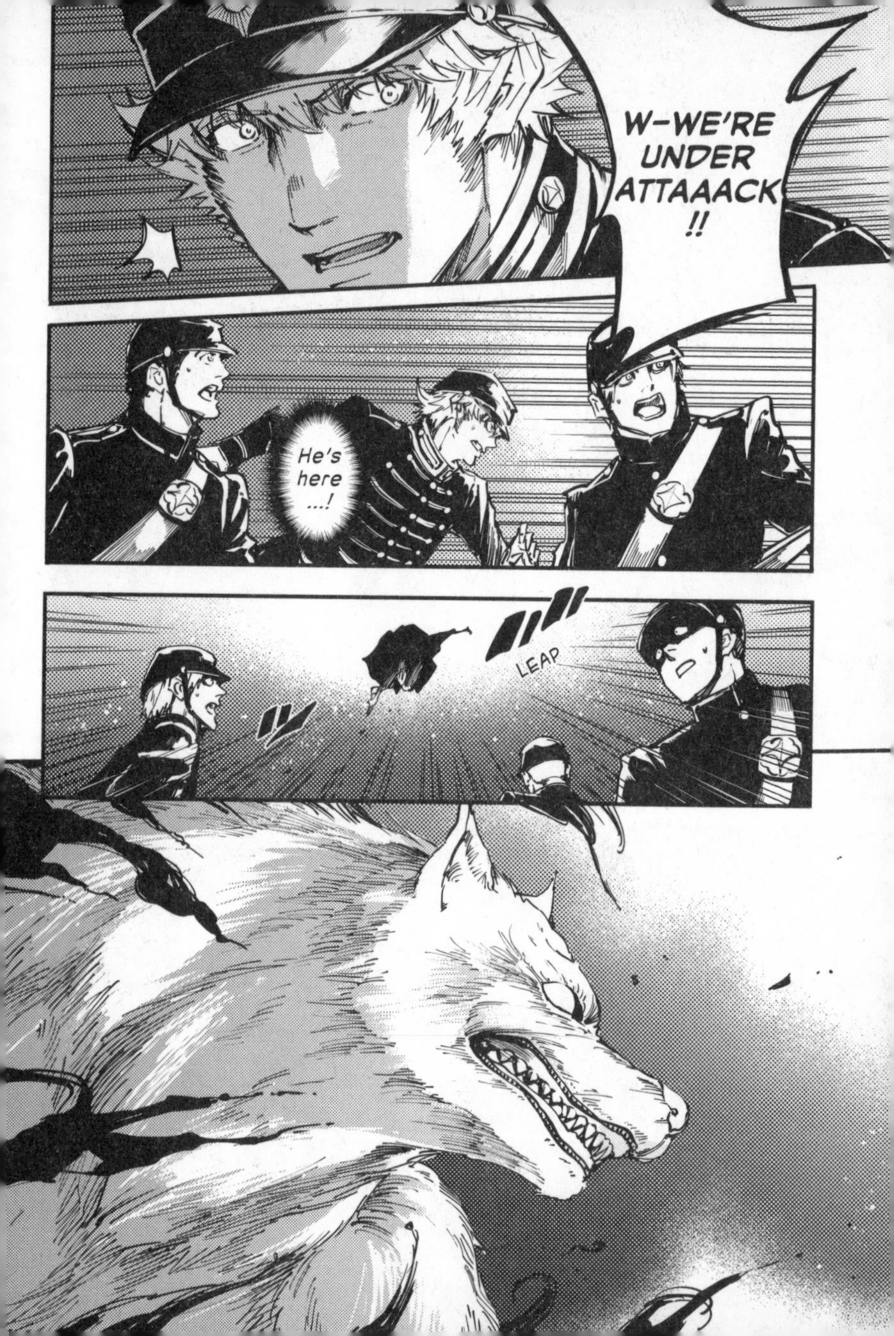
W-WE'RE UNDER ATTAAACK !!
He's here ...!
LEAP

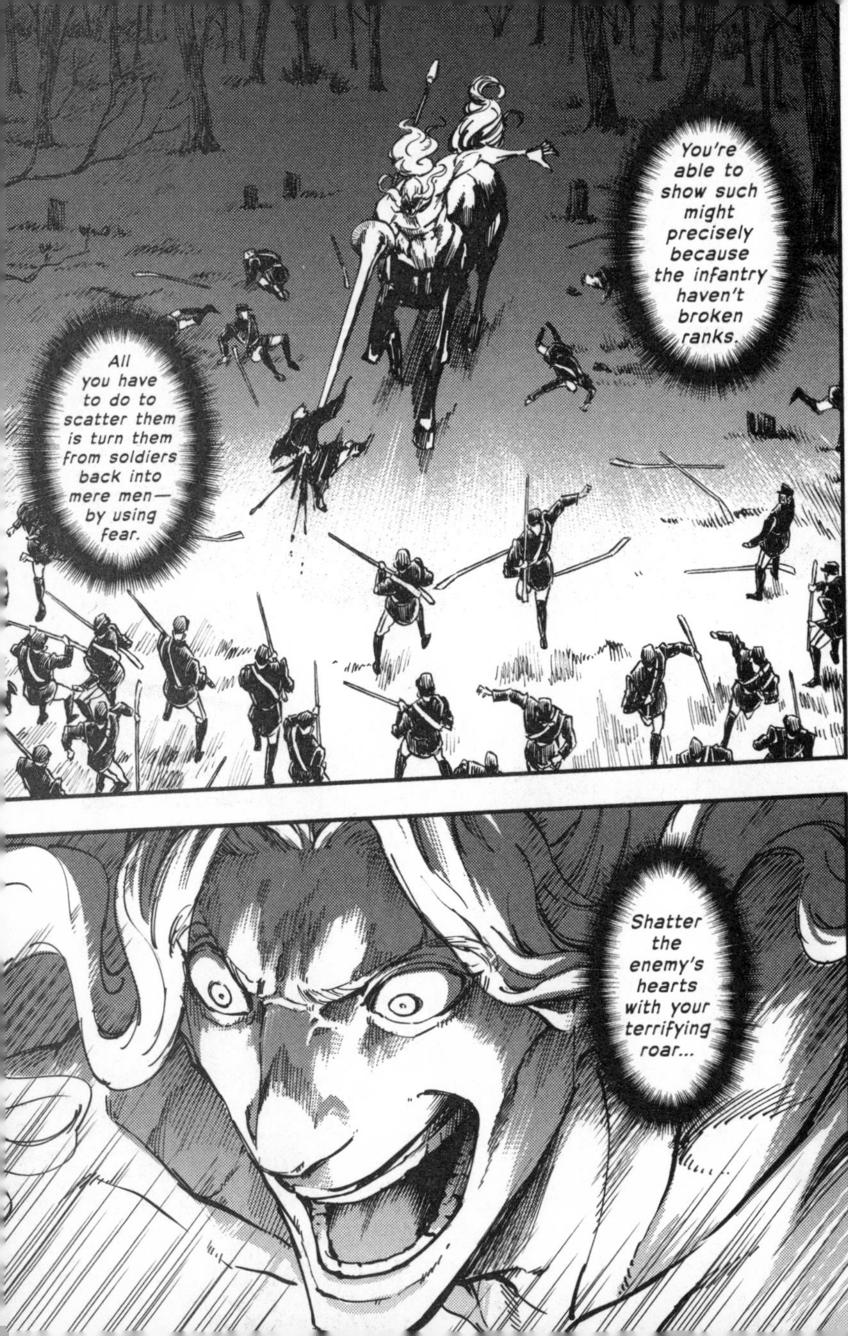
You're able to show such might precisely because the infantry haven't broken ranks.
All you have to do to scatter them is turn them from soldiers back into mere men—by using fear.
Shatter the enemy's hearts with your terrifying roar...

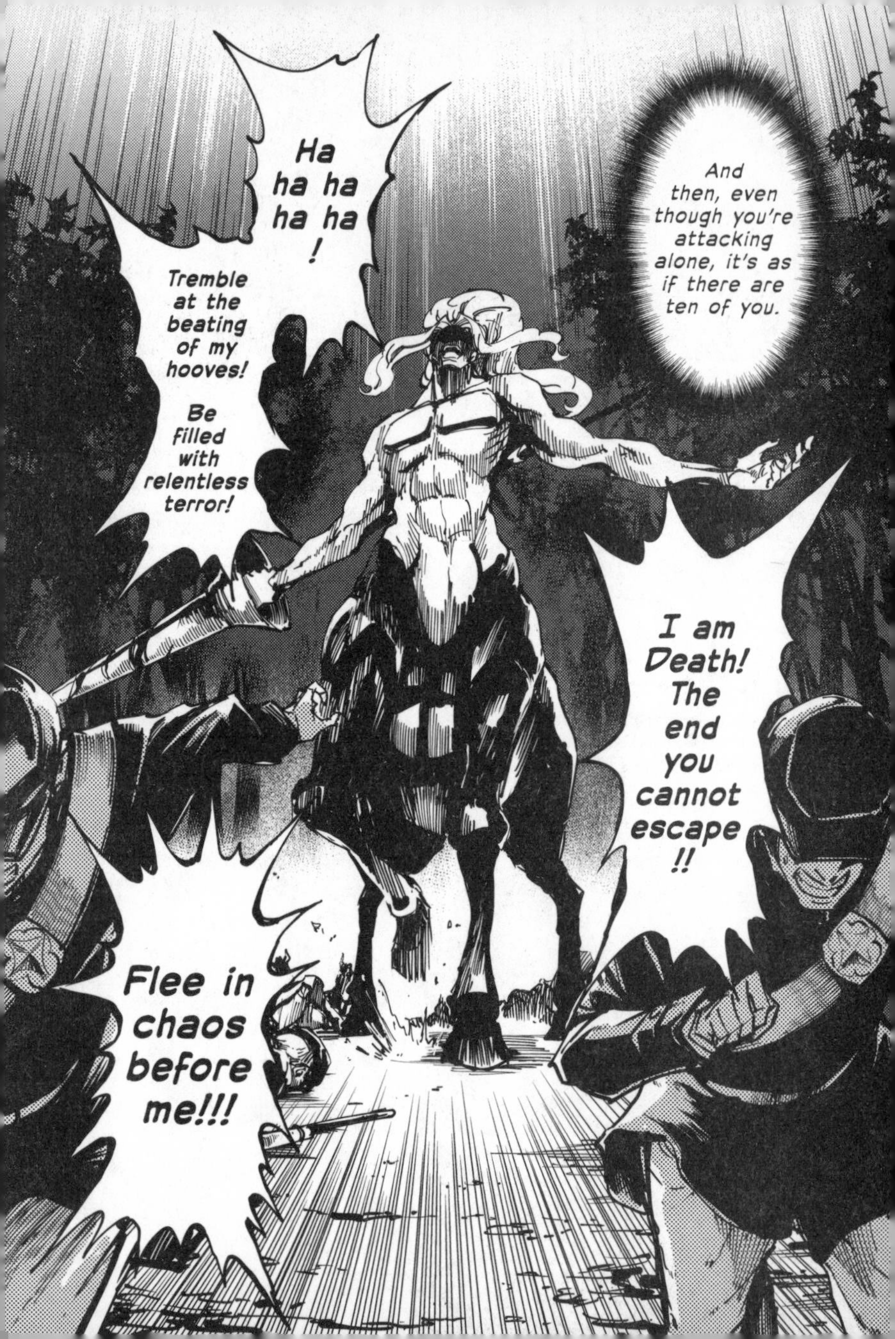
And then, even though you're attacking alone, it's as if there are ten of you.
Ha ha ha ha ha!
Tremble at the beating of my hooves!
Be filled with relentless terror!
I am Death! The end you cannot escape!!
Flee in chaos before me!!!

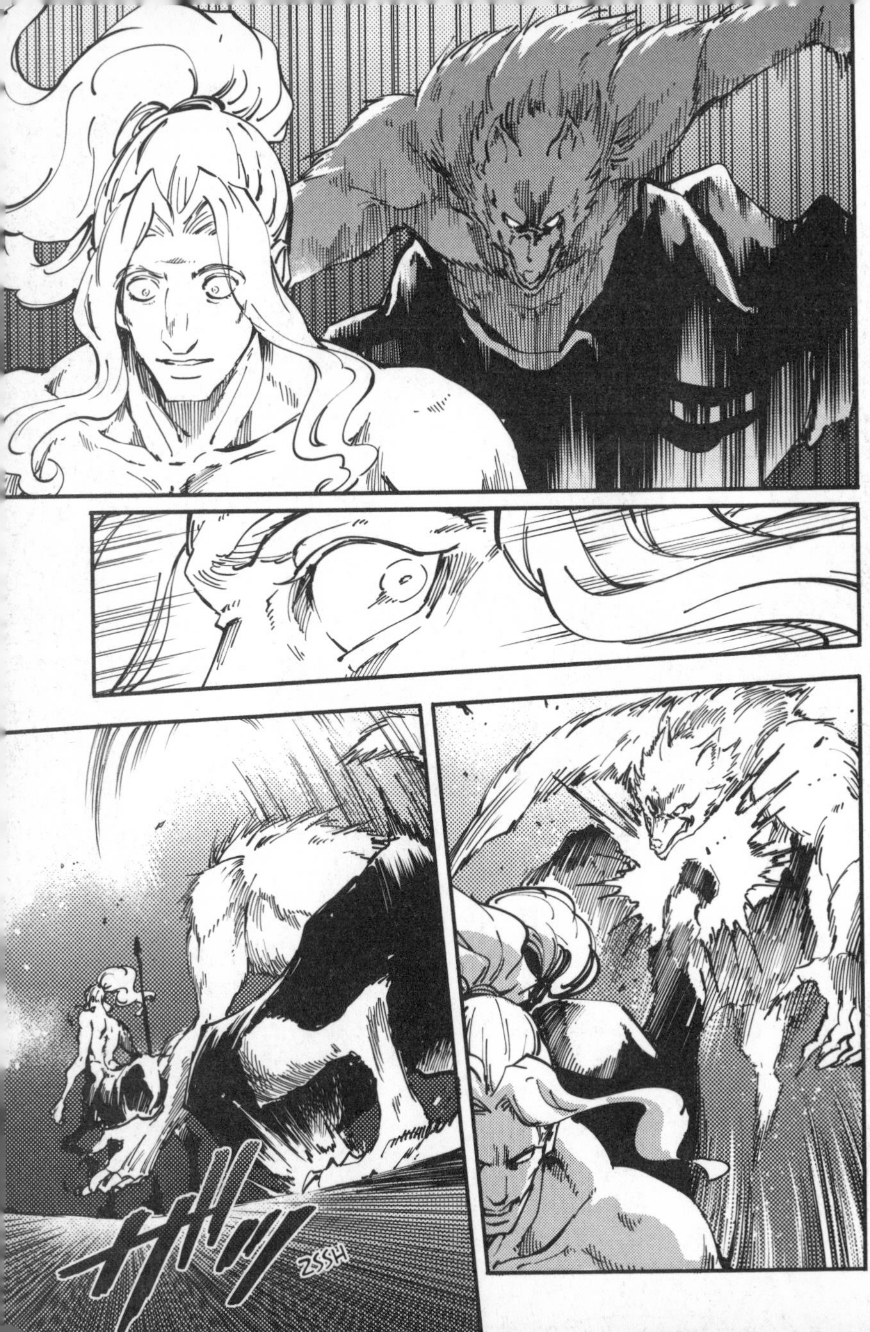
ZSSH

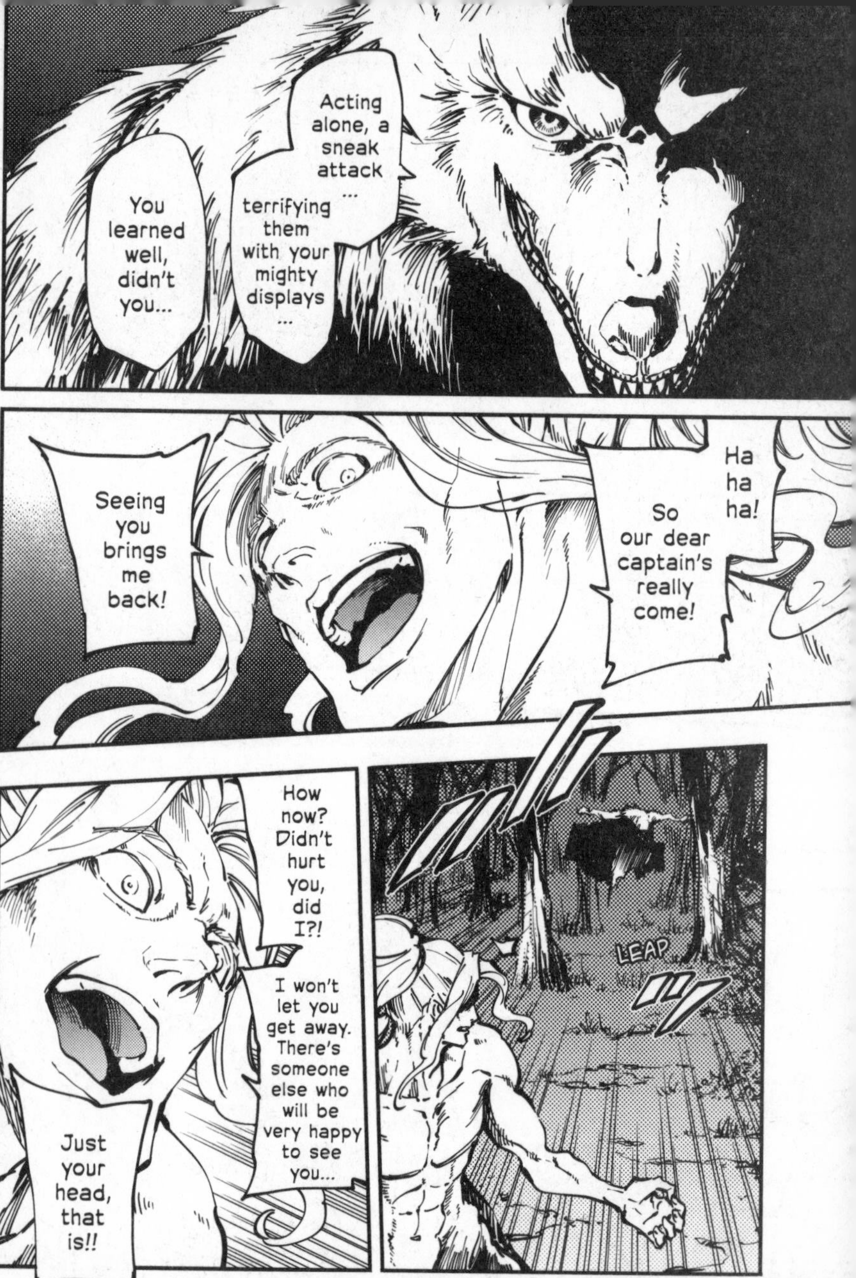
Acting alone, a sneak attack ...
terrifying them with your mighty displays ...
You learned well, didn't you...
Ha ha ha!
So our dear captain's really come!
Seeing you brings me back!
LEAP
How now? Didn't hurt you, did I?!
I won't let you get away. There's someone else who will be very happy to see you...
Just your head, that is!!

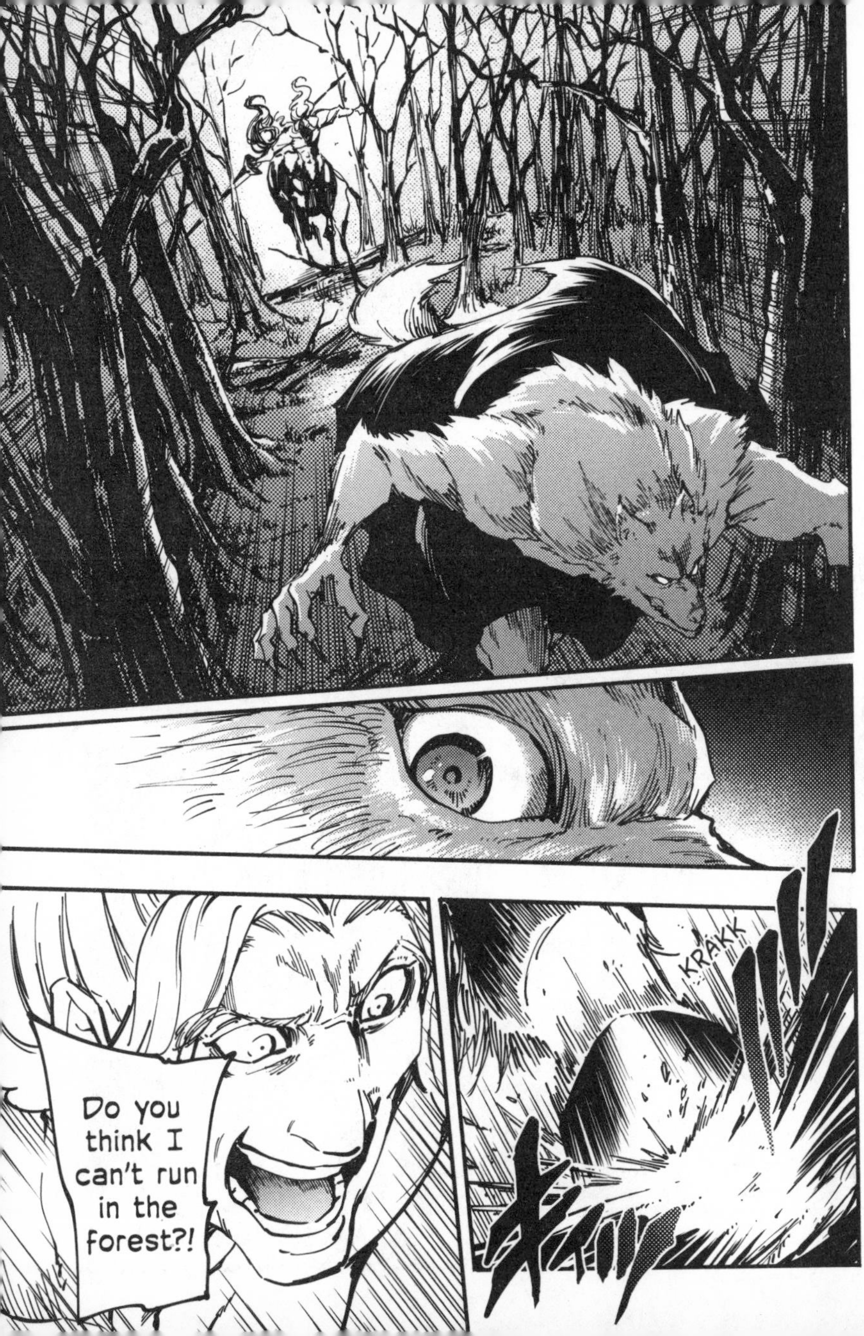
KRAKK
Do you think I can't run in the forest?!

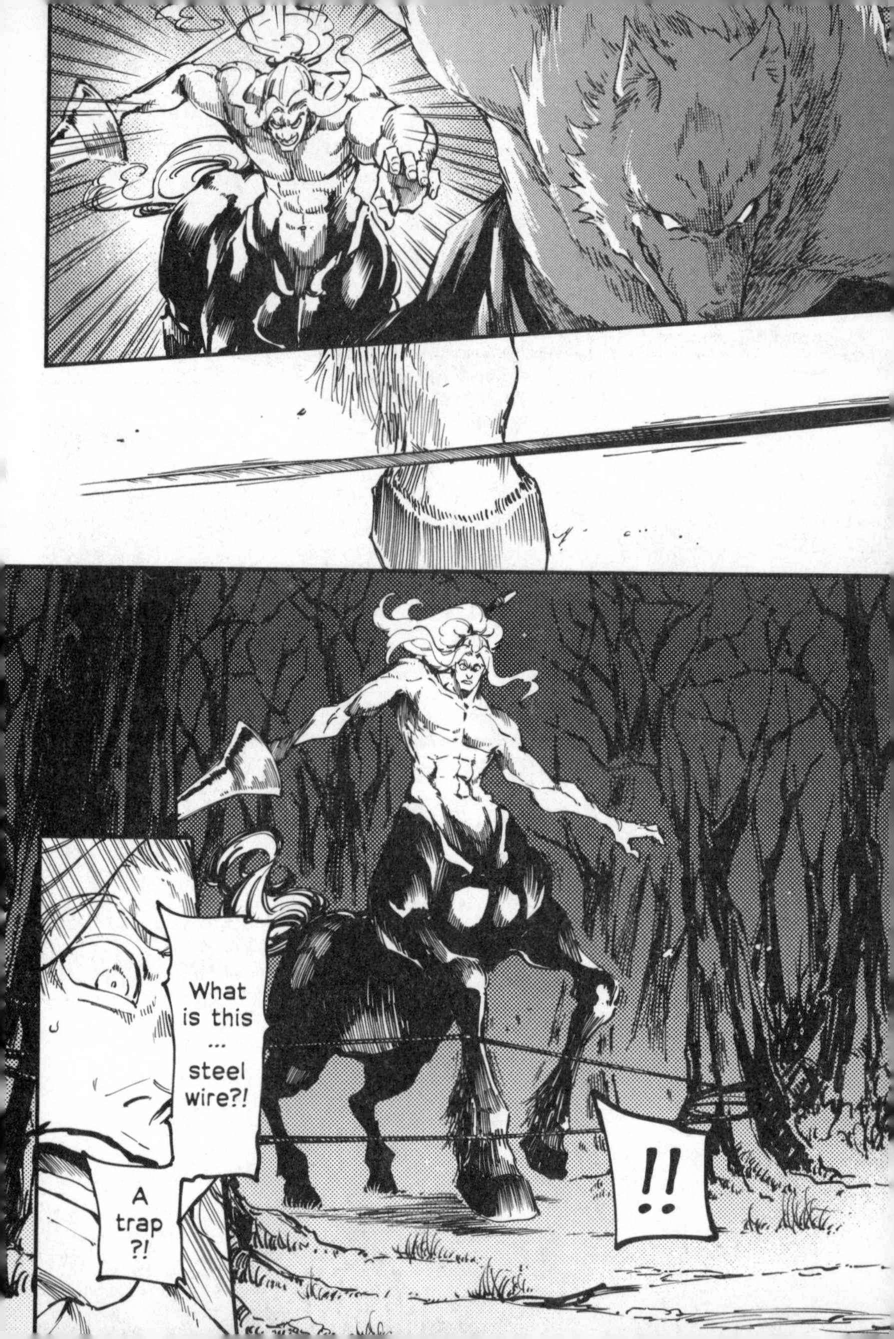
!!
What is this ... steel wire?!
A trap ?!

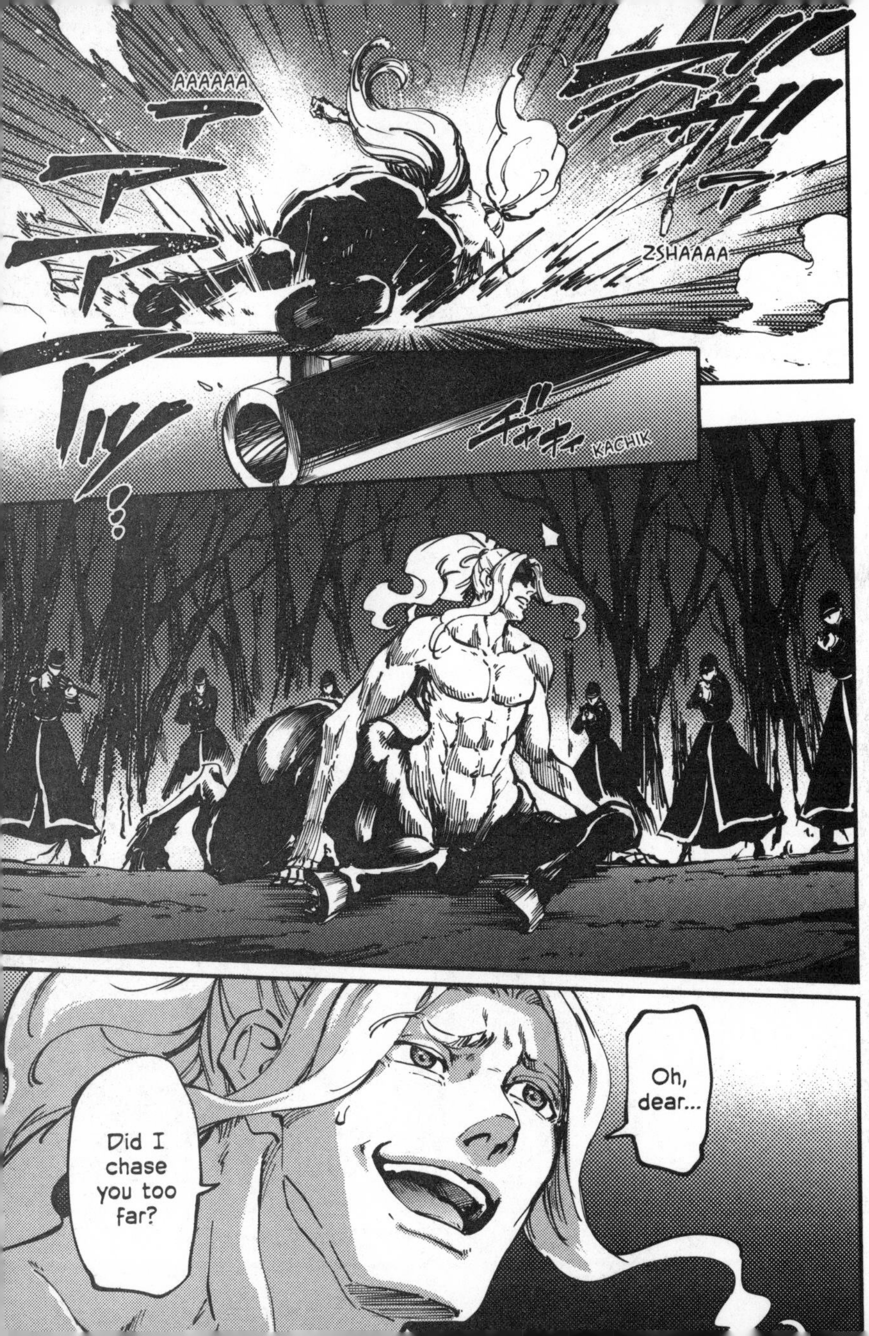
ZSHAAAA
AAAAAA
KACHIK
Oh, dear...
Did I chase you too far?

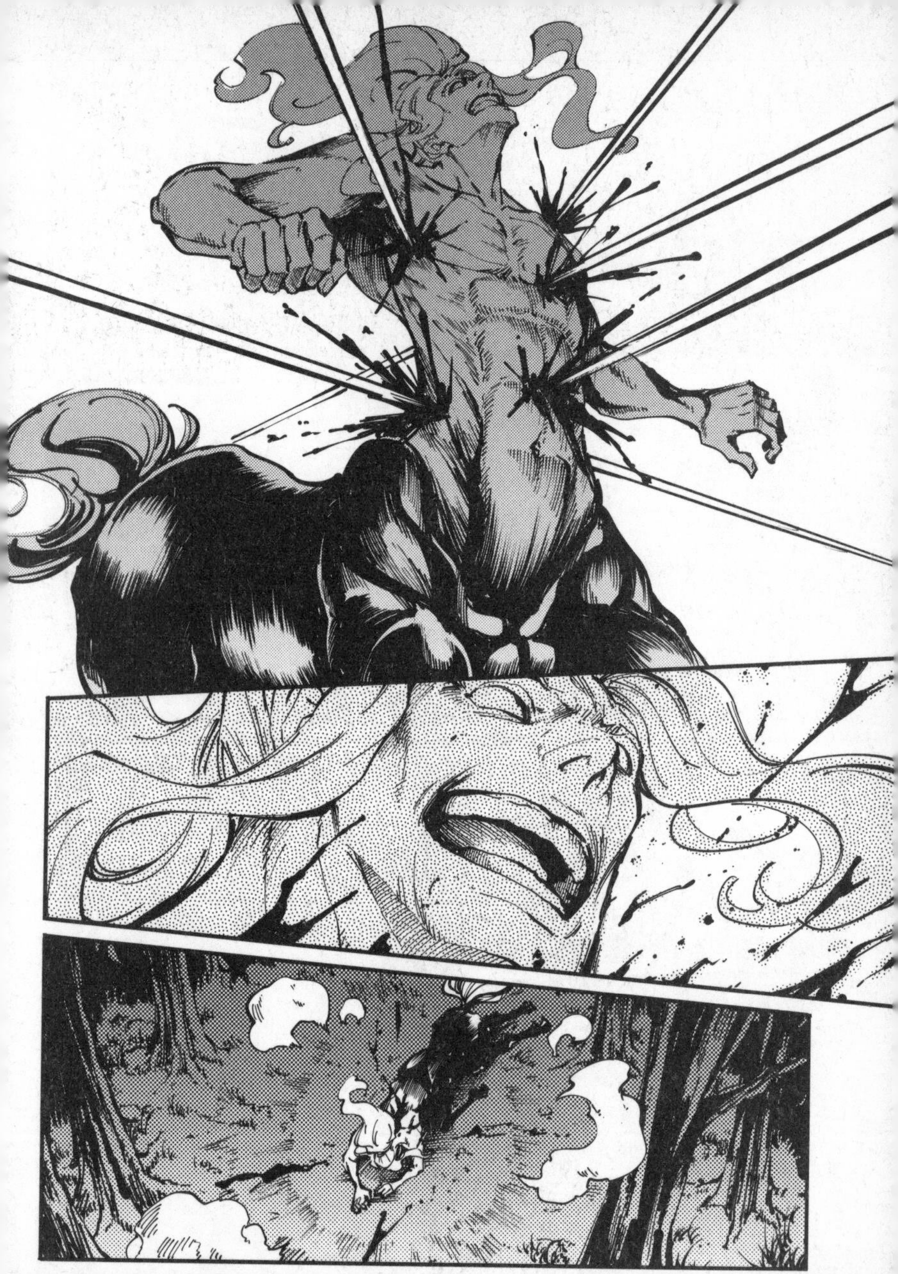

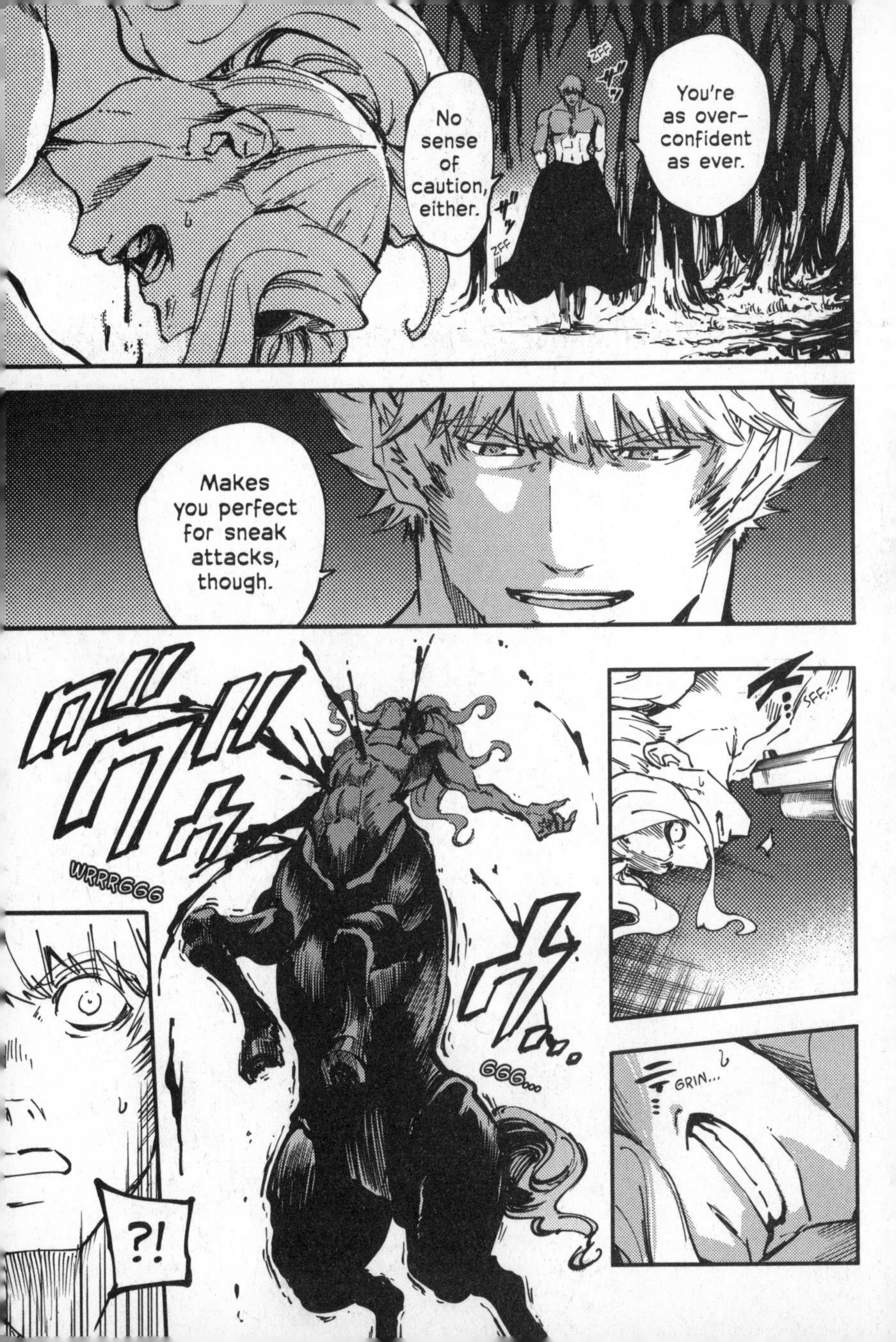
ZFF
You're as over-confident as ever.
No sense of caution, either.
ZFF
Makes you perfect for sneak attacks, though.
SFF...
GRIN...
WRRRGGG
GGG...
?!

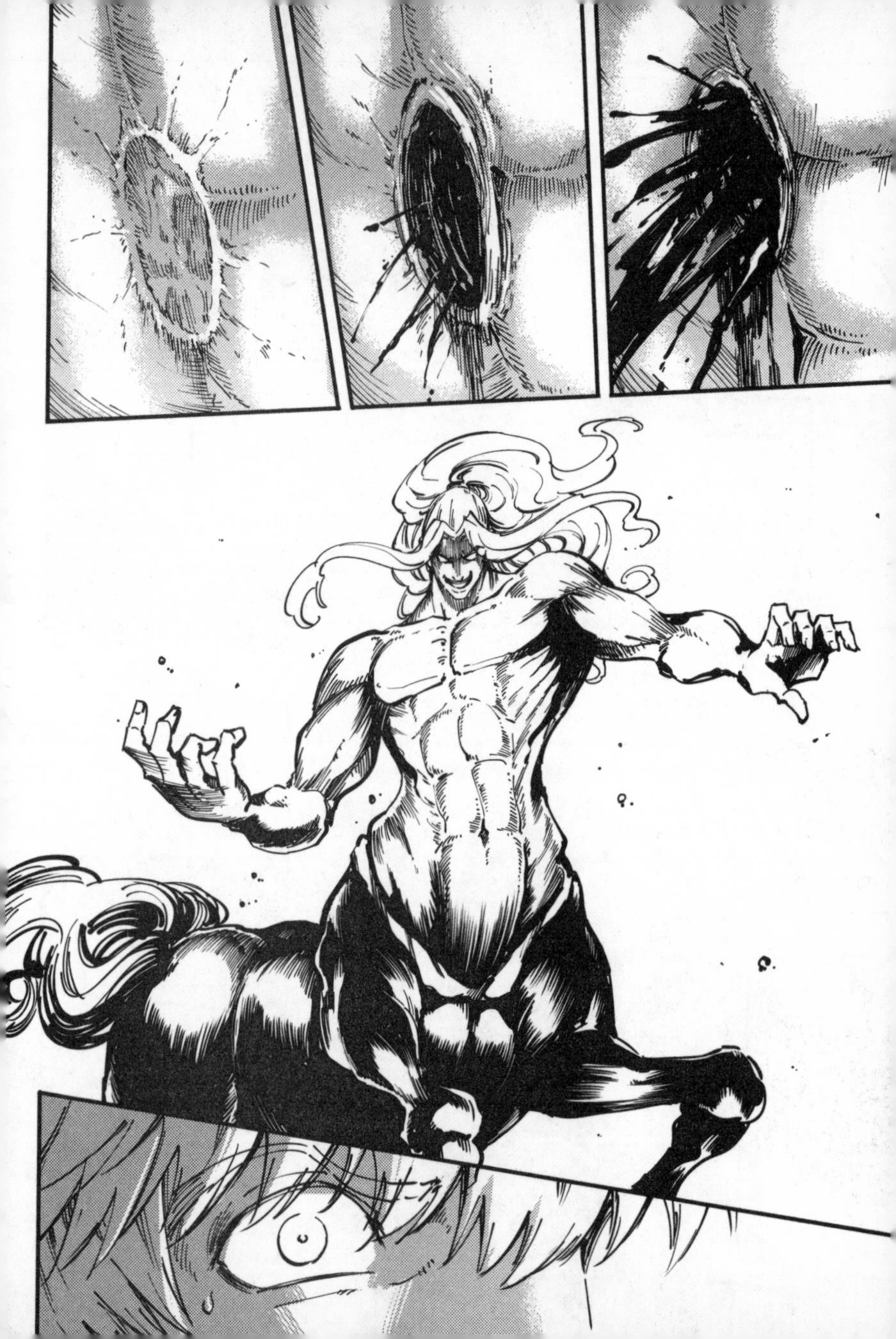

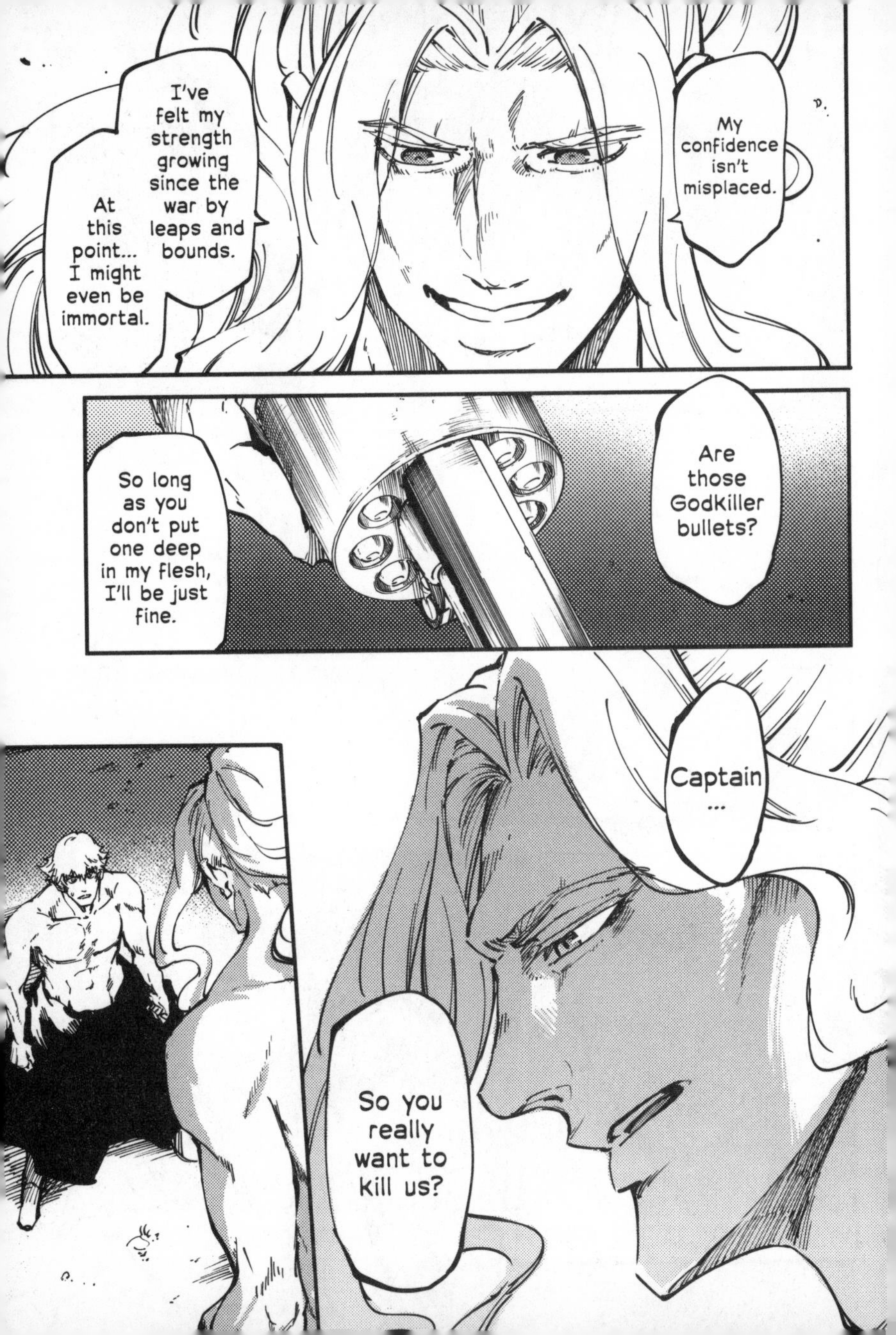
My confidence isn't misplaced.
I've felt my strength growing since the war by leaps and bounds.
At this point... I might even be immortal.
Are those GodKiller bullets?
So long as you don't put one deep in my flesh, I'll be just fine.
Captain...
So you really want to kill us?

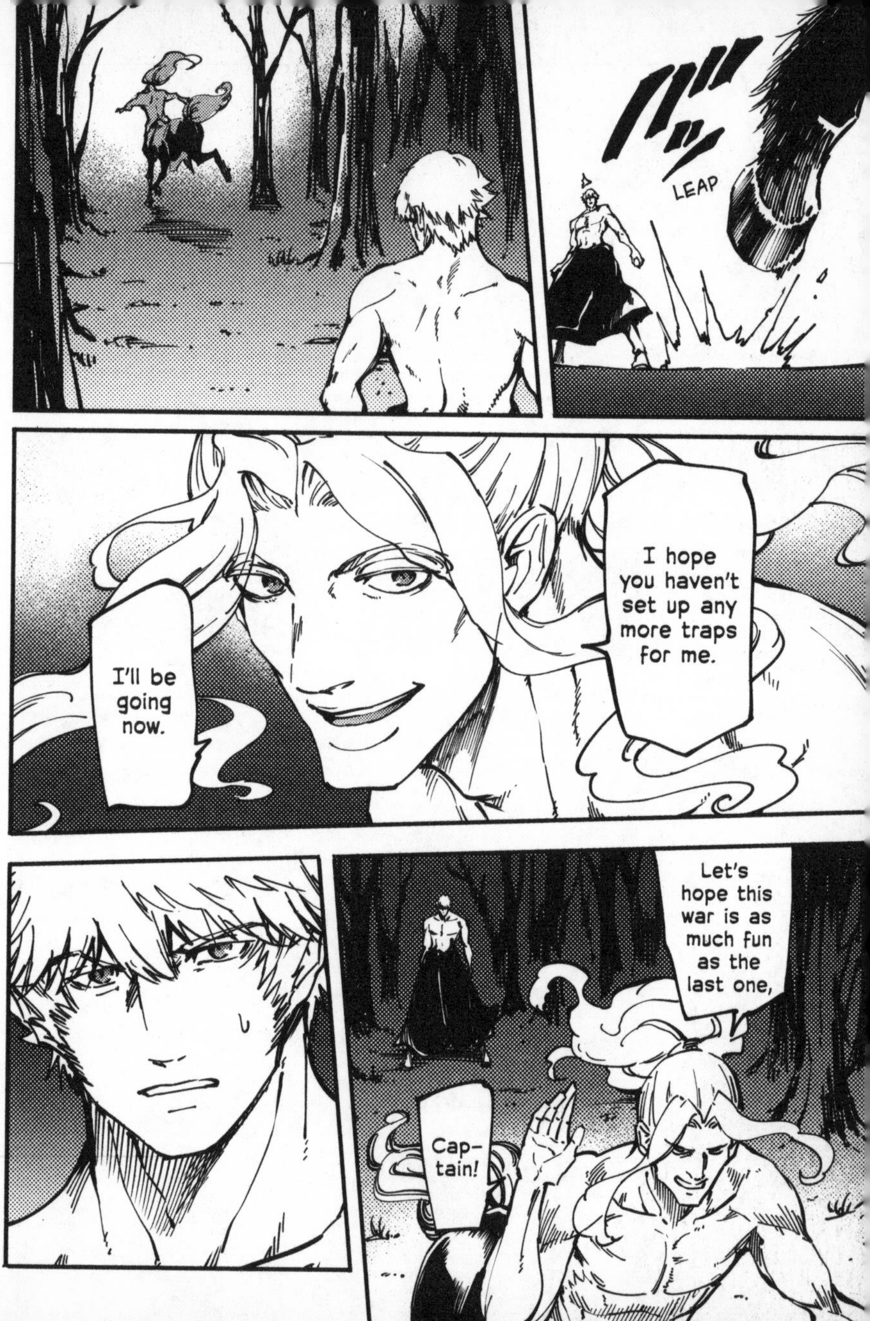
LEAP
I hope you haven't set up any more traps for me.
I'll be going now.
Let's hope this war is as much fun as the last one,
Cap-tain!

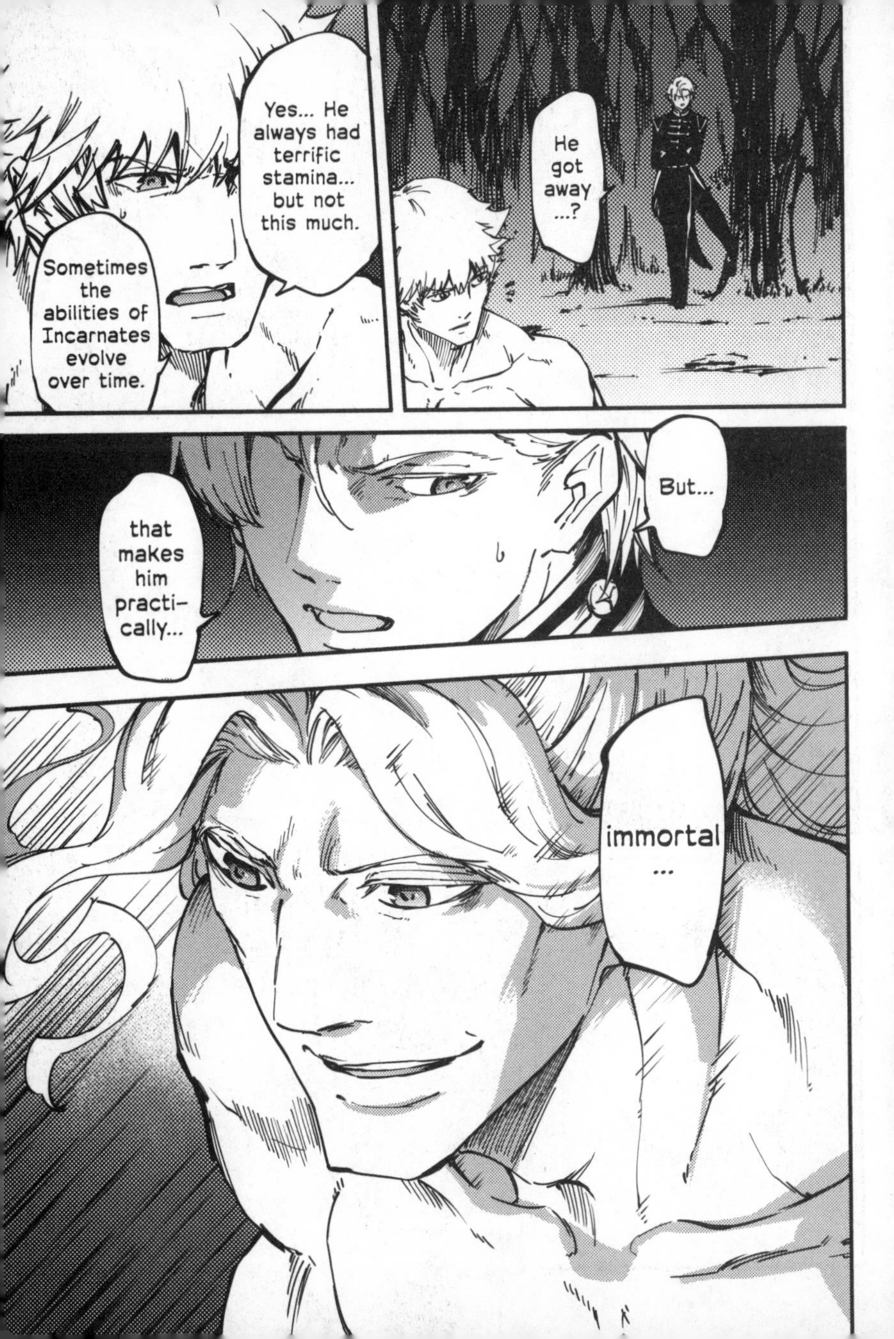
He got away ...?
Yes... He always had terrific stamina... but not this much.
Sometimes the abilities of Incarnates evolve over time.
But...
that makes him practi- cally...
immortal ...

To the Abandoned
Sacred Beasts

Chapter 25: Immortal Beast (Pt. 2)

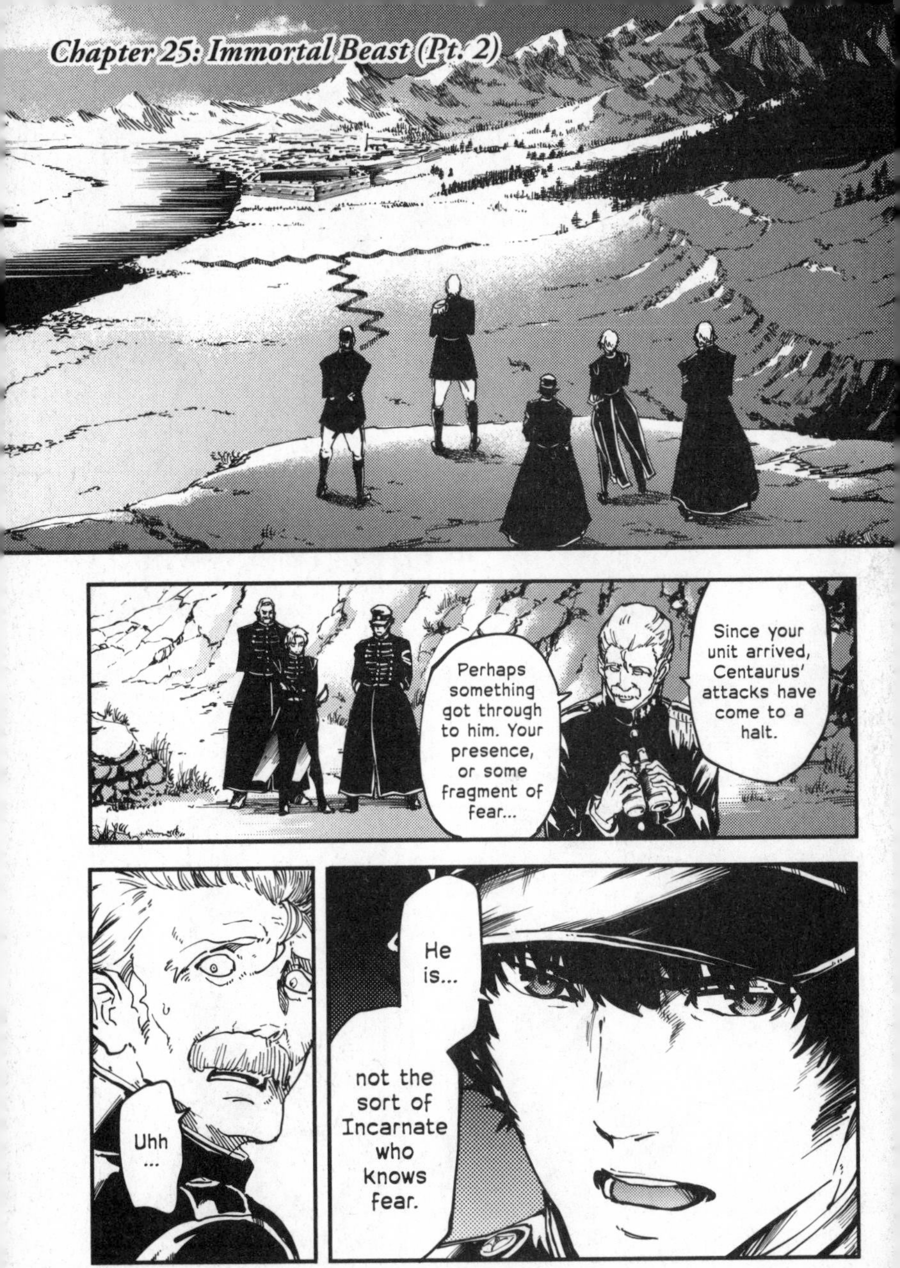
Since your unit arrived, Centaurus' attacks have come to a halt.
Perhaps something got through to him. Your presence, or some fragment of fear...
He is...
not the sort of Incarnate who knows fear.
Uhh ...

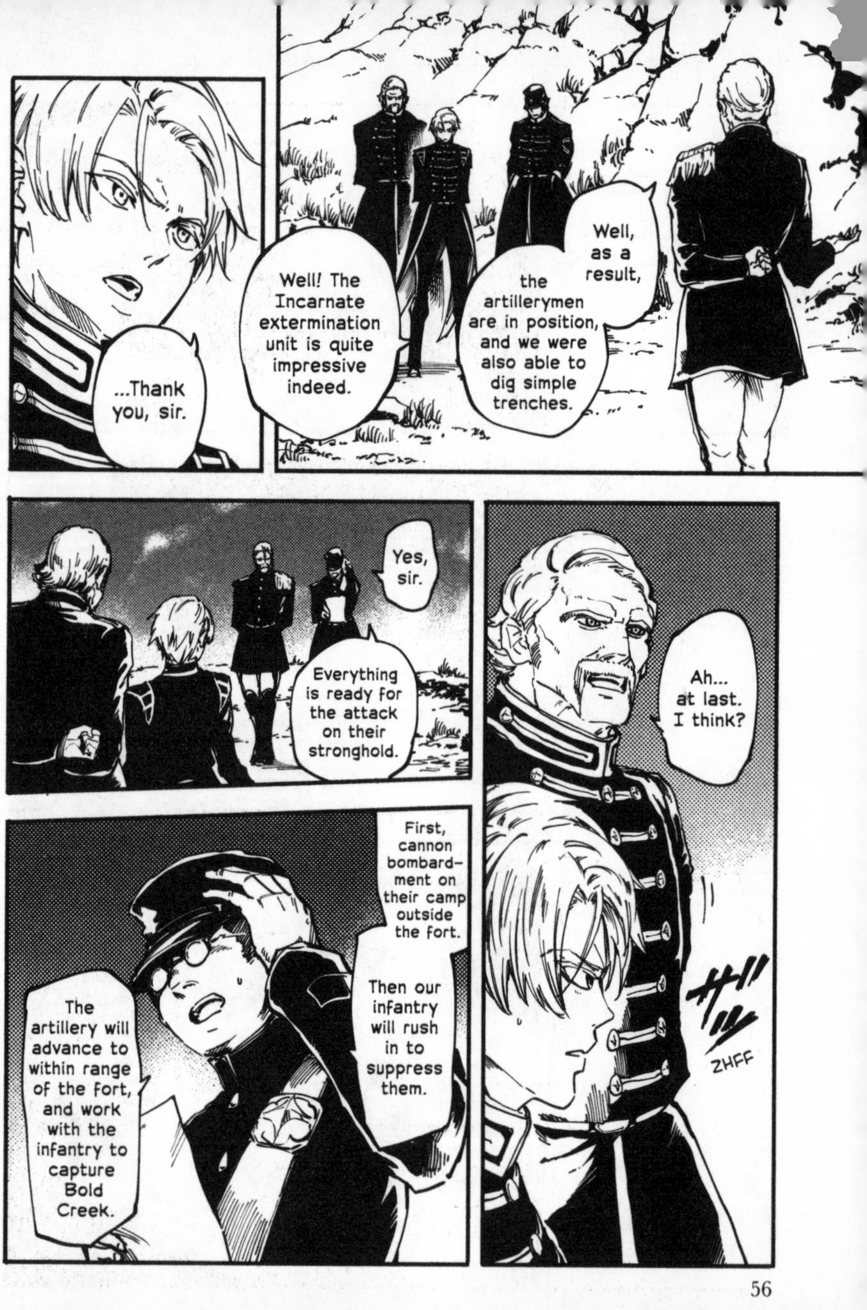
Well, as a result, the artillerymen are in position, and we were also able to dig simple trenches.
Well! The Incarnate extermination unit is quite impressive indeed.
...Thank you, sir.
Ah... at last. I think?
ZHFF
Yes, sir.
Everything is ready for the attack on their stronghold.
First, cannon bombard-ment on their camp outside the fort.
Then our infantry will rush in to suppress them.
The artillery will advance to within range of the fort, and work with the infantry to capture Bold Creek.

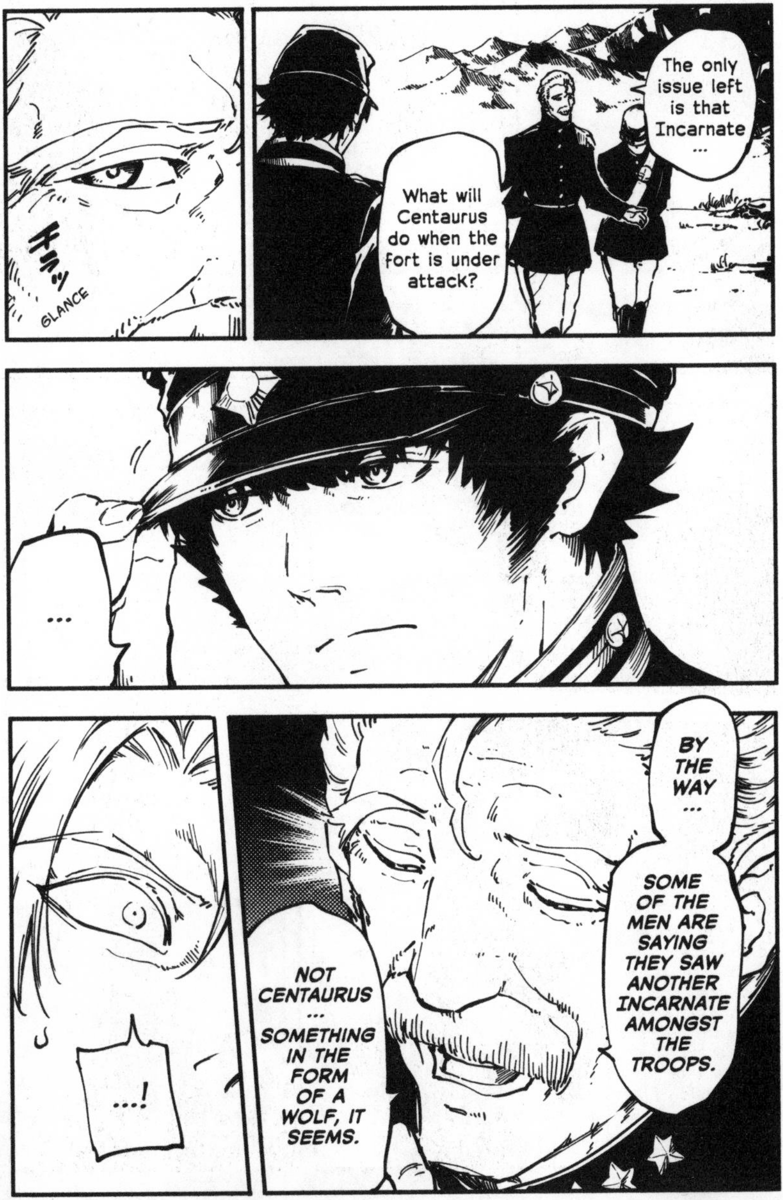
The only issue left is that Incarnate ...
What will Centaurus do when the fort is under attack?
チラッ
GLANCE
...
BY THE WAY ...
SOME OF THE MEN ARE SAYING THEY SAW ANOTHER INCARNATE AMONGST THE TROOPS.
NOT CENTAURUS ... SOMETHING IN THE FORM OF A WOLF, IT SEEMS.
...!

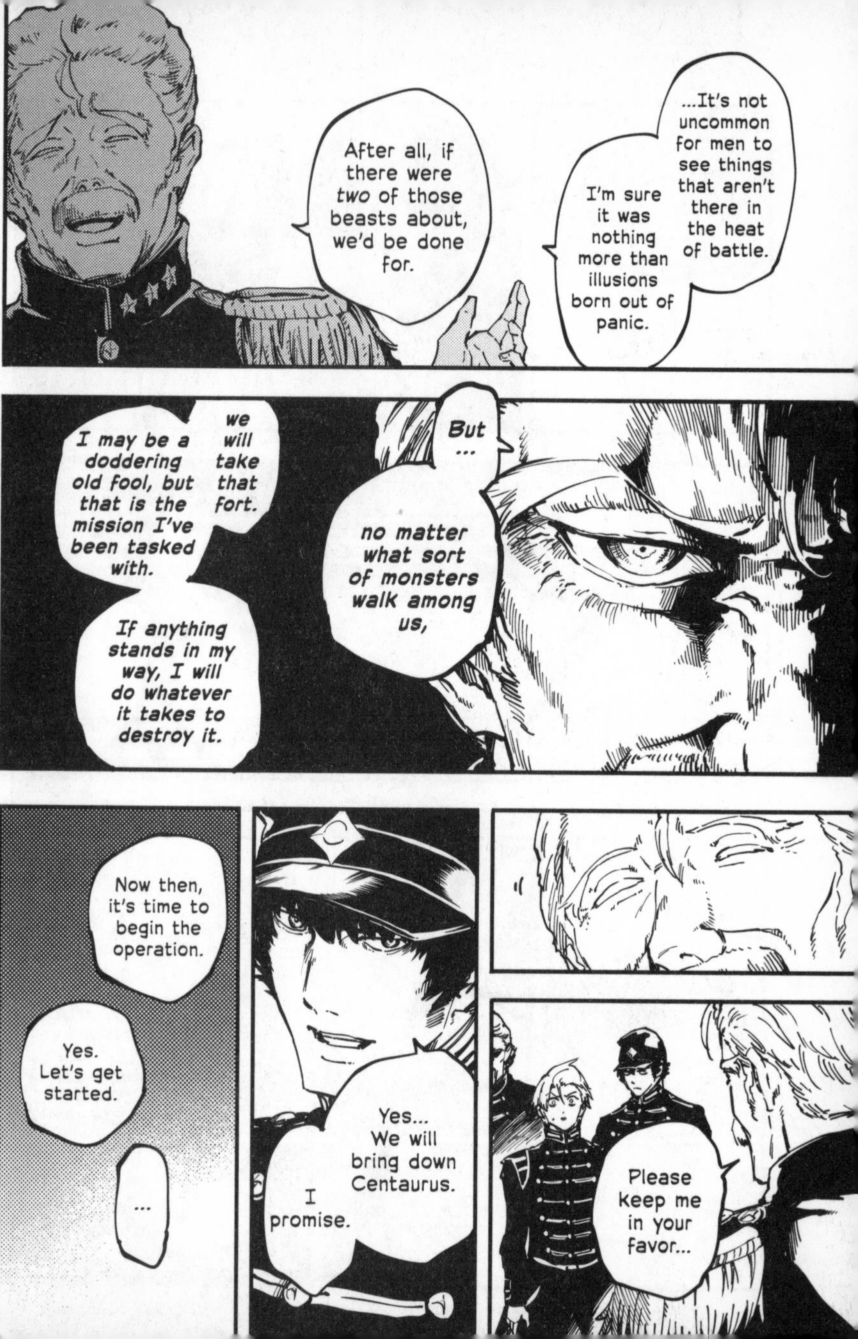
...It's not uncommon for men to see things that aren't there in the heat of battle.
I'm sure it was nothing more than illusions born out of panic.
After all, if there were *two* of those beasts about, we'd be done for.
But...
no matter what sort of monsters walk among us,
we will take that fort.
I may be a doddering old fool, but that is the mission I've been tasked with.
If anything stands in my way, I will do whatever it takes to destroy it.
Please keep me in your favor...
Yes... We will bring down Centaurus.
I promise.
Now then, it's time to begin the operation.
Yes. Let's get started.
...

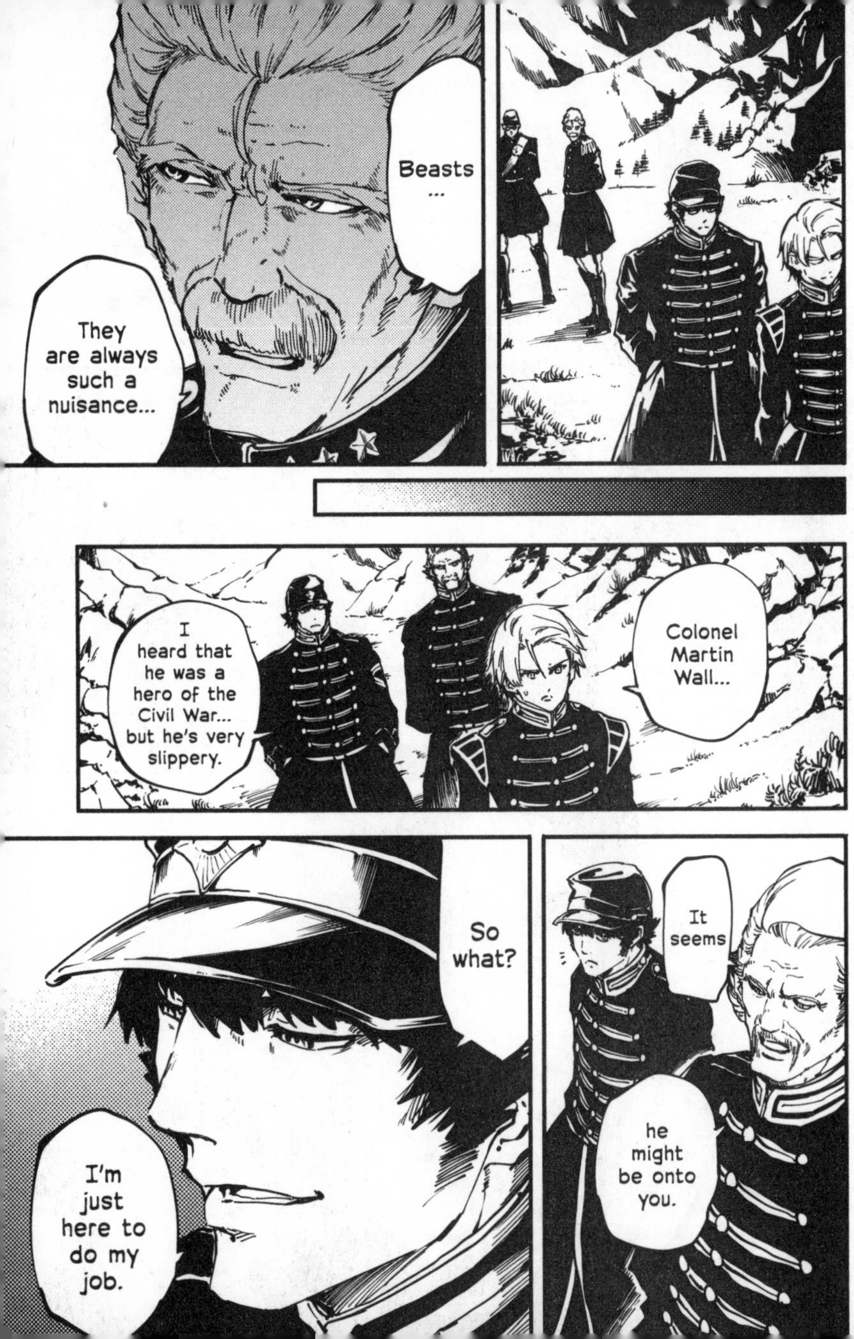
Beasts ...
They are always such a nuisance...
Colonel Martin Wall...
I heard that he was a hero of the Civil War... but he's very slippery.
It seems
he might be onto you.
So what?
I'm just here to do my job.

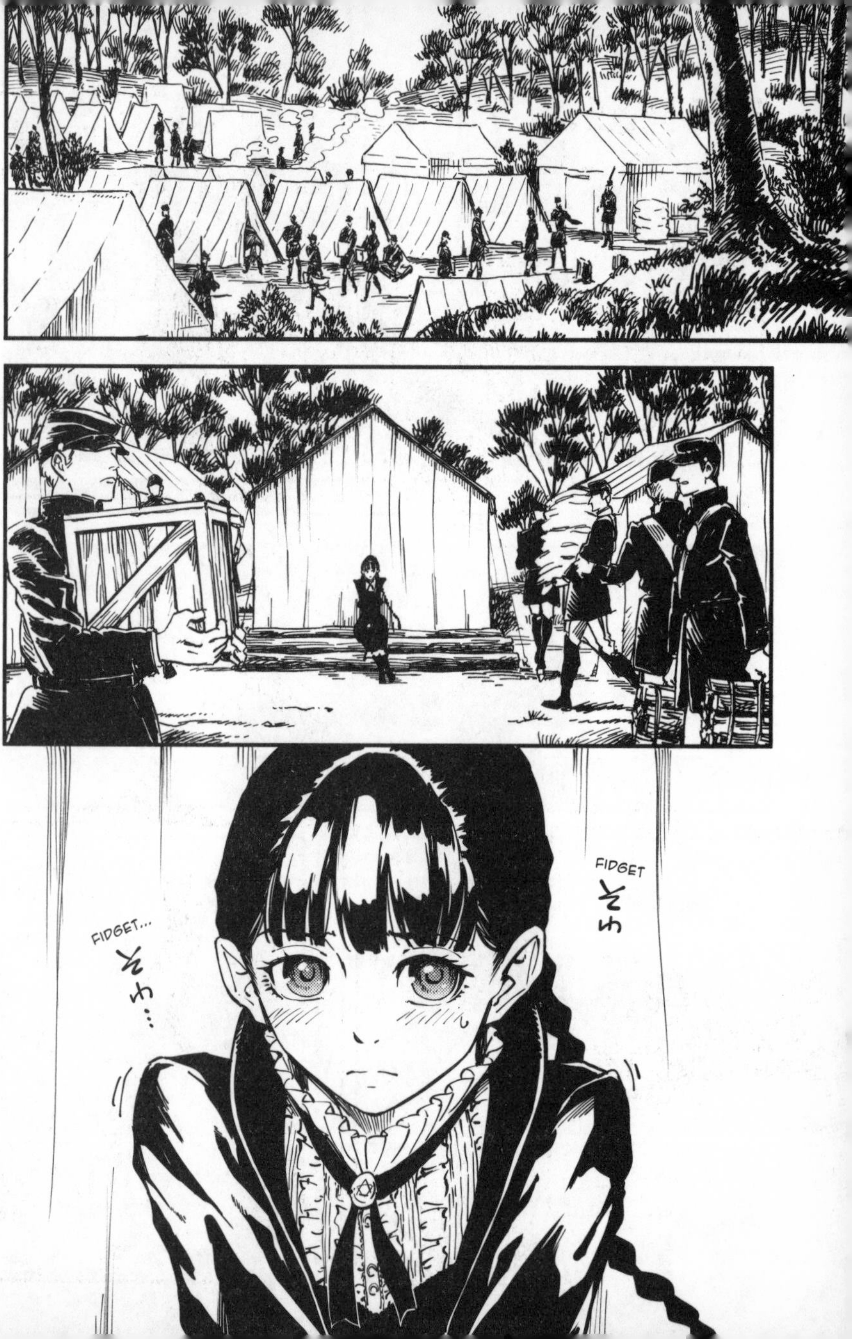
FIDGET
そわ
FIDGET...
そわ...

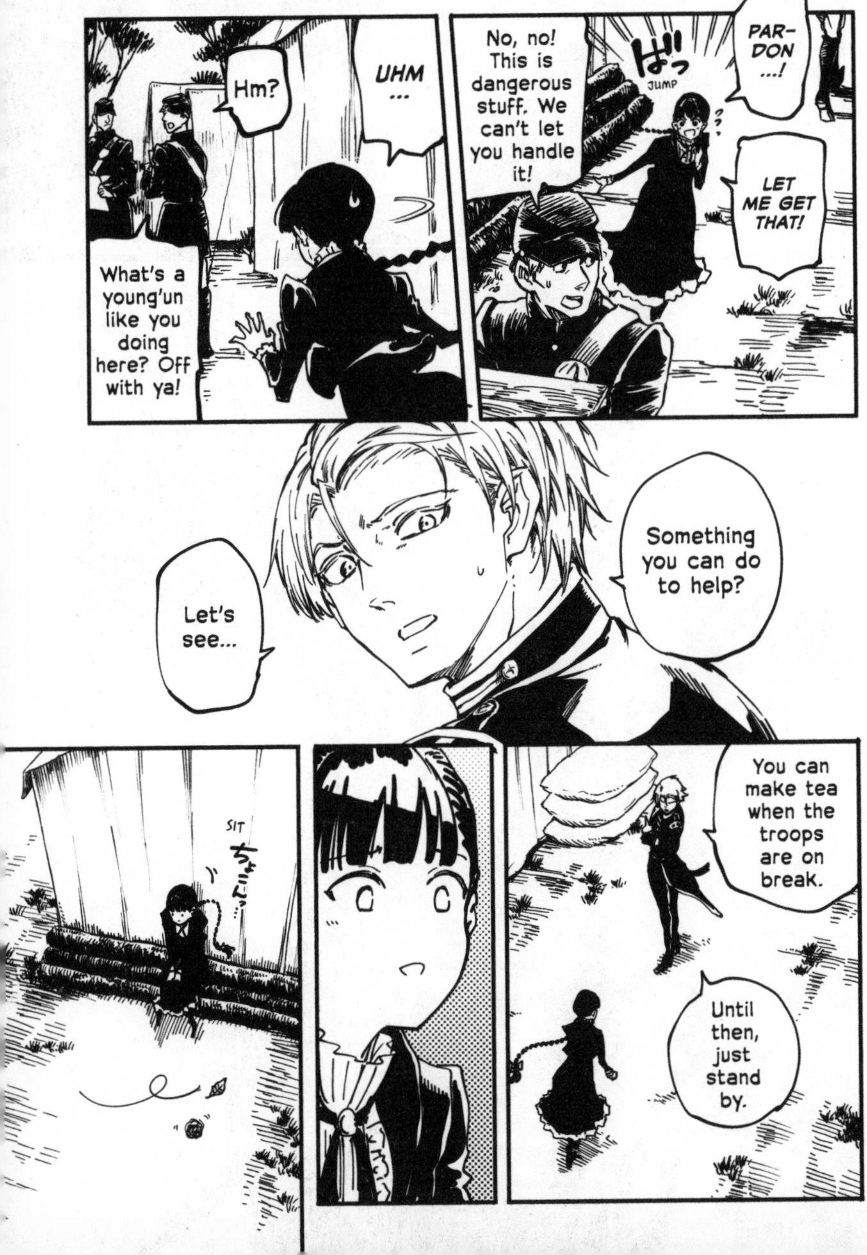
PAR-DON ...!
ぱっ
JUMP
LET ME GET THAT!
No, no! This is dangerous stuff. We can't let you handle it!
UHM ...
Hm?
What's a young'un like you doing here? Off with ya!
Something you can do to help?
Let's see...
You can make tea when the troops are on break.
Until then, just stand by.
SIT
ちょこんっ

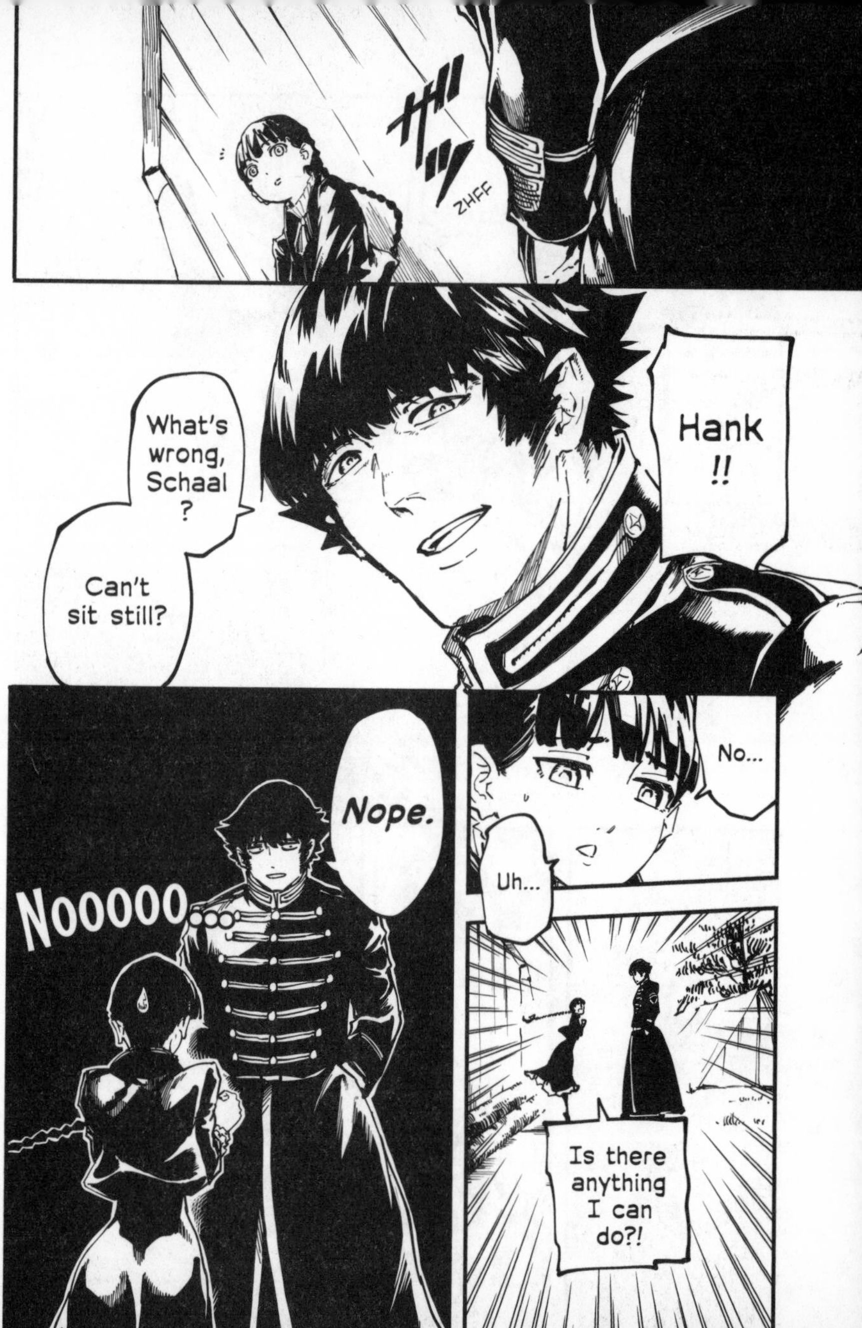
ZHFF
Hank !!
What's wrong, Schaal ?
Can't sit still?
No...
Uh...
Is there anything I can do?!
Nope.
Nooooo...

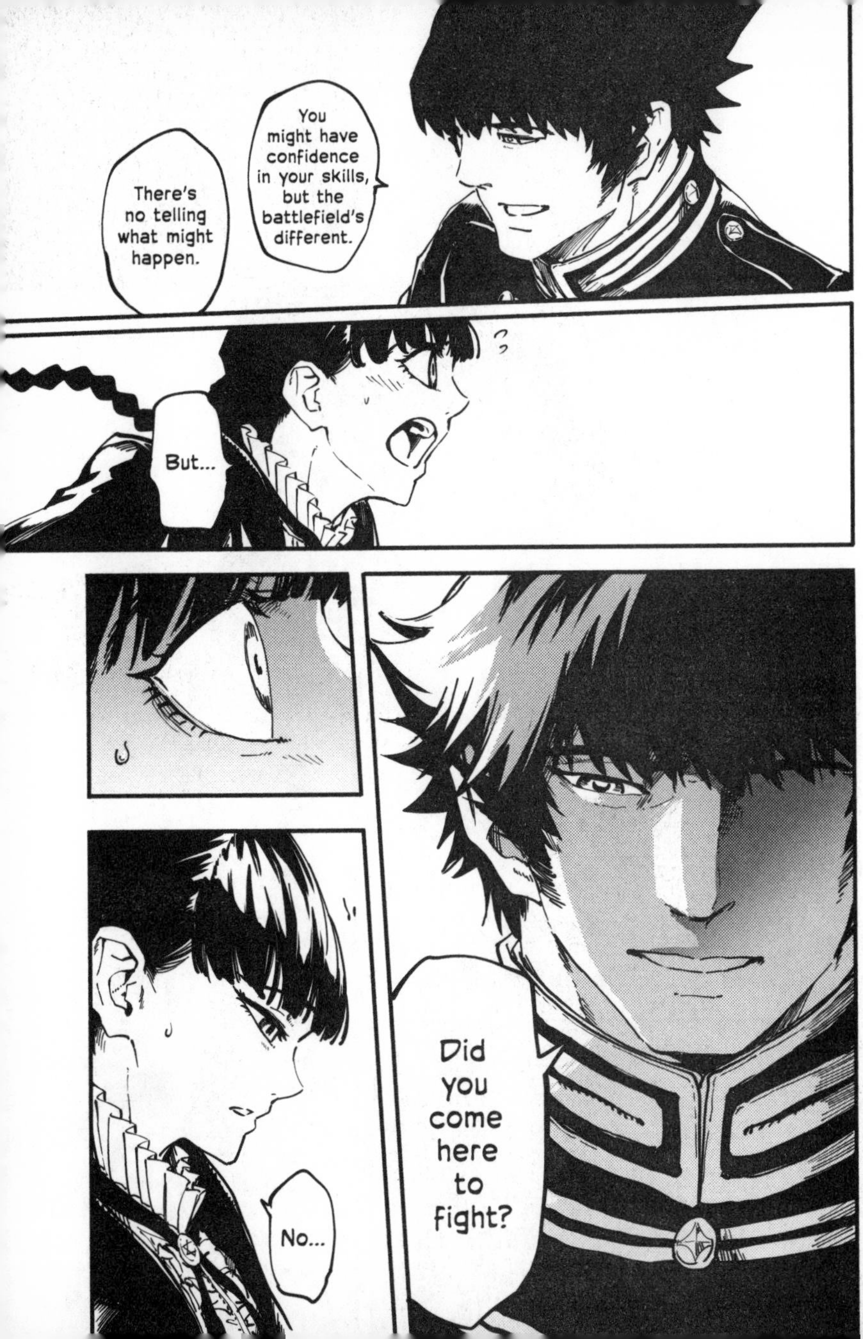
You might have confidence in your skills, but the battlefield's different.
There's no telling what might happen.
But...
Did you come here to fight?
No...

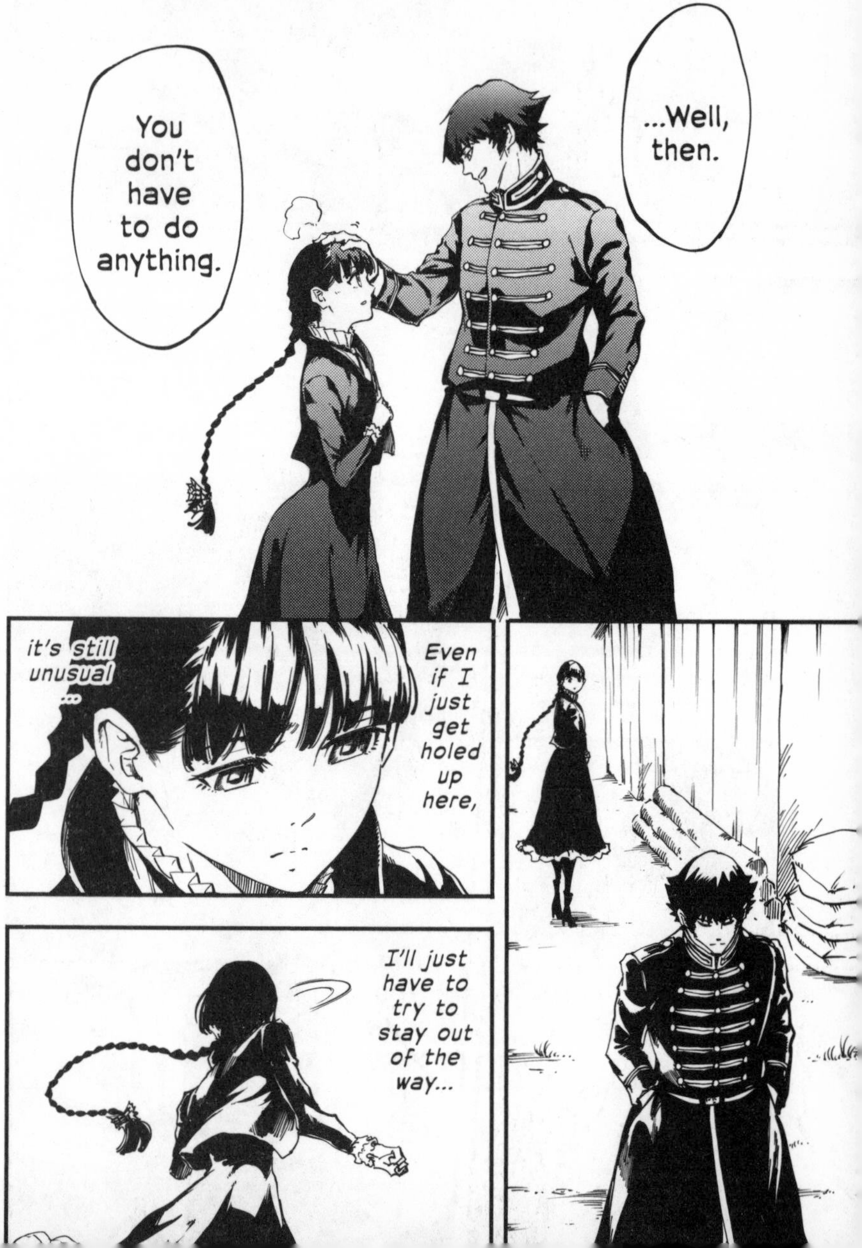
...Well, then.
You don't have to do anything.
Even if I just get holed up here,
it's still unusual...
I'll just have to try to stay out of the way...

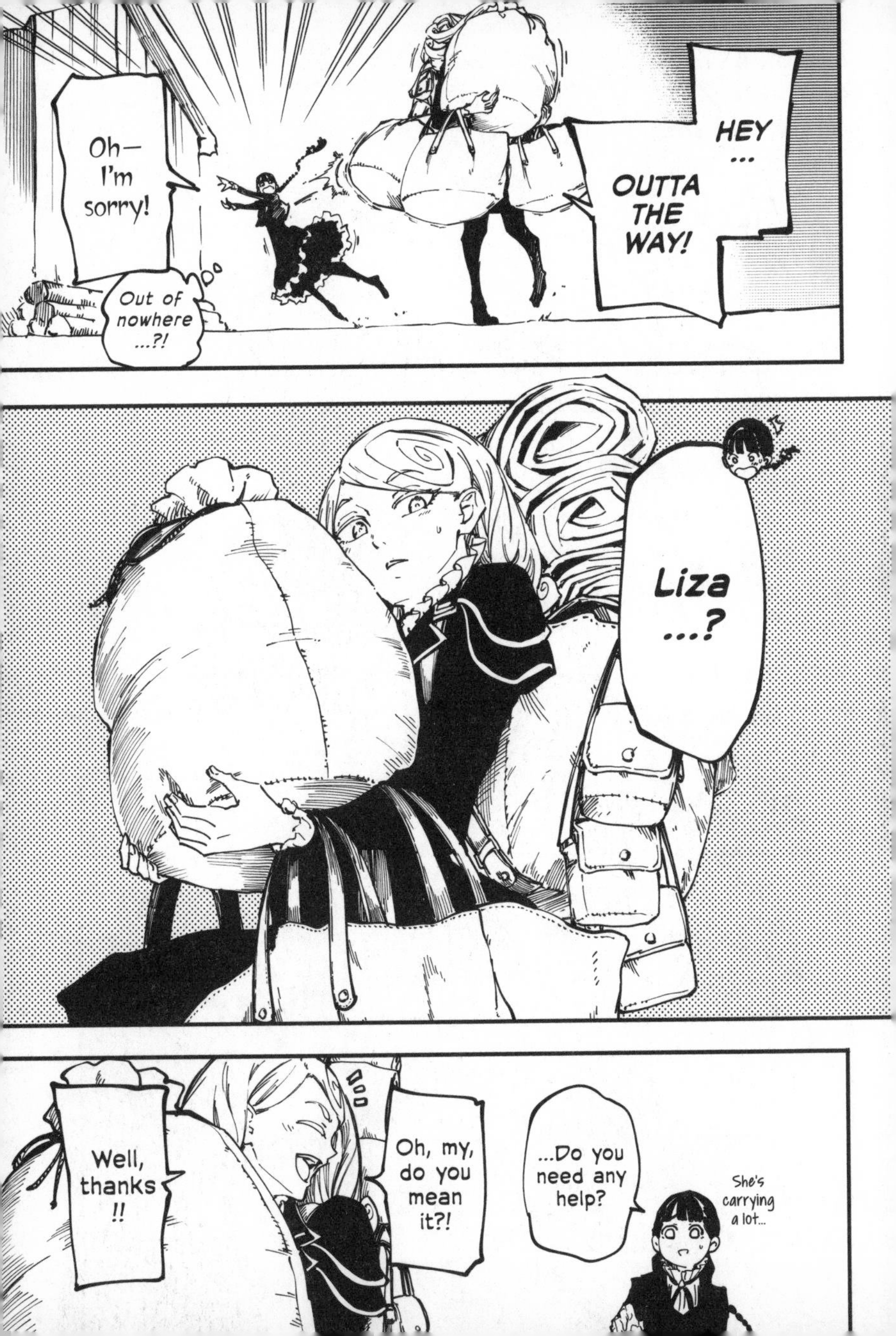
HEY ... OUTTA THE WAY!
Oh— I'm sorry!
Out of nowhere ...?!
Liza ...?
She's carrying a lot...
...Do you need any help?
Oh, my, do you mean it?!
Well, thanks !!

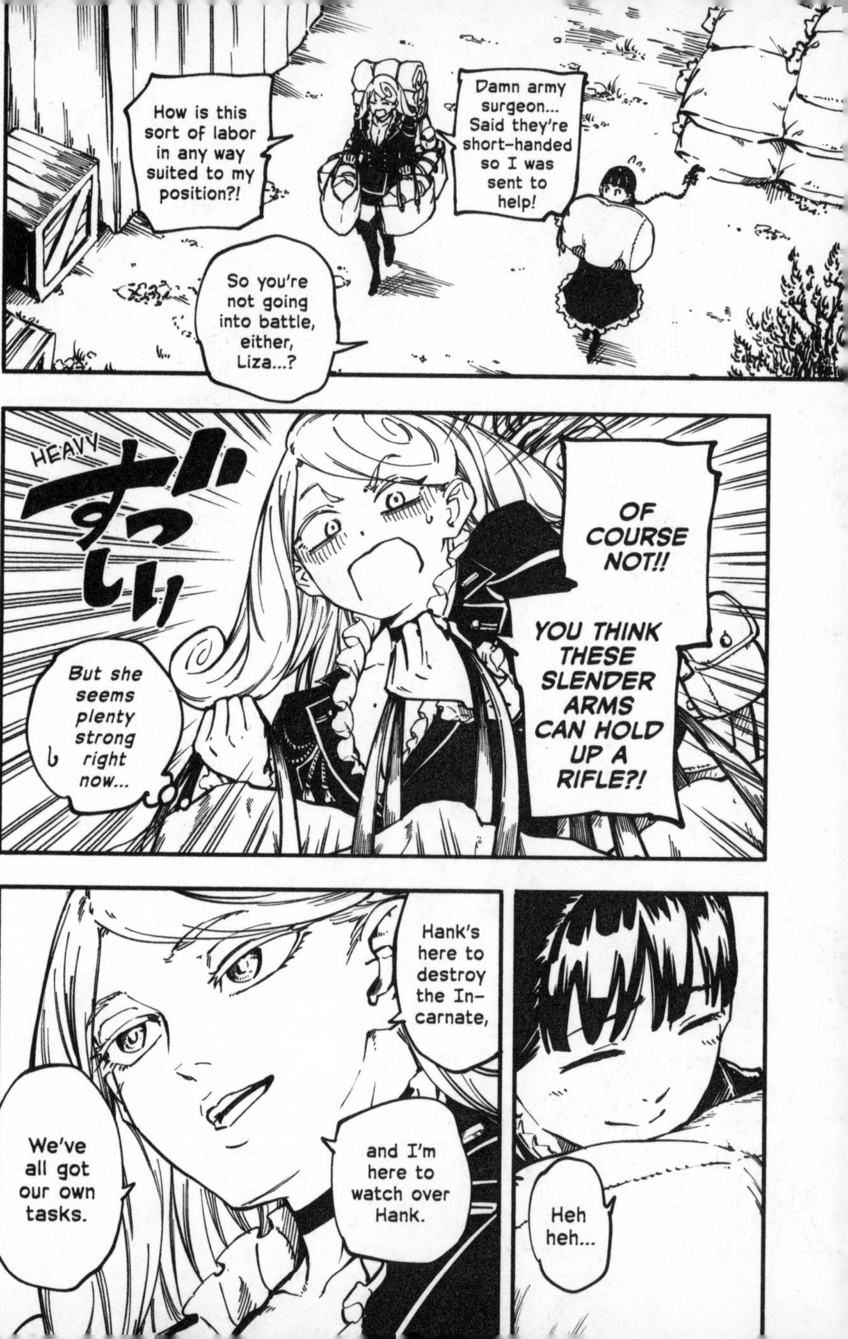
Damn army surgeon... Said they're short-handed so I was sent to help!
How is this sort of labor in any way suited to my position?!
So you're not going into battle, either, Liza...?
OF COURSE NOT!!
YOU THINK THESE SLENDER ARMS CAN HOLD UP A RIFLE?!
HEAVY
But she seems plenty strong right now...
Heh heh...
Hank's here to destroy the In-carnate,
and I'm here to watch over Hank.
We've all got our own tasks.

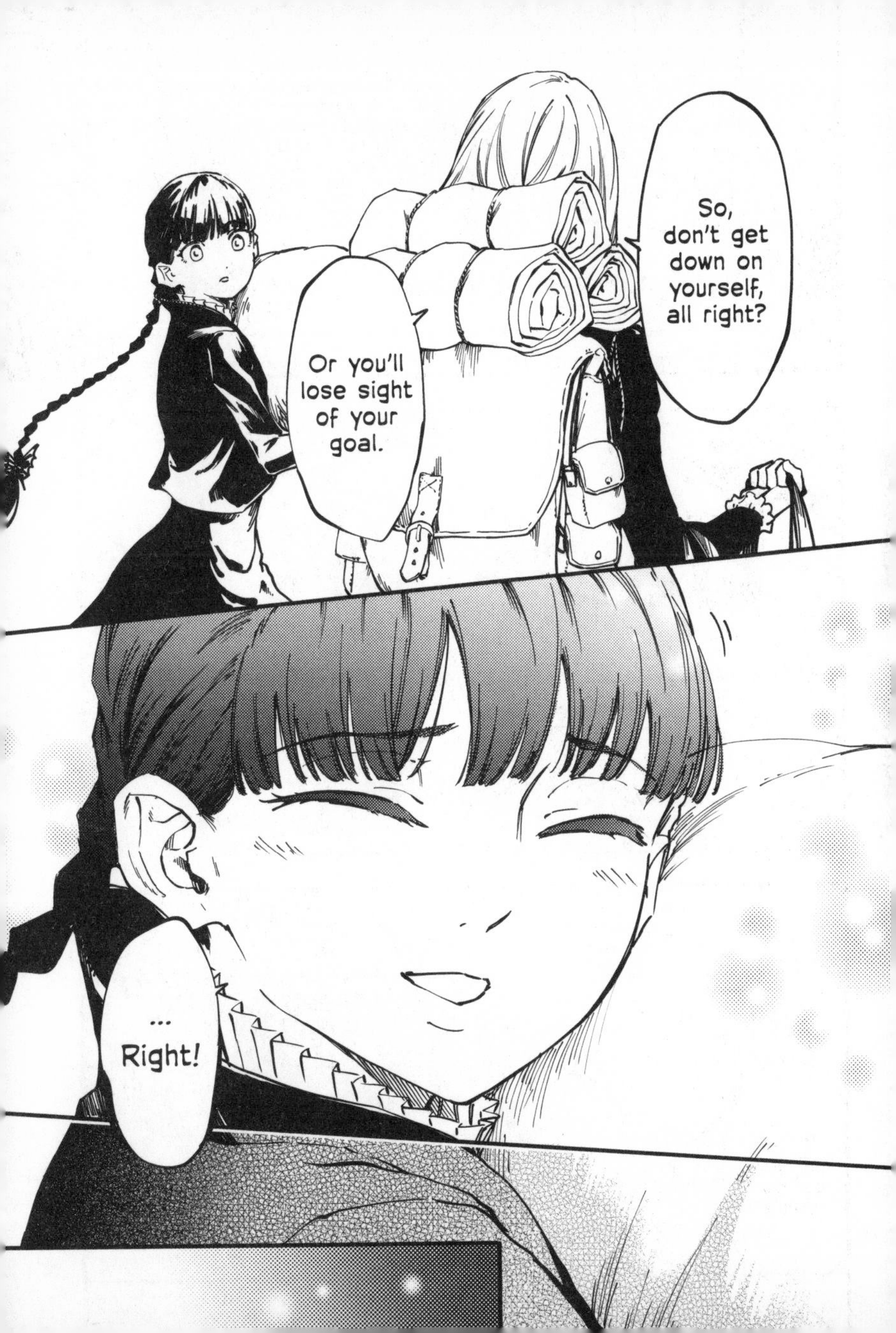
So, don't get down on yourself, all right?
Or you'll lose sight of your goal.
... Right!

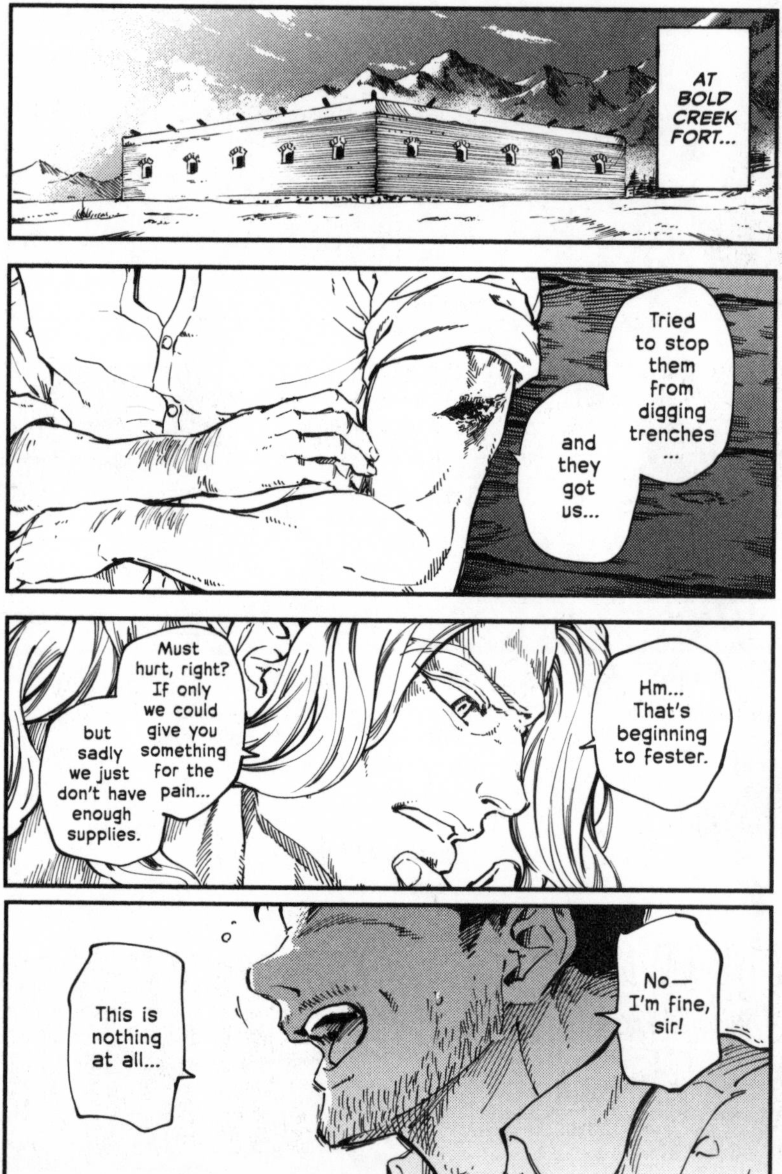
AT BOLD CREEK FORT...
Tried to stop them from digging trenches ...
and they got us...
Hm... That's beginning to fester.
Must hurt, right? If only we could give you something for the pain...
but sadly we just don't have enough supplies.
No— I'm fine, sir!
This is nothing at all...

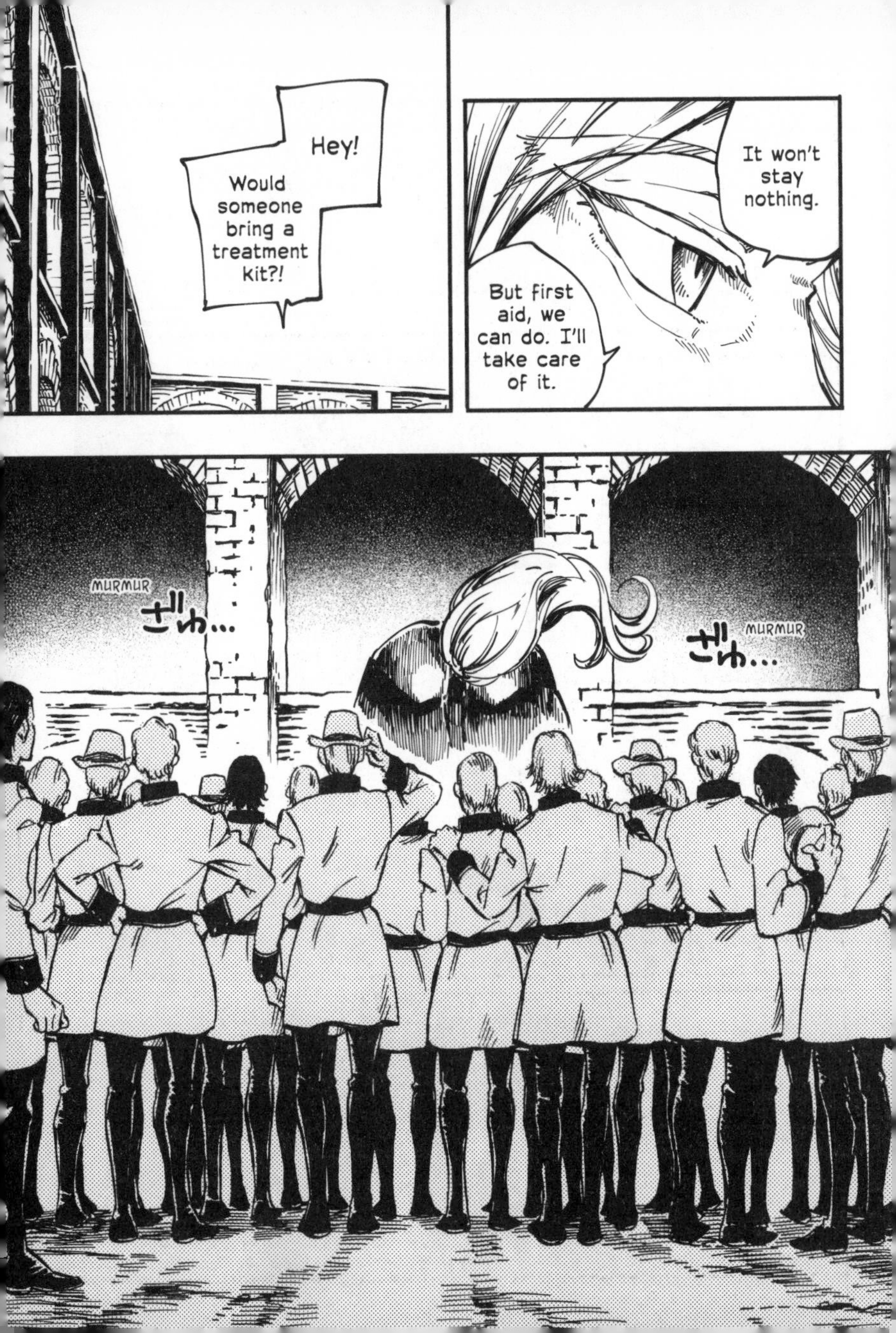
It won't stay nothing.
But first aid, we can do. I'll take care of it.
Hey!
Would someone bring a treatment kit?!
MURMUR
ざわ…
MURMUR
ざわ…

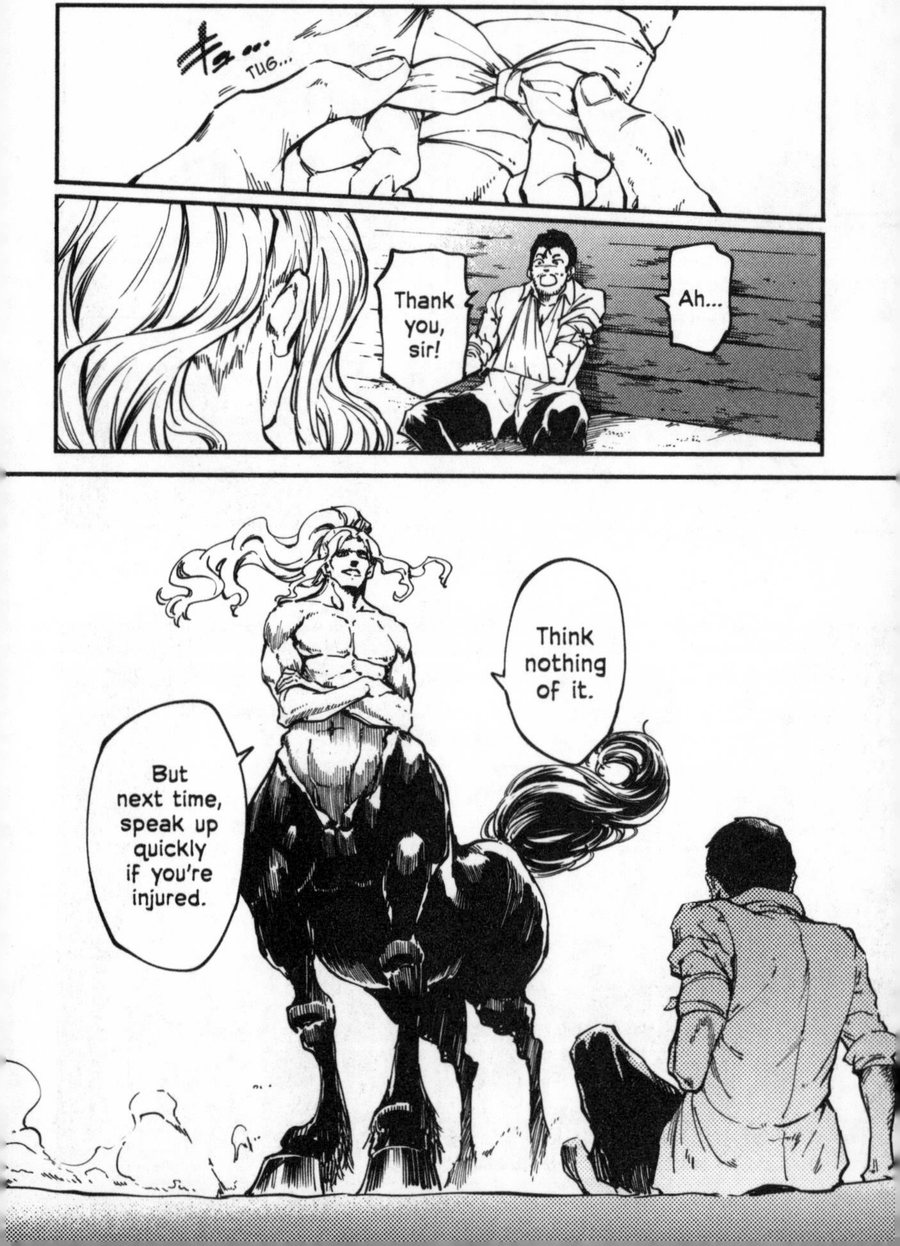
TUG...
Ah...
Thank you, sir!
Think nothing of it.
But next time, speak up quickly if you're injured.

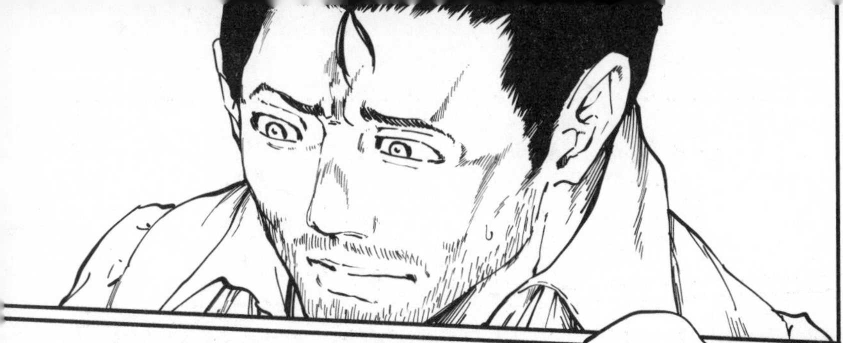

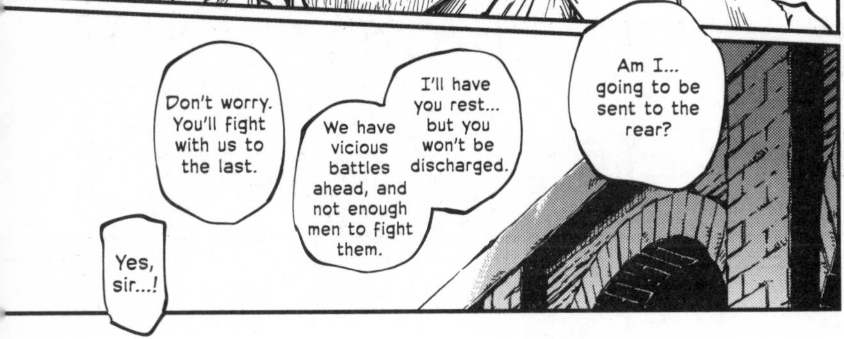
Am I... going to be sent to the rear?
I'll have you rest... but you won't be discharged.
We have vicious battles ahead, and not enough men to fight them.
Don't worry. You'll fight with us to the last.
Yes, sir...!

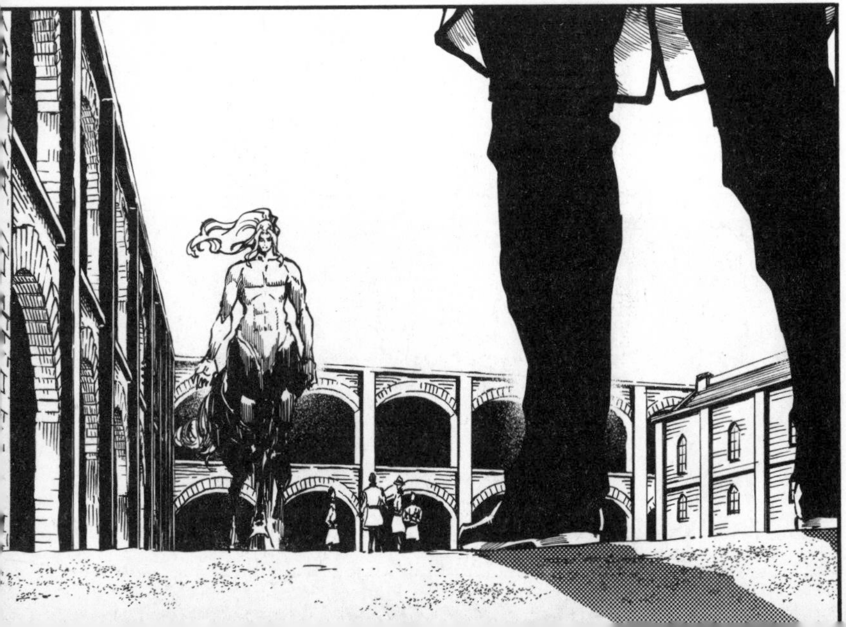

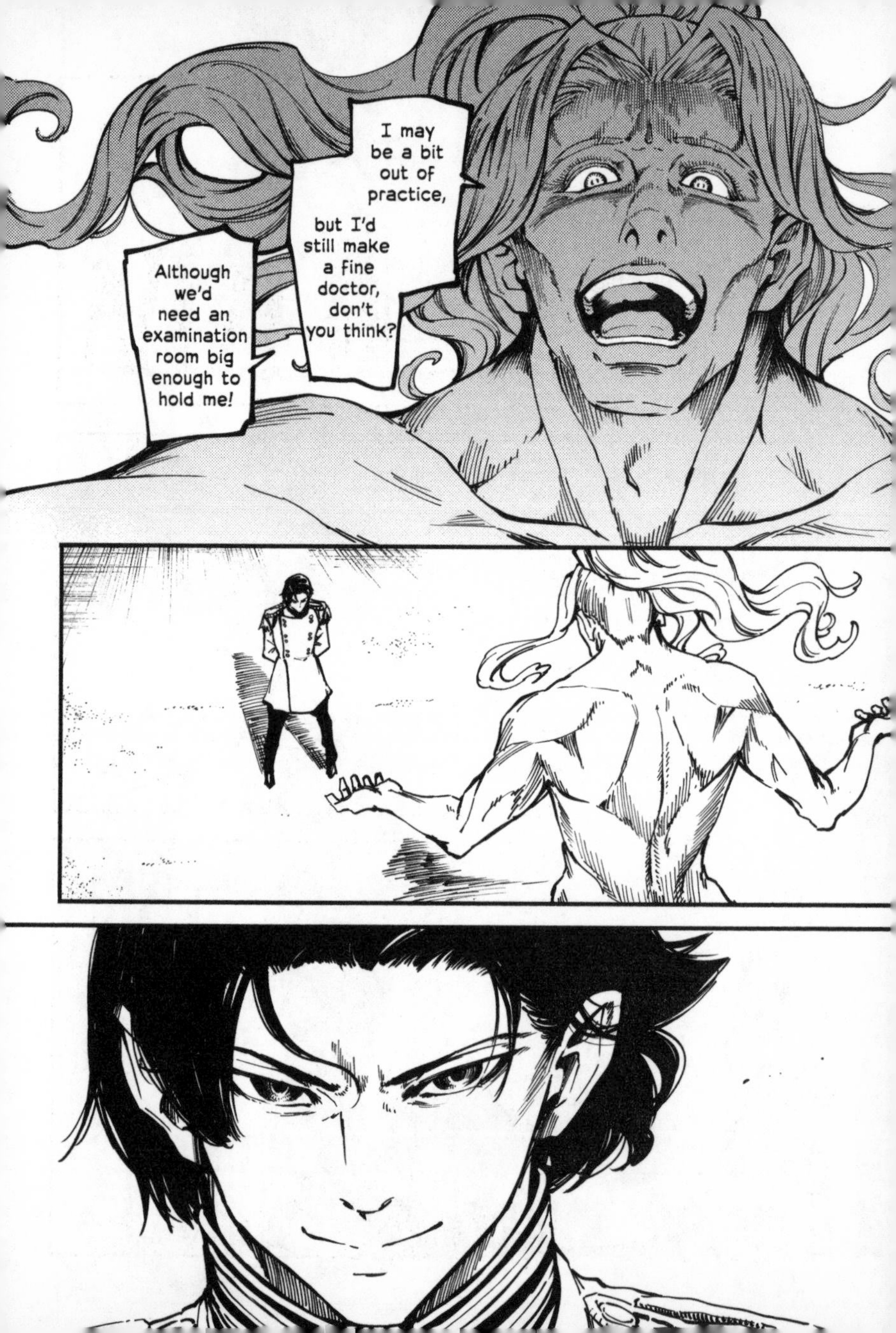
I may be a bit out of practice,
but I'd still make a fine doctor, don't you think?
Although we'd need an examination room big enough to hold me!

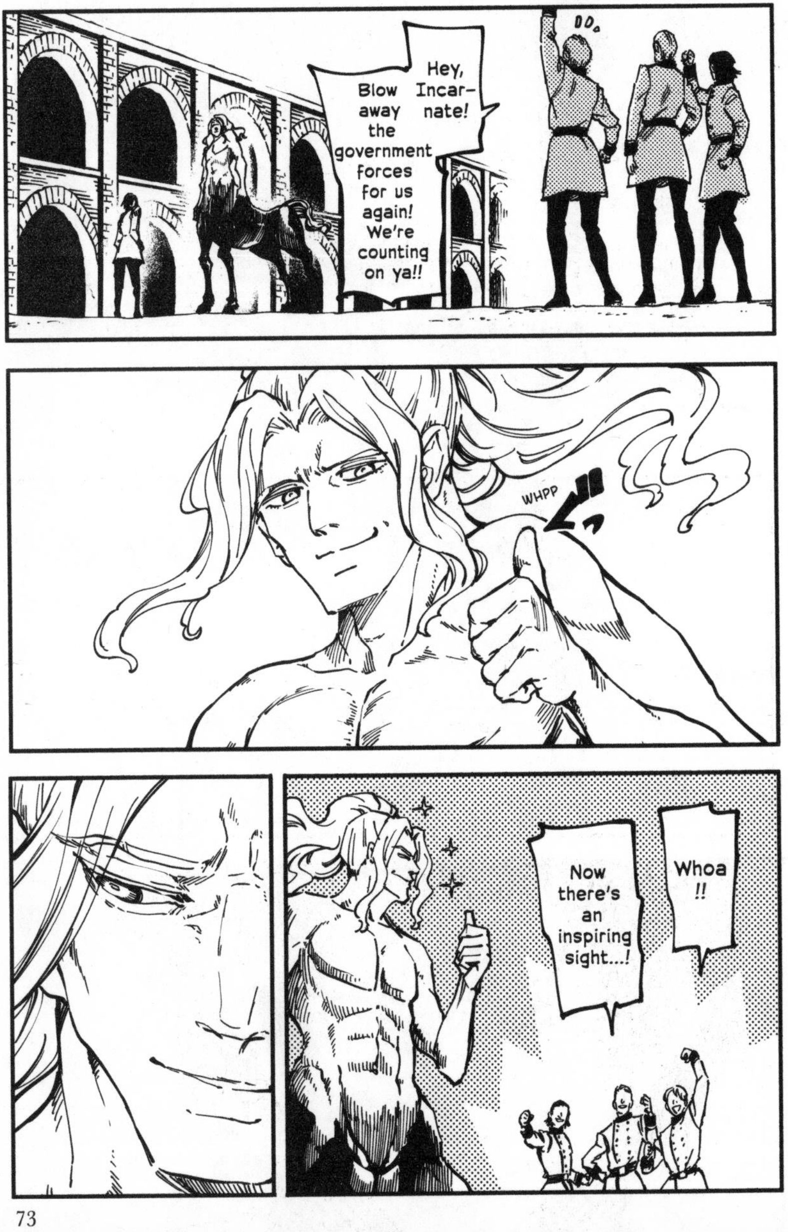
Hey, Incarnate! Blow away the government forces for us again! We're counting on ya!!
WHPP
Whoa !!
Now there's an inspiring sight...!

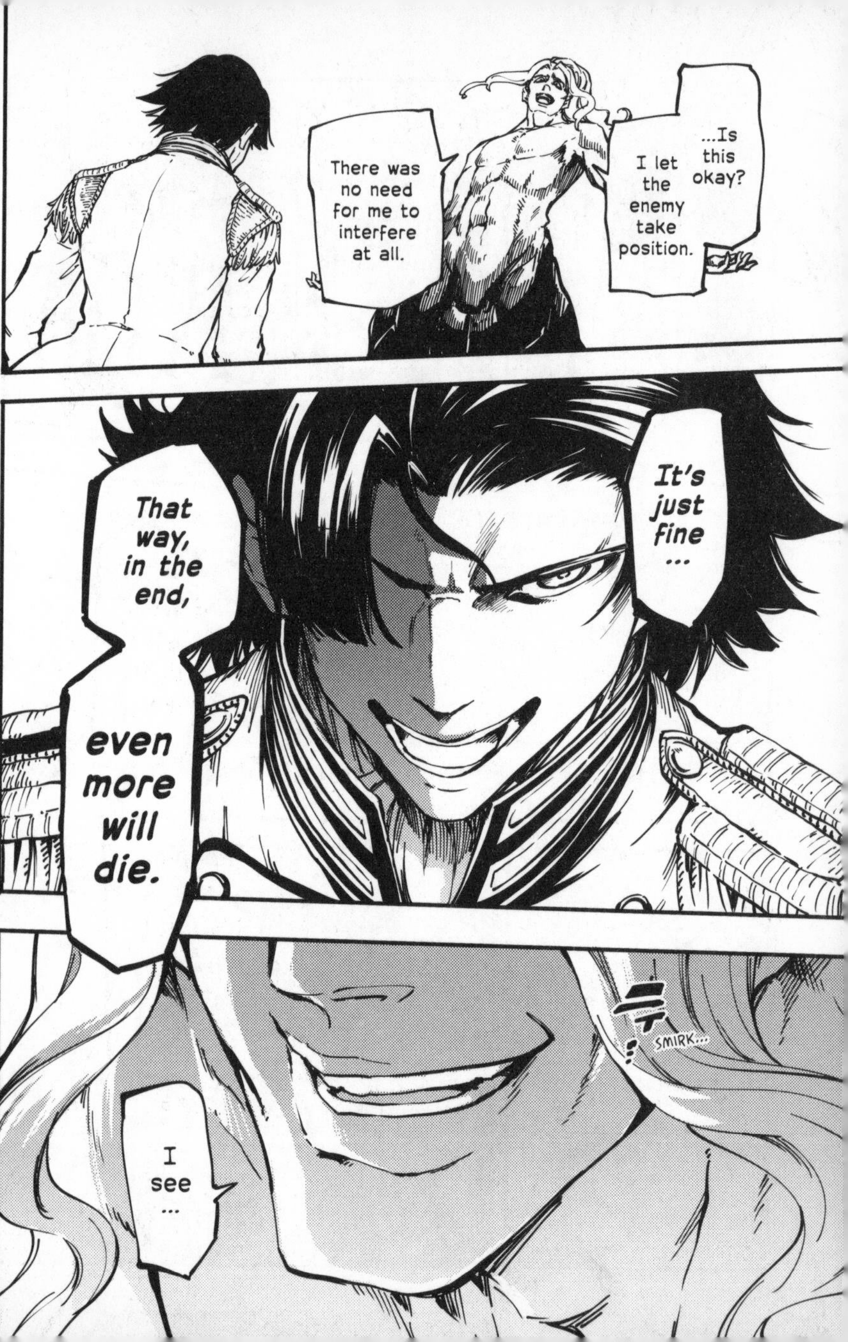
...Is this okay?
I let the enemy take position.
There was no need for me to interfere at all.
It's just fine ...
That way, in the end,
even more will die.
SMIRK...
I see ...

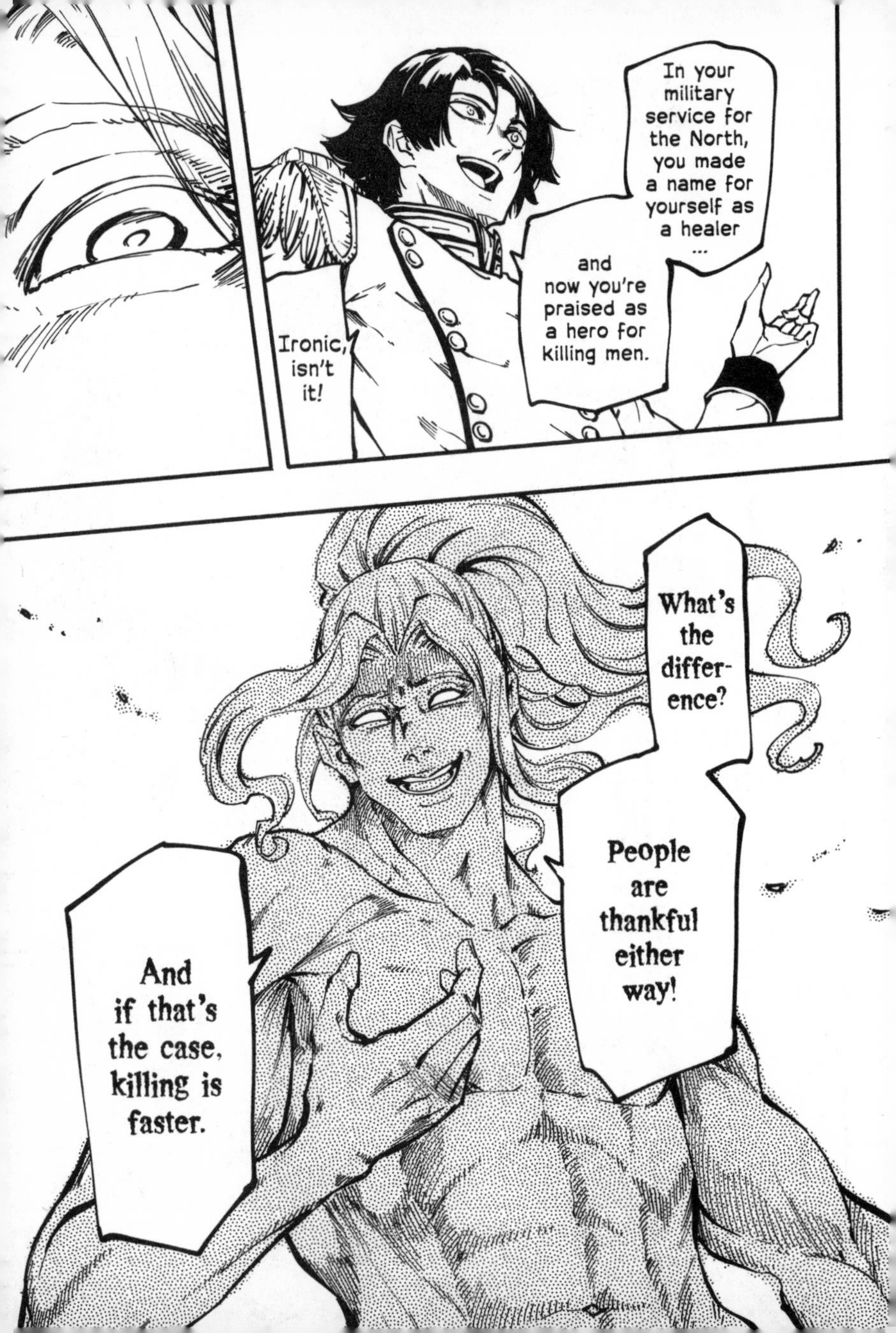
In your military service for the North, you made a name for yourself as a healer ...
and now you're praised as a hero for killing men.
Ironic, isn't it!
What's the differ-ence?
People are thankful either way!
And if that's the case, killing is faster.

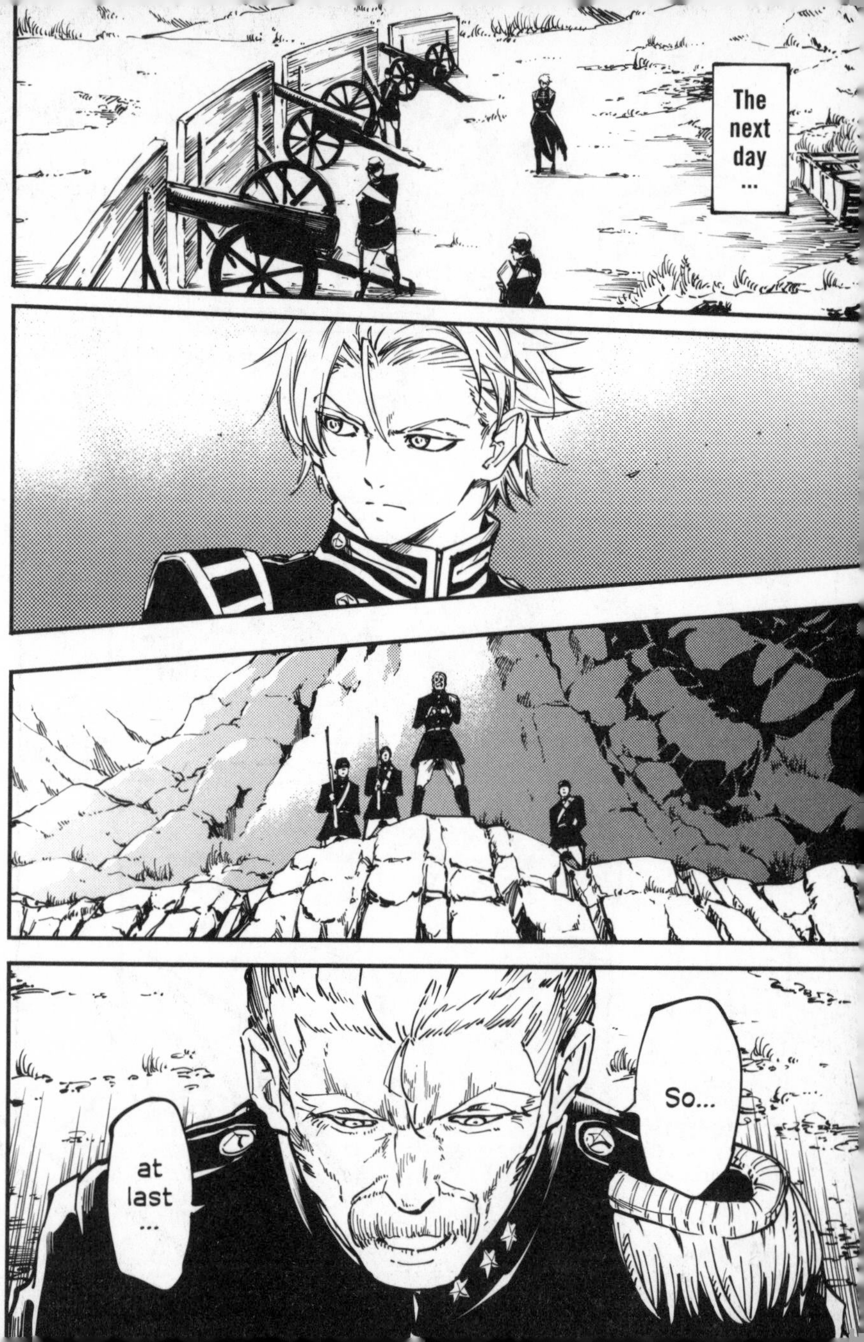
The next day ...
So...
at last ...

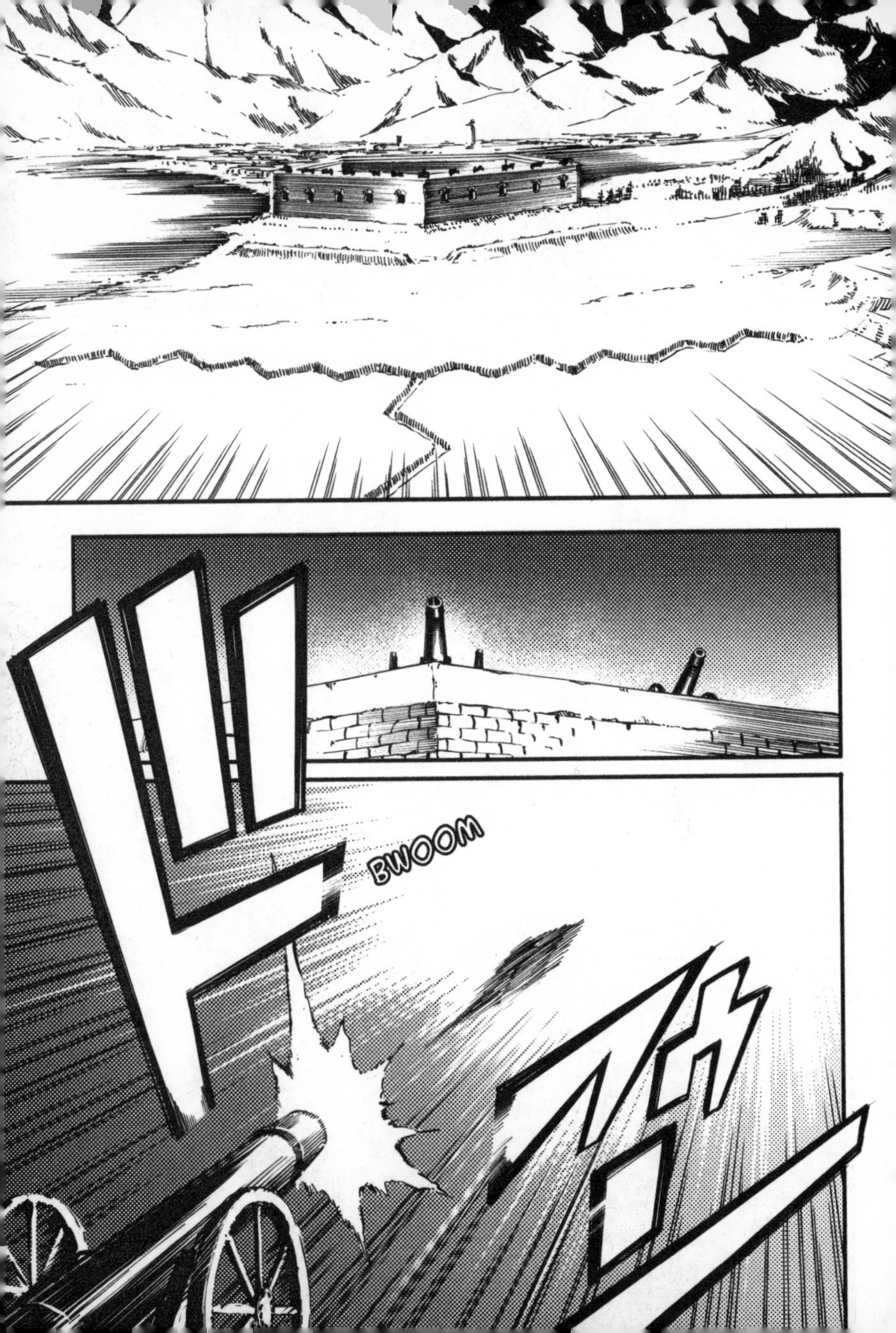
BWOOM

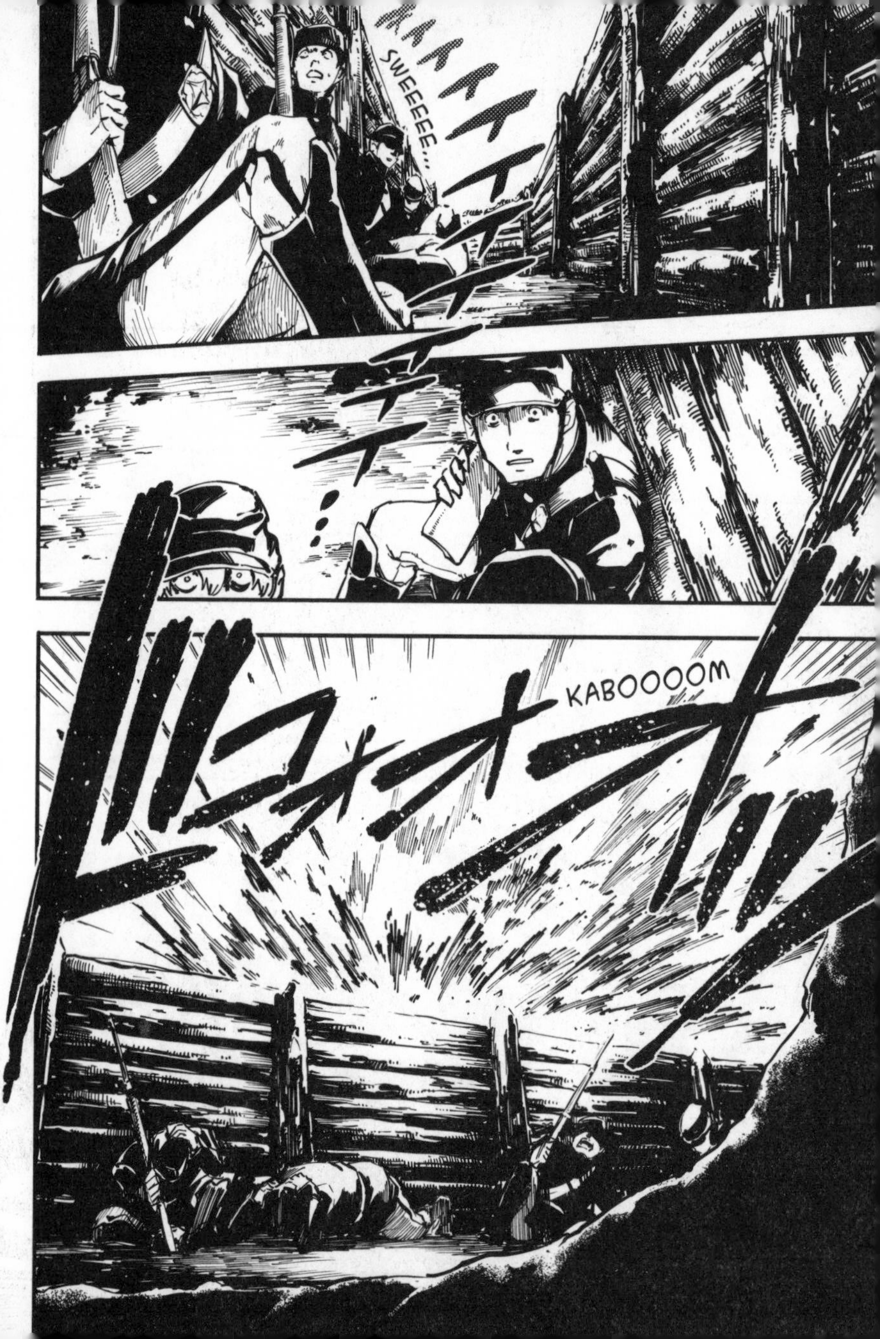
SWEEEEEE...
KABOOOOM

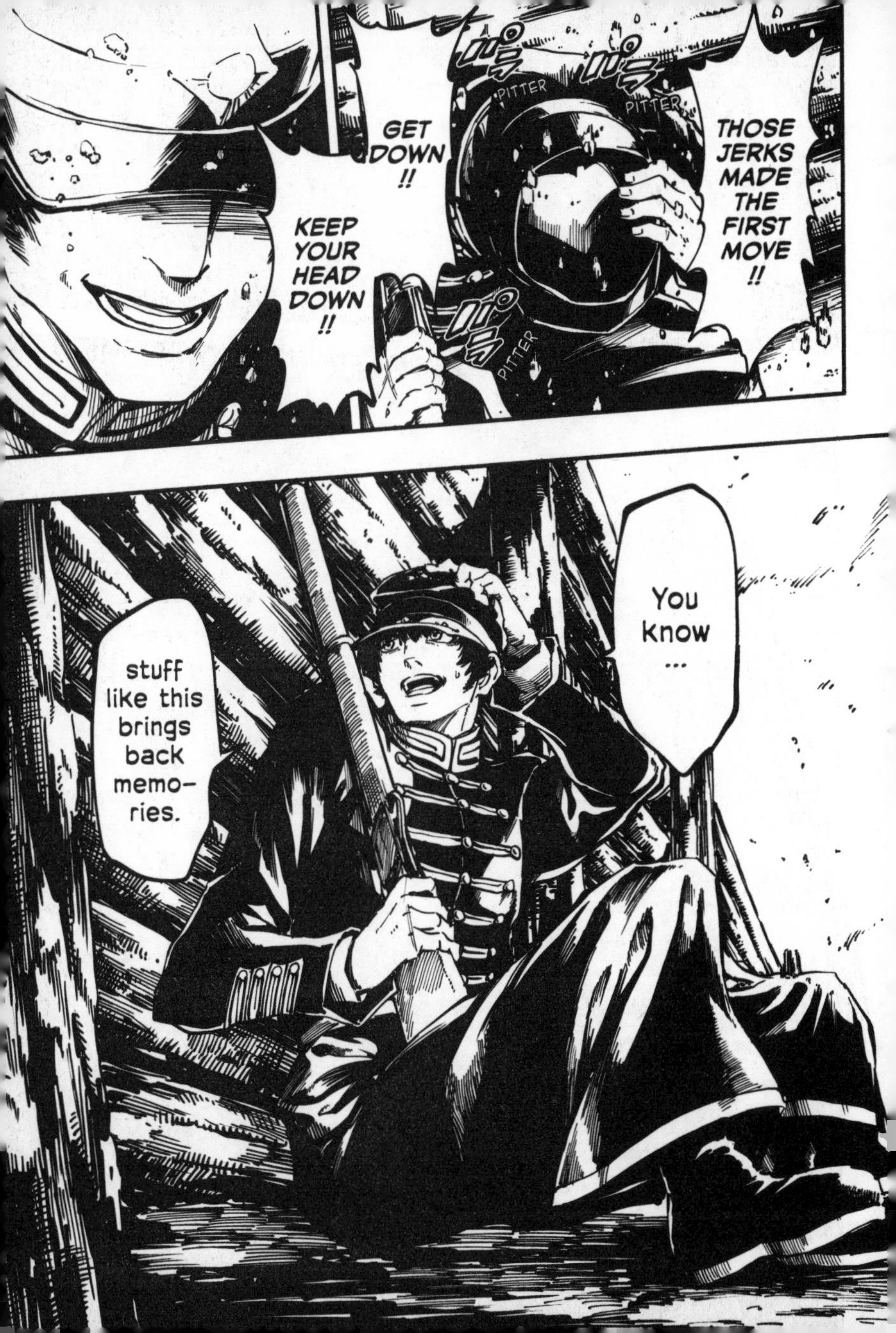
THOSE JERKS MADE THE FIRST MOVE!!
PITTER PITTER
GET DOWN!!
KEEP YOUR HEAD DOWN!!
PITTER
You know...
stuff like this brings back memo-ries.

To the Abandoned
Sacred Beasts

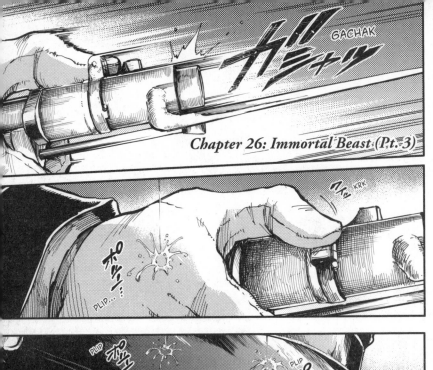

GACHAK

Chapter 26: Immortal Beast (Pt. 3)

KRK

PLIP...

PLIP

PLIP

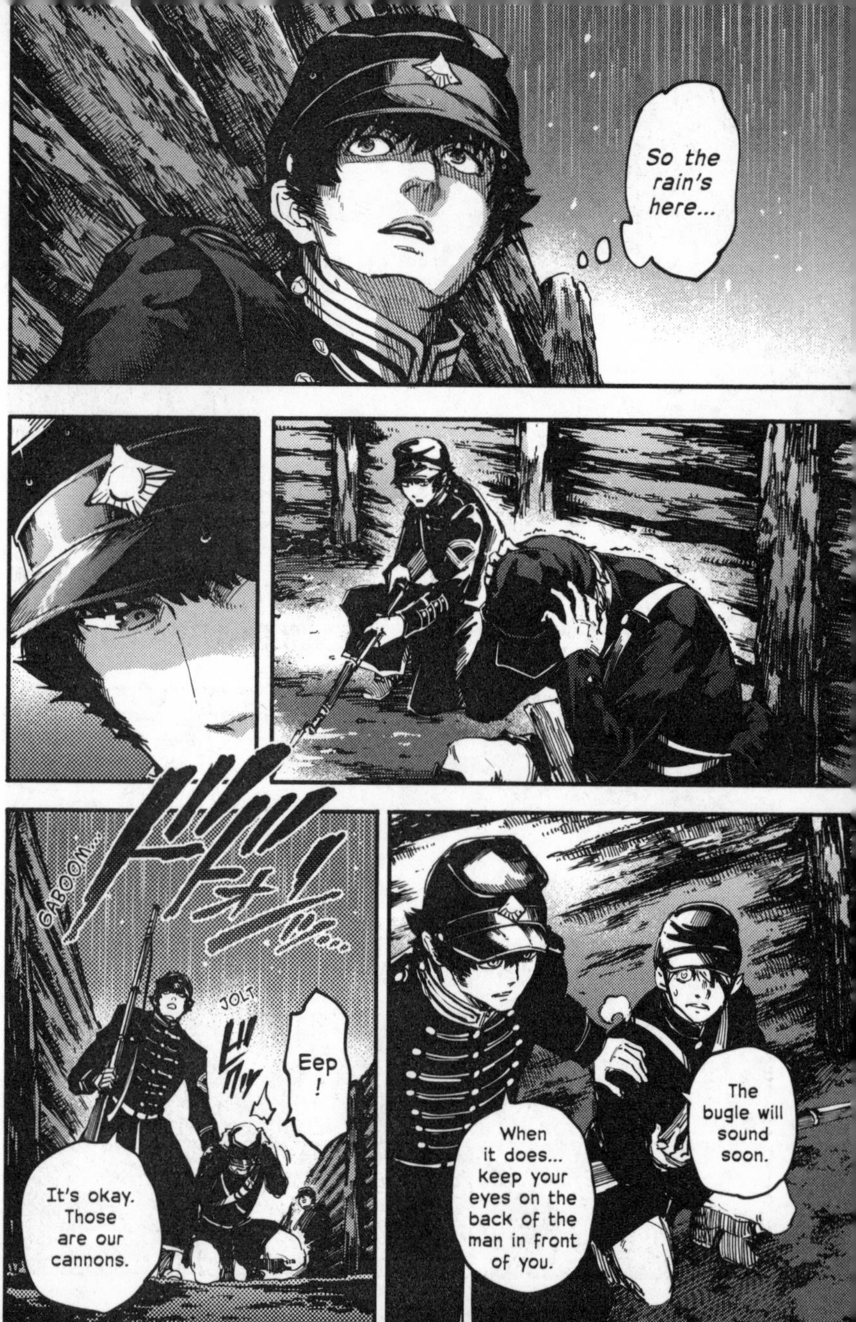
So the rain's here...
The bugle will sound soon.
When it does... keep your eyes on the back of the man in front of you.
GABOOM...
JOLT
Eep!
It's okay. Those are our cannons.

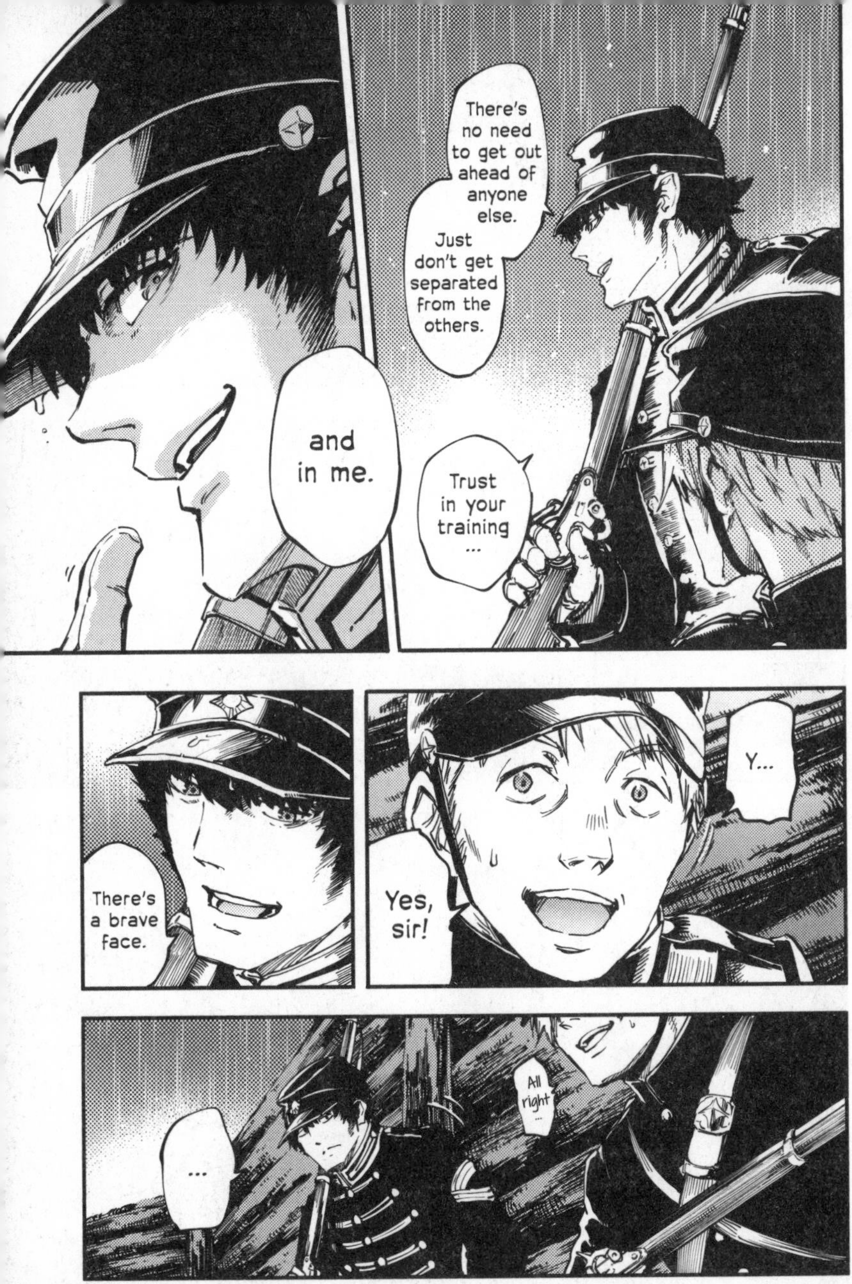
There's no need to get out ahead of anyone else.
Just don't get separated from the others.
Trust in your training ...
and in me.
Y...
Yes, sir!
There's a brave face.
All right ...
...

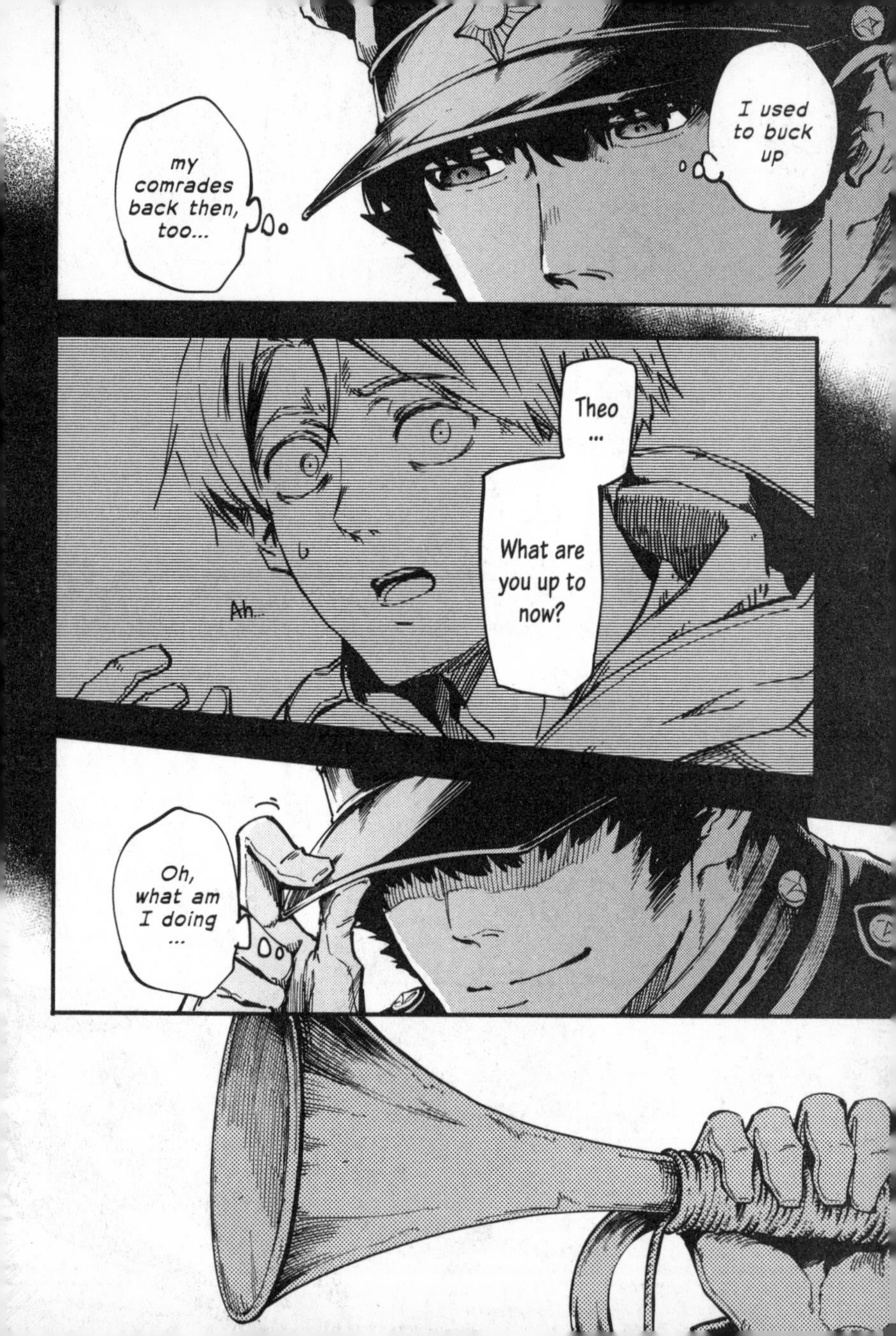
I used to buck up
my comrades back then, too...
Theo ...
What are you up to now?
Ah...
Oh, what am I doing ...

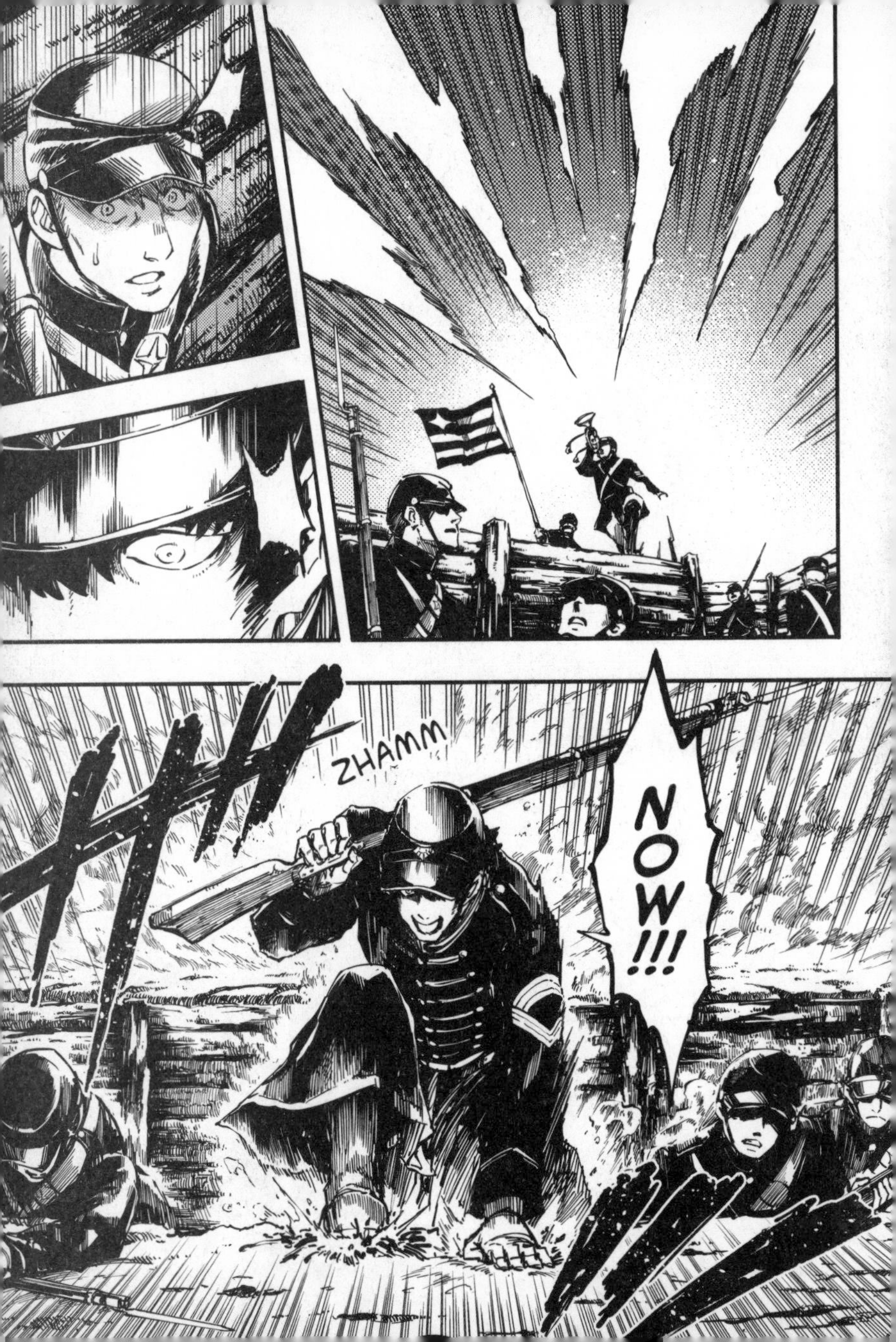
ZHAMM
NOW!!!

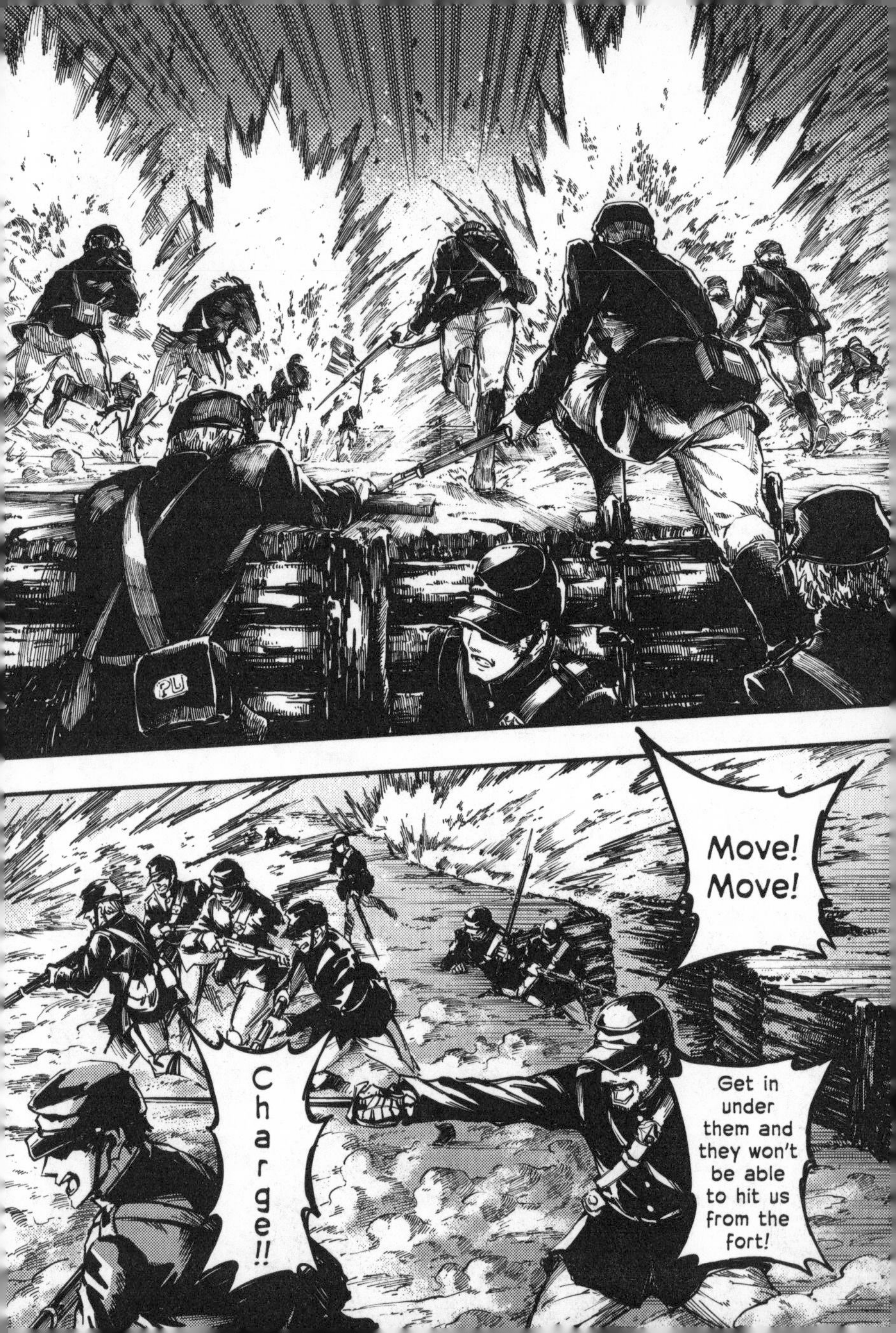
PU
Move! Move!
Get in under them and they won't be able to hit us from the fort!
Charge!!

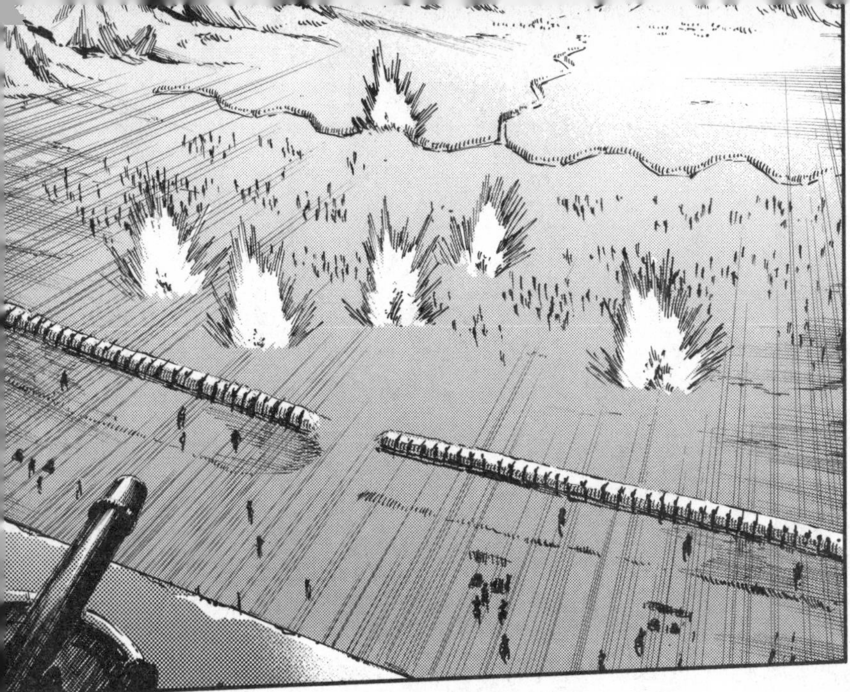

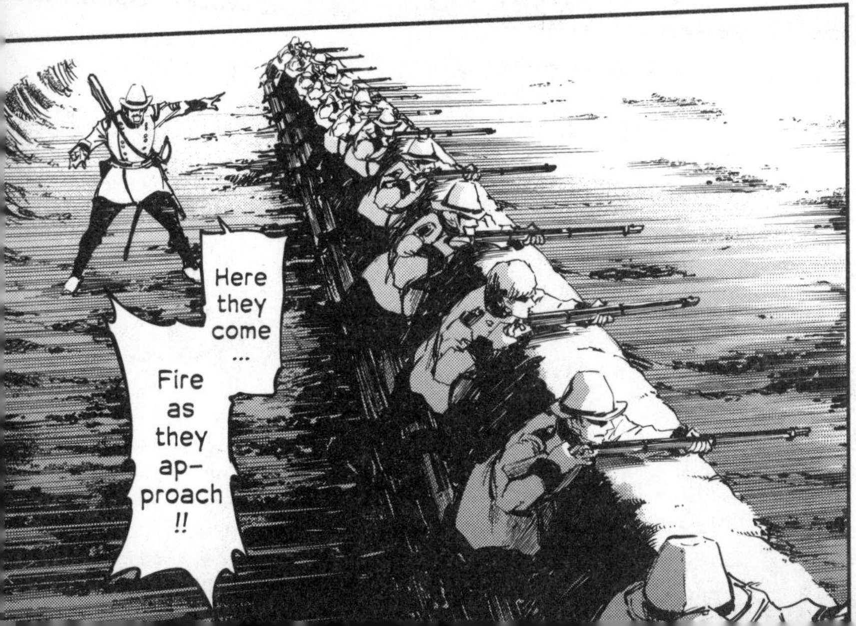
Here they come ... Fire as they ap-proach !!

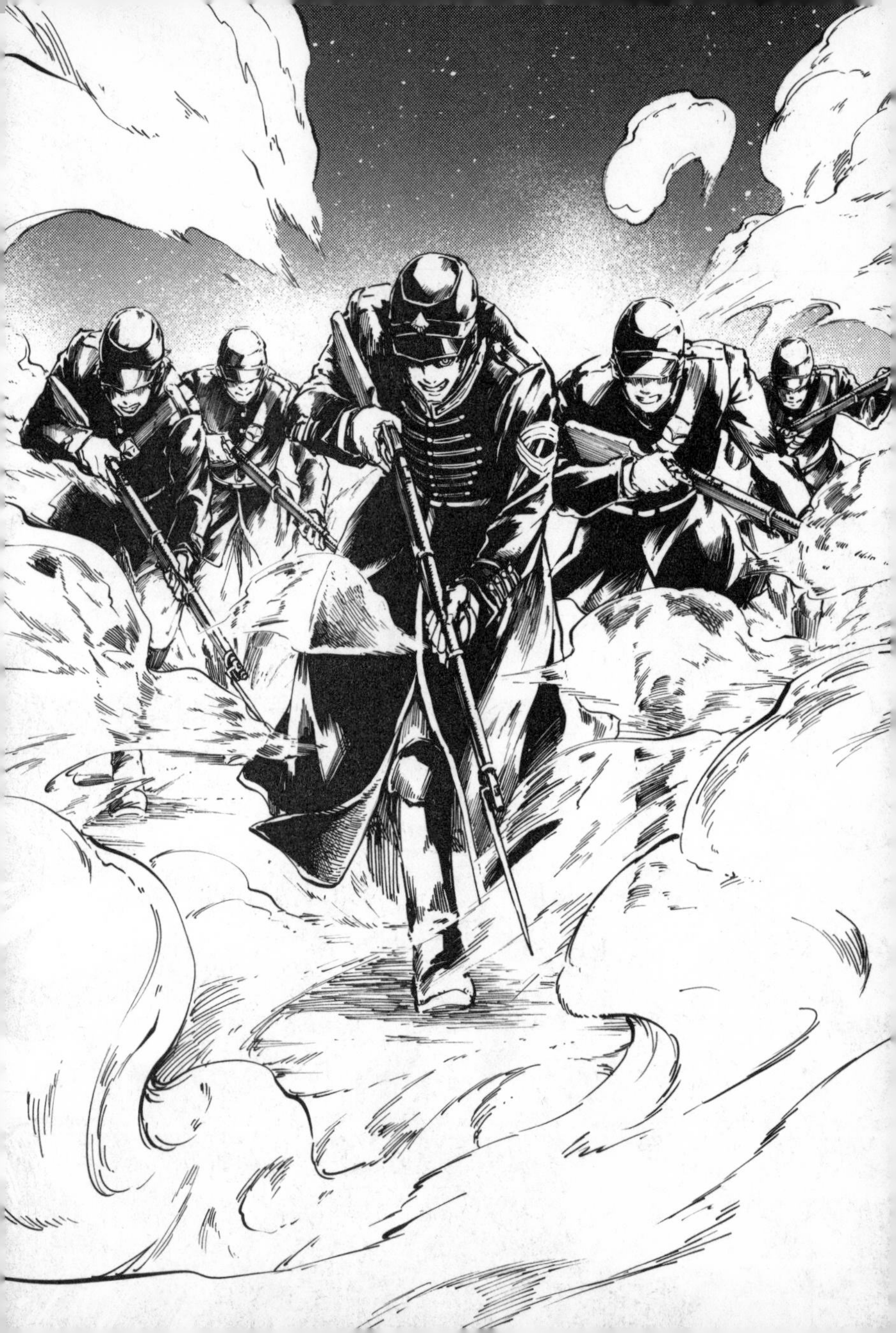

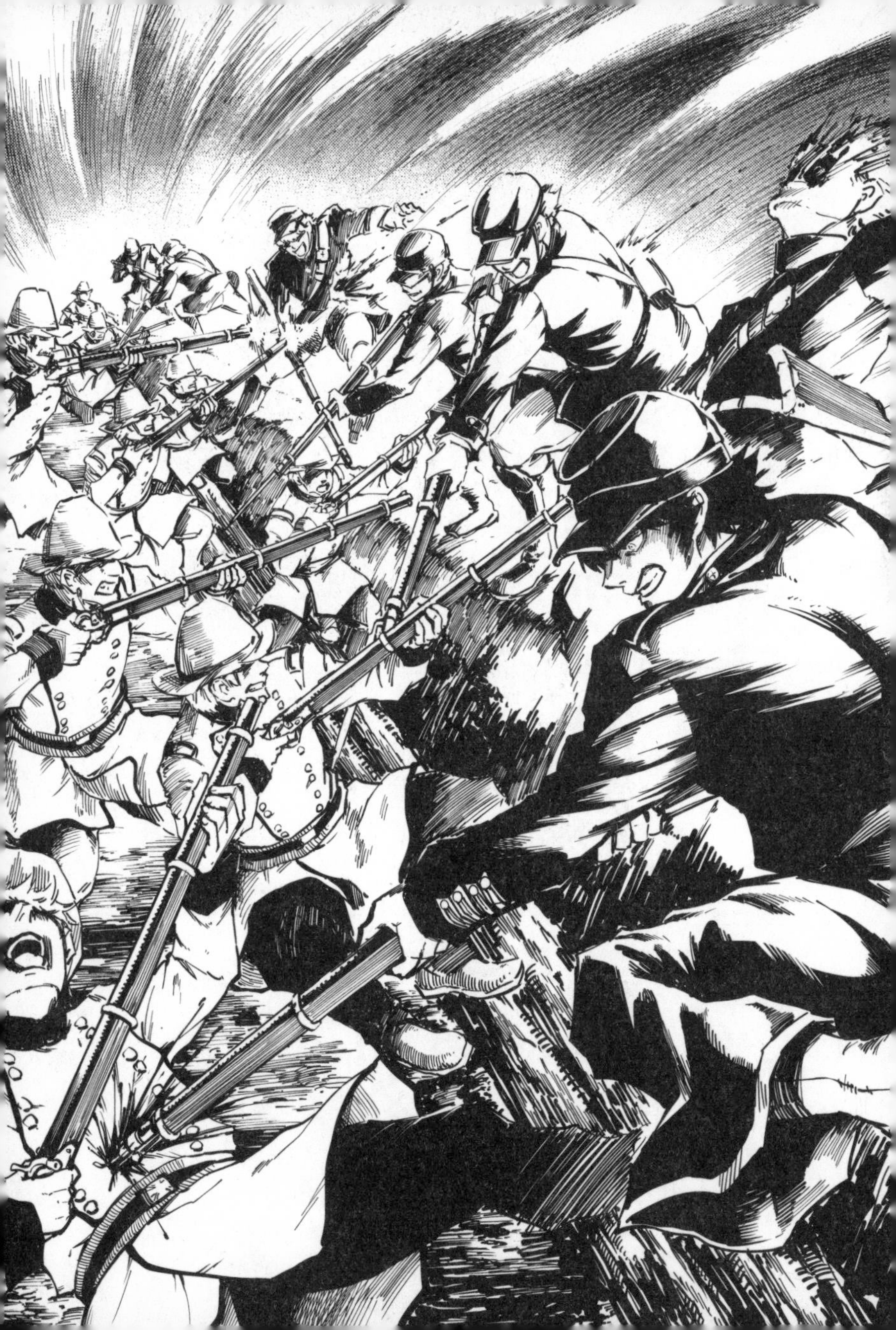

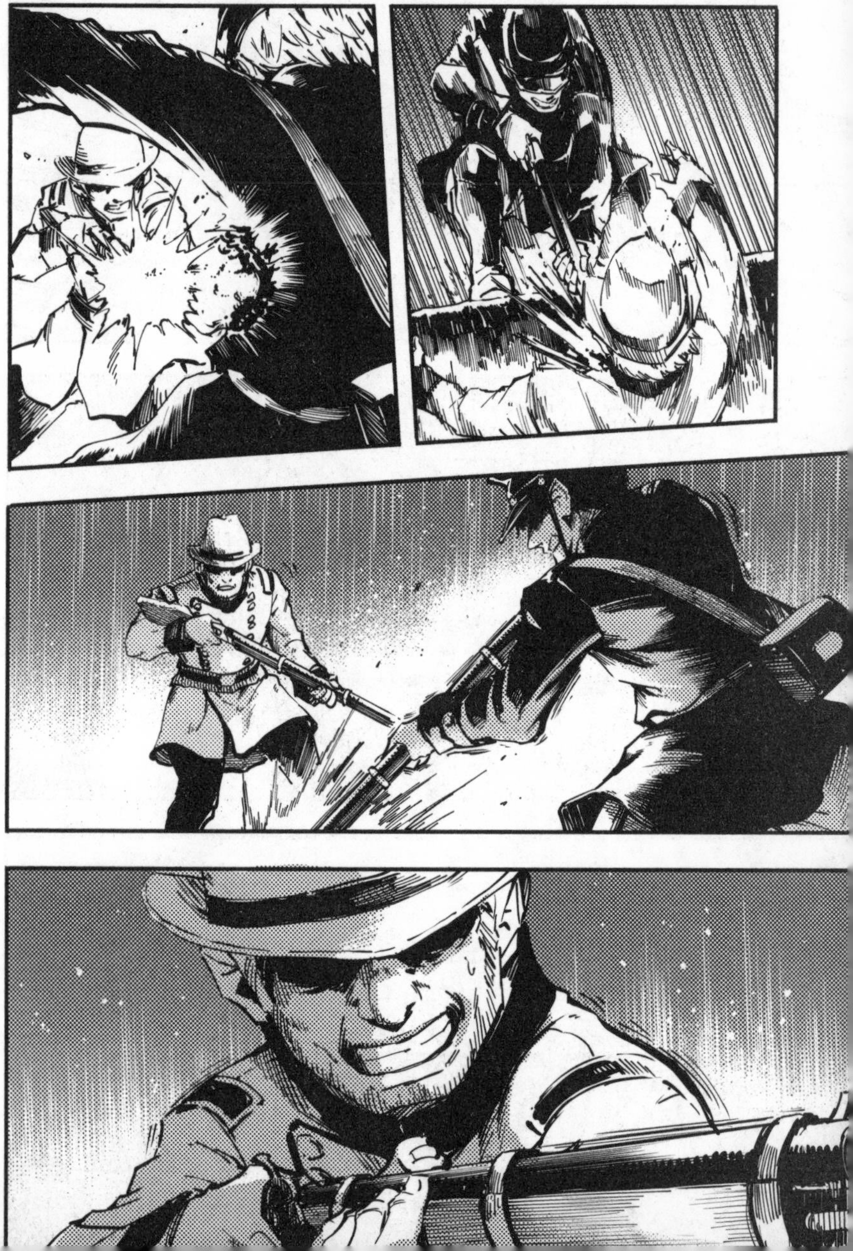

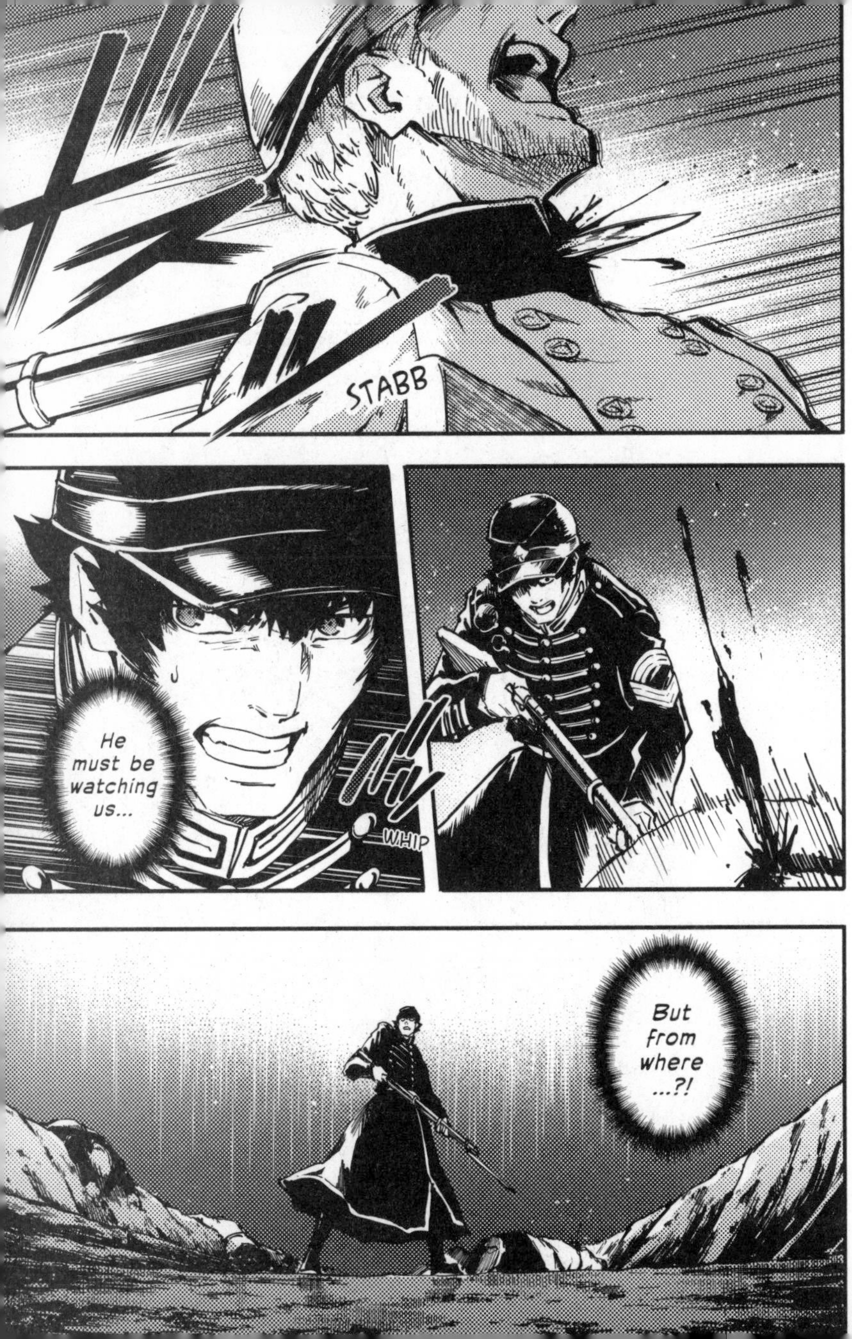
STABB
WHIP
He must be watching us...
But from where ...?!

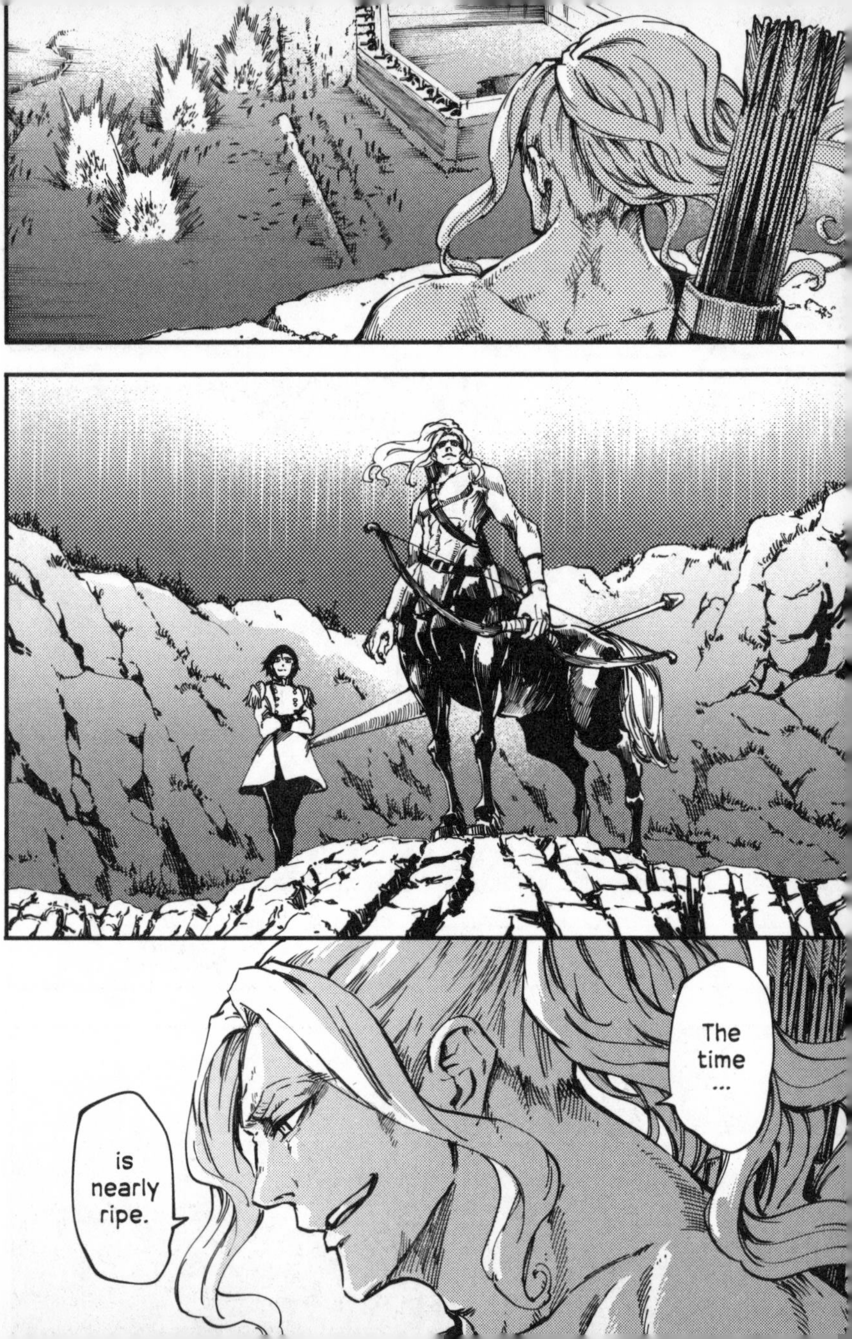
The time ...
is nearly ripe.

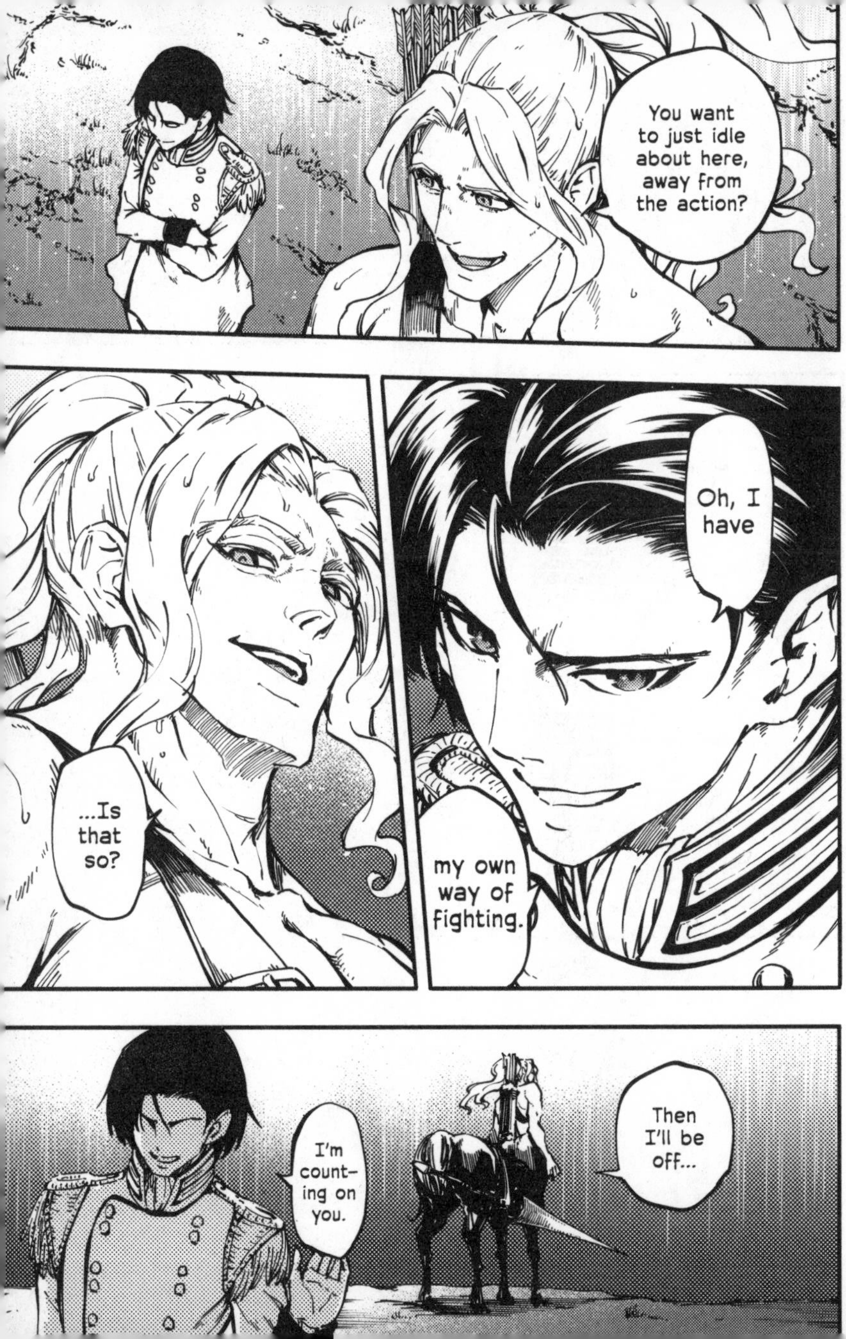
You want to just idle about here, away from the action?
Oh, I have
my own way of fighting.
...Is that so?
Then I'll be off...
I'm count-ing on you.

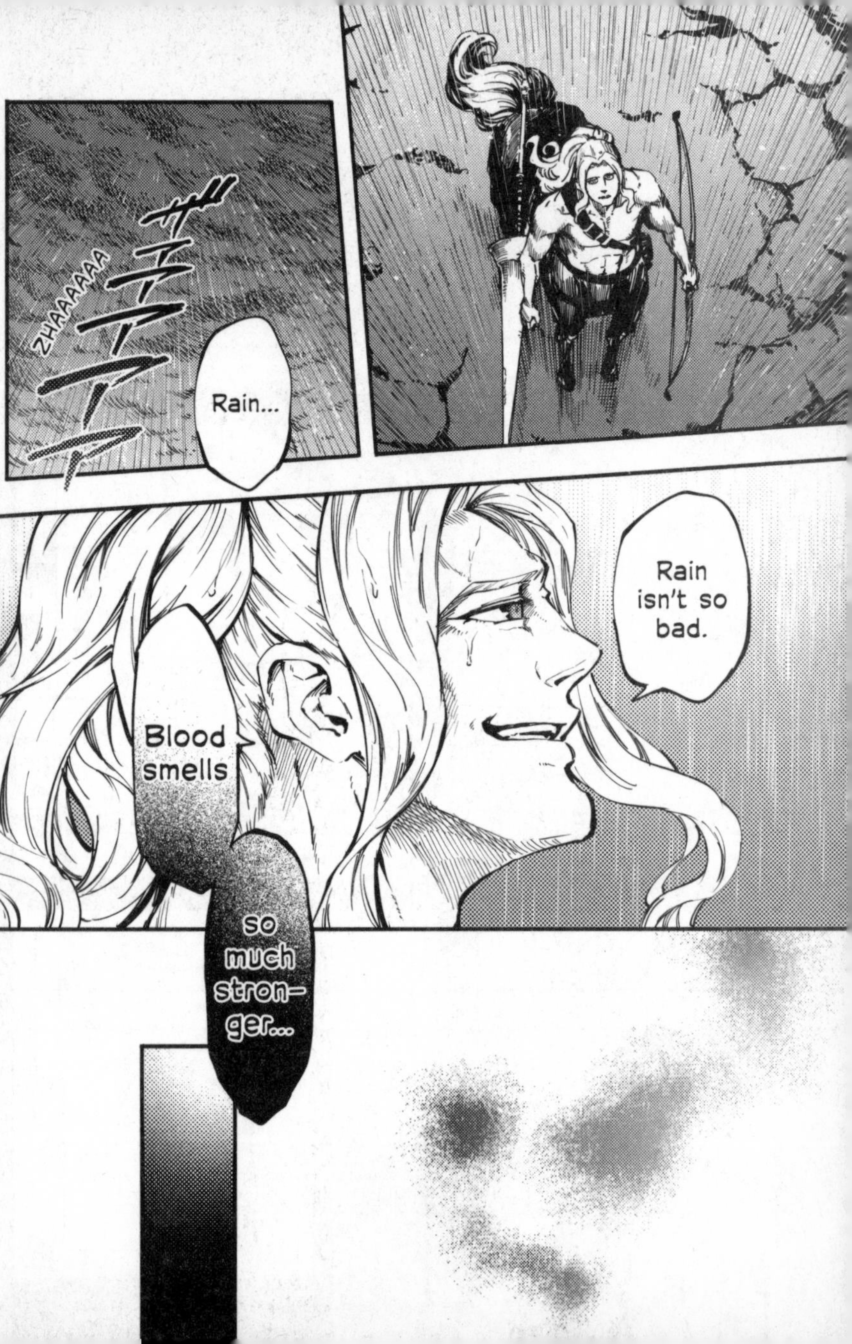
ZHAAAAAA
Rain...
Rain isn't so bad.
Blood smells
so much stronger...

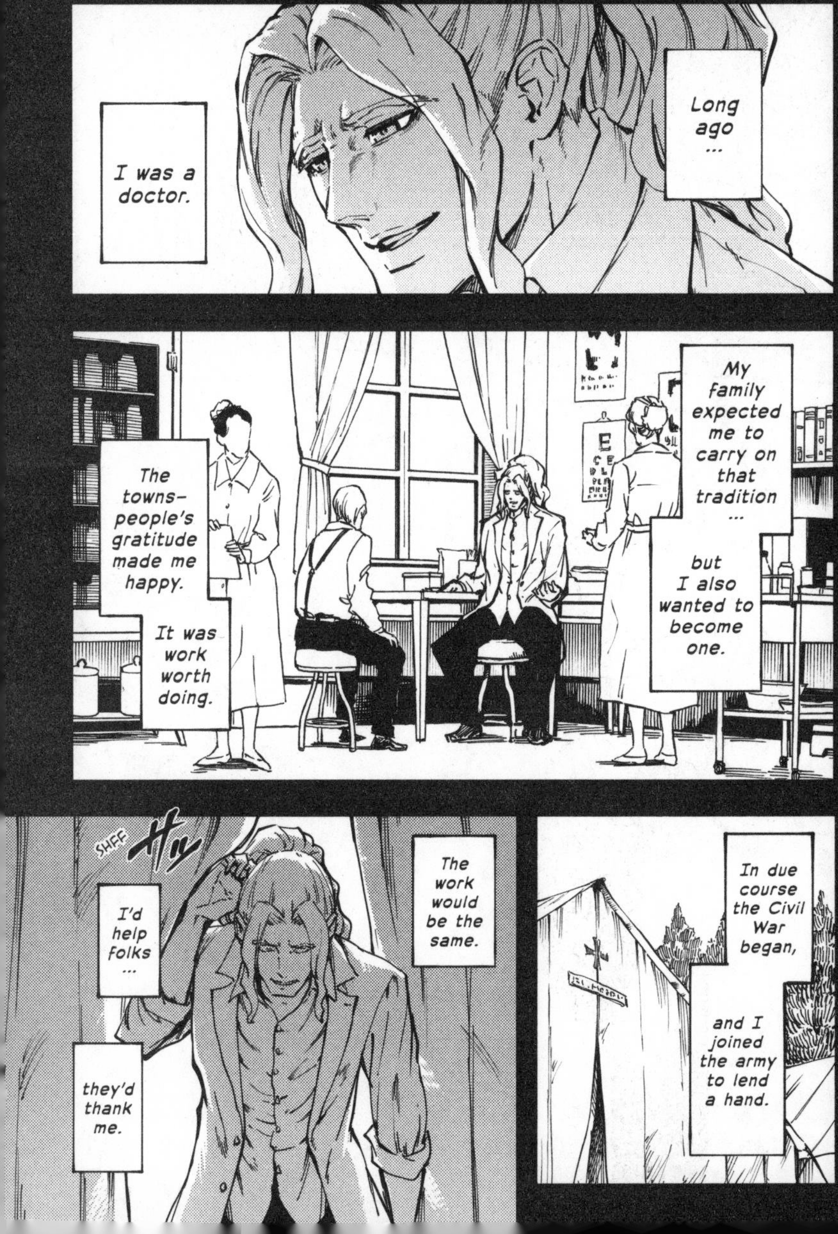

Long ago ...
I was a doctor.
My family expected me to carry on that tradition ...
but I also wanted to become one.
The towns-people's gratitude made me happy.
It was work worth doing.
In due course the Civil War began,
and I joined the army to lend a hand.
SHFF
The work would be the same.
I'd help folks ...
they'd thank me.

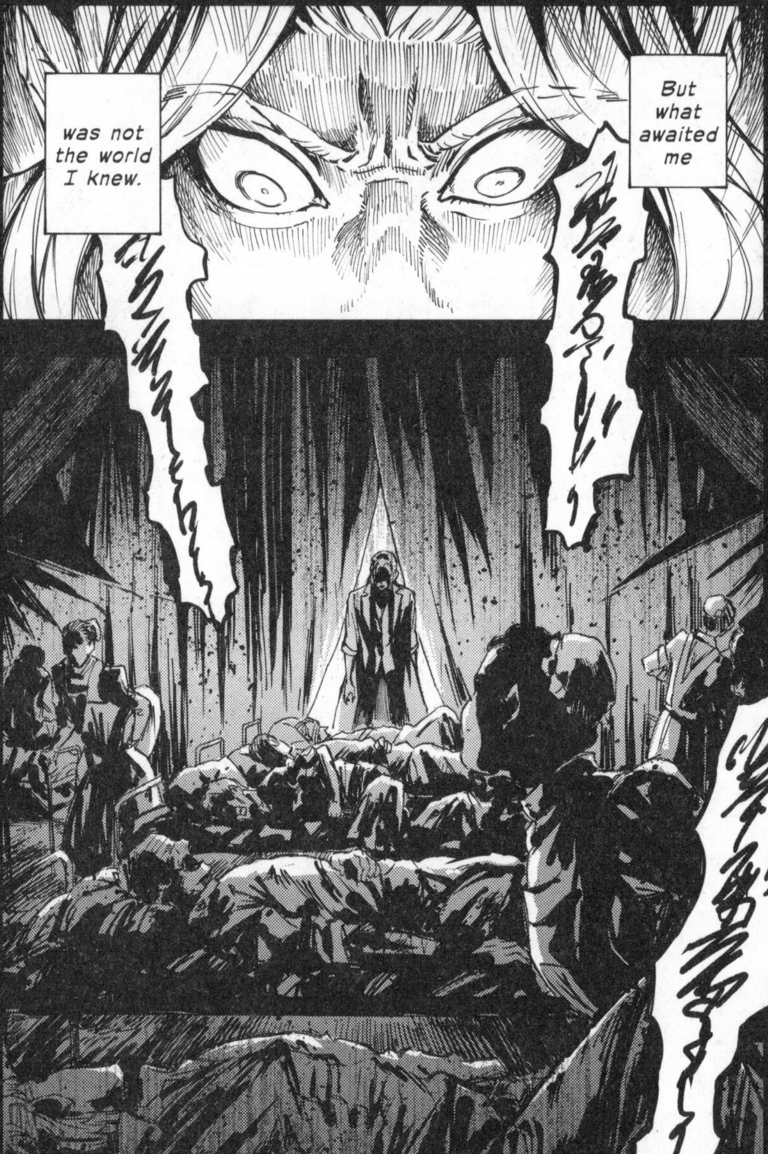
But what awaited me
was not the world I knew.

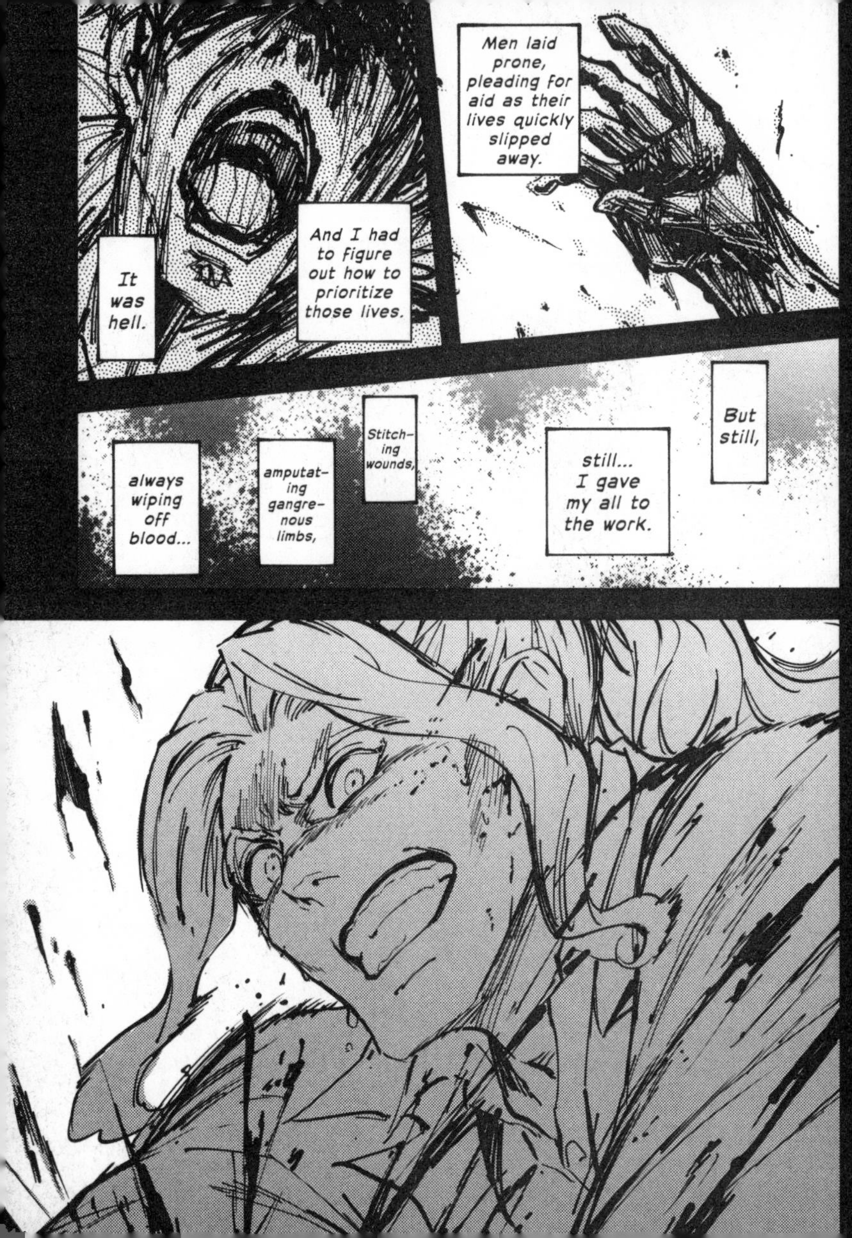
Men laid prone, pleading for aid as their lives quickly slipped away.
And I had to figure out how to prioritize those lives.
It was hell.
But still,
still... I gave my all to the work.
Stitching wounds,
amputating gangrenous limbs,
always wiping off blood...

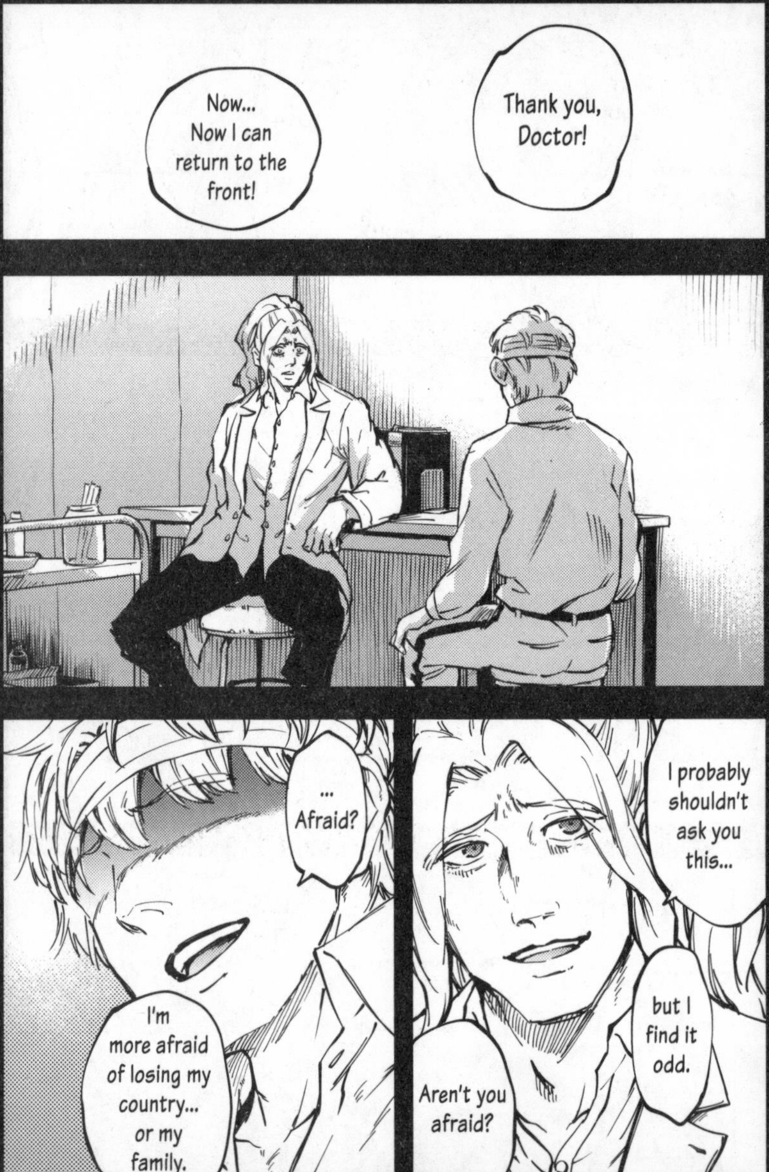
Thank you, Doctor!
Now... Now I can return to the front!
I probably shouldn't ask you this...
but I find it odd.
Aren't you afraid?
... Afraid?
I'm more afraid of losing my country... or my family.

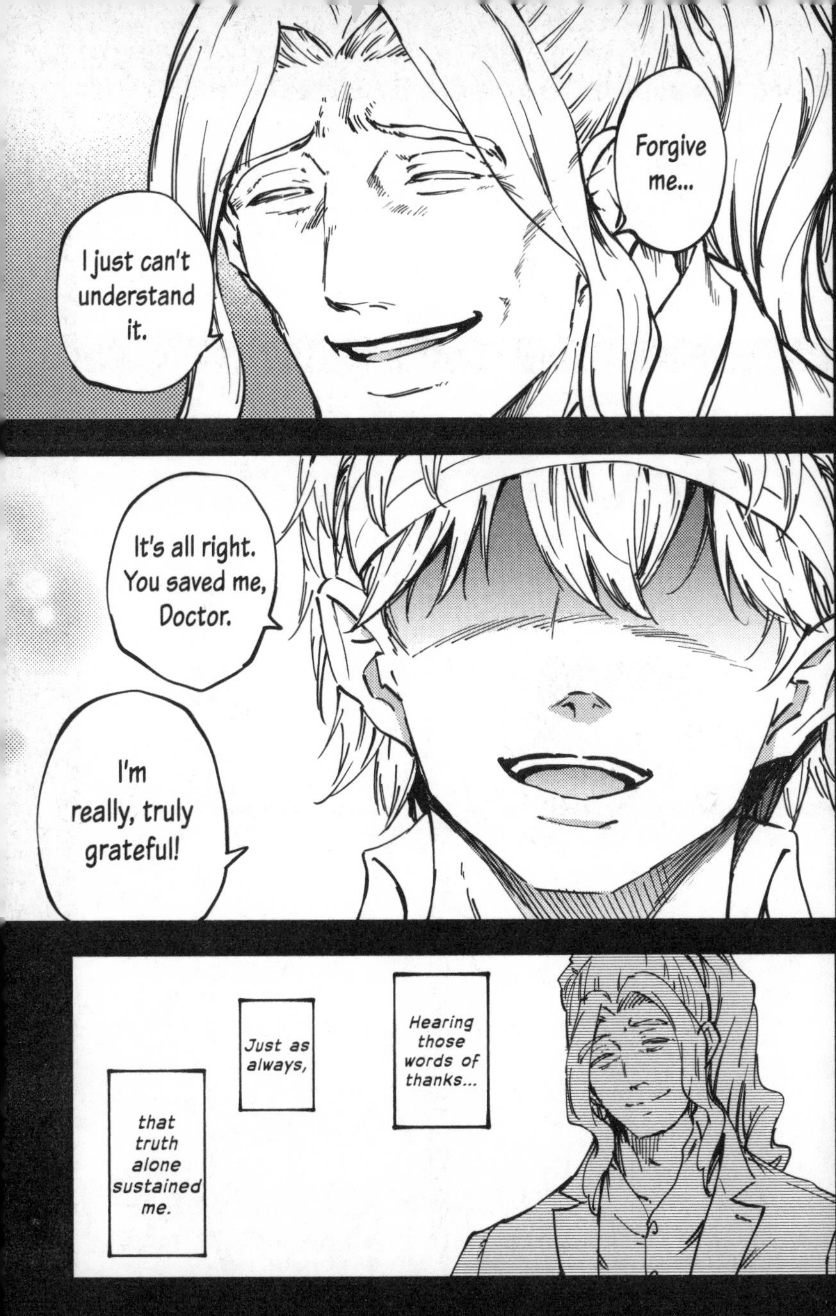
Forgive me...
I just can't understand it.
It's all right. You saved me, Doctor.
I'm really, truly grateful!
Hearing those words of thanks...
Just as always,
that truth alone sustained me.

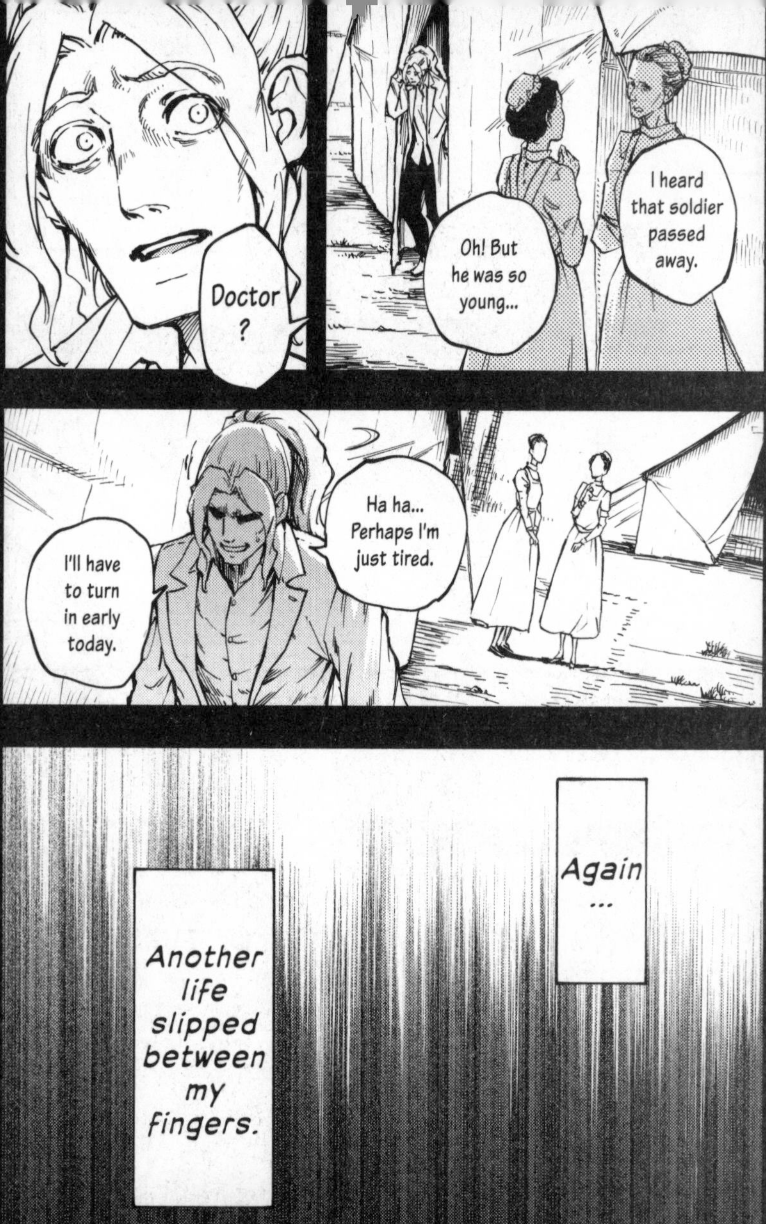
I heard that soldier passed away.
Oh! But he was so young...
Doctor ?
Ha ha... Perhaps I'm just tired.
I'll have to turn in early today.
Again ...
Another life slipped between my fingers.

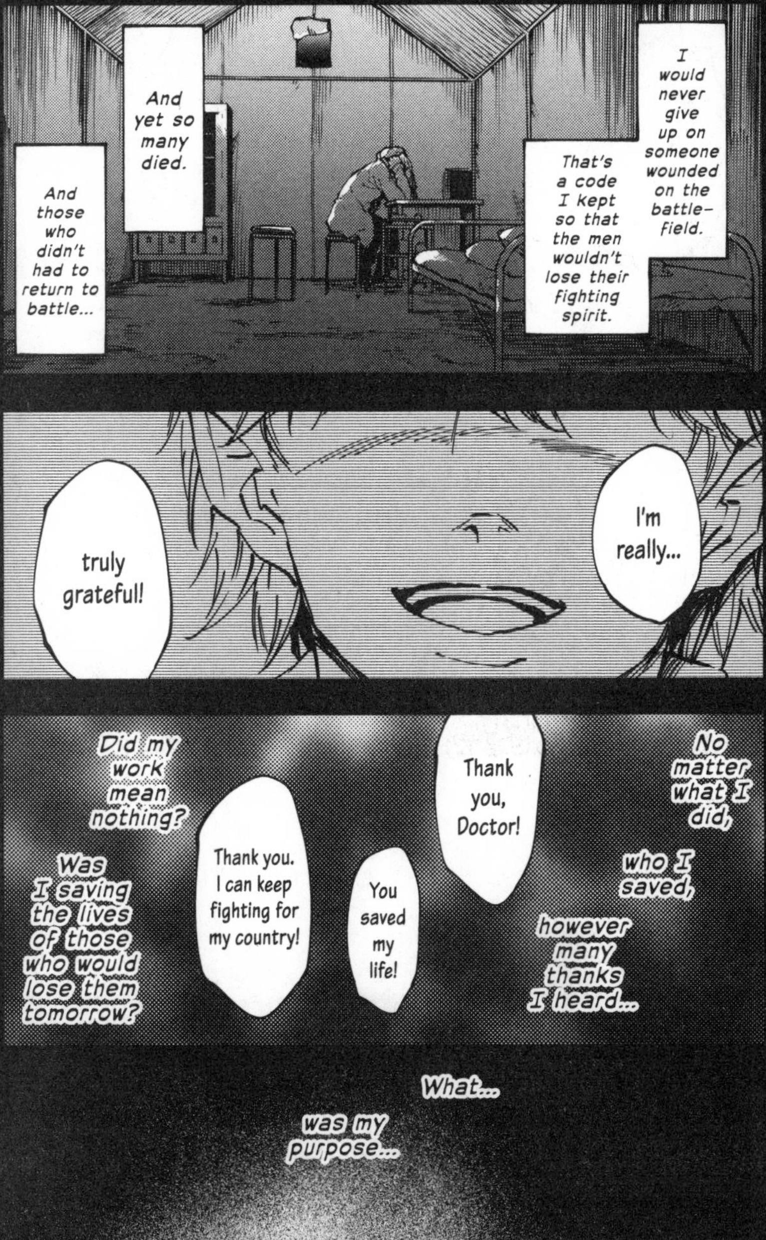

I would never give up on someone wounded on the battlefield.
That's a code I kept so that the men wouldn't lose their fighting spirit.
And yet so many died.
And those who didn't had to return to battle...
I'm really...
truly grateful!
No matter what I did,
who I saved,
however many thanks I heard...
Thank you, Doctor!
You saved my life!
Thank you. I can keep fighting for my country!
Did my work mean nothing?
Was I saving the lives of those who would lose them tomorrow?
What...
was my purpose...

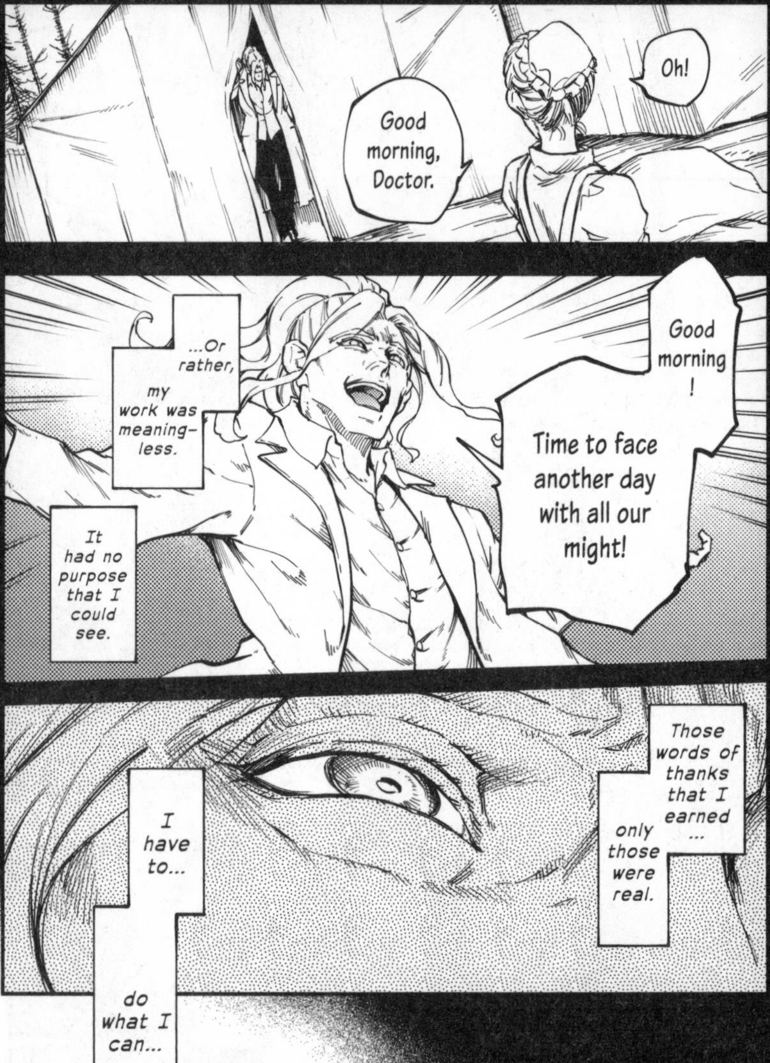

Oh!
Good morning, Doctor.
Good morning!
Time to face another day with all our might!
...Or rather, my work was meaning-less.
It had no purpose that I could see.
Those words of thanks that I earned...
only those were real.
I have to...
do what I can...

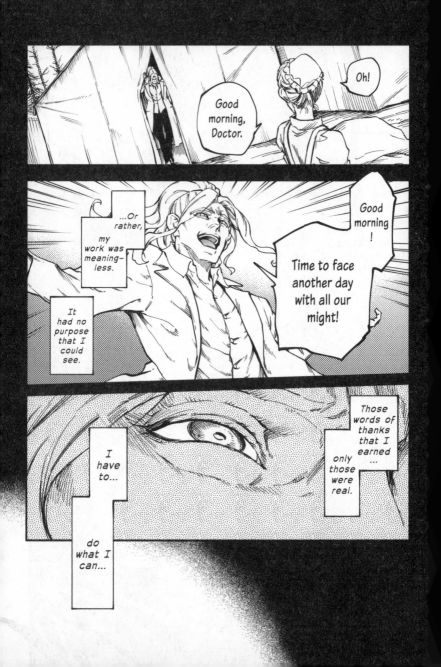

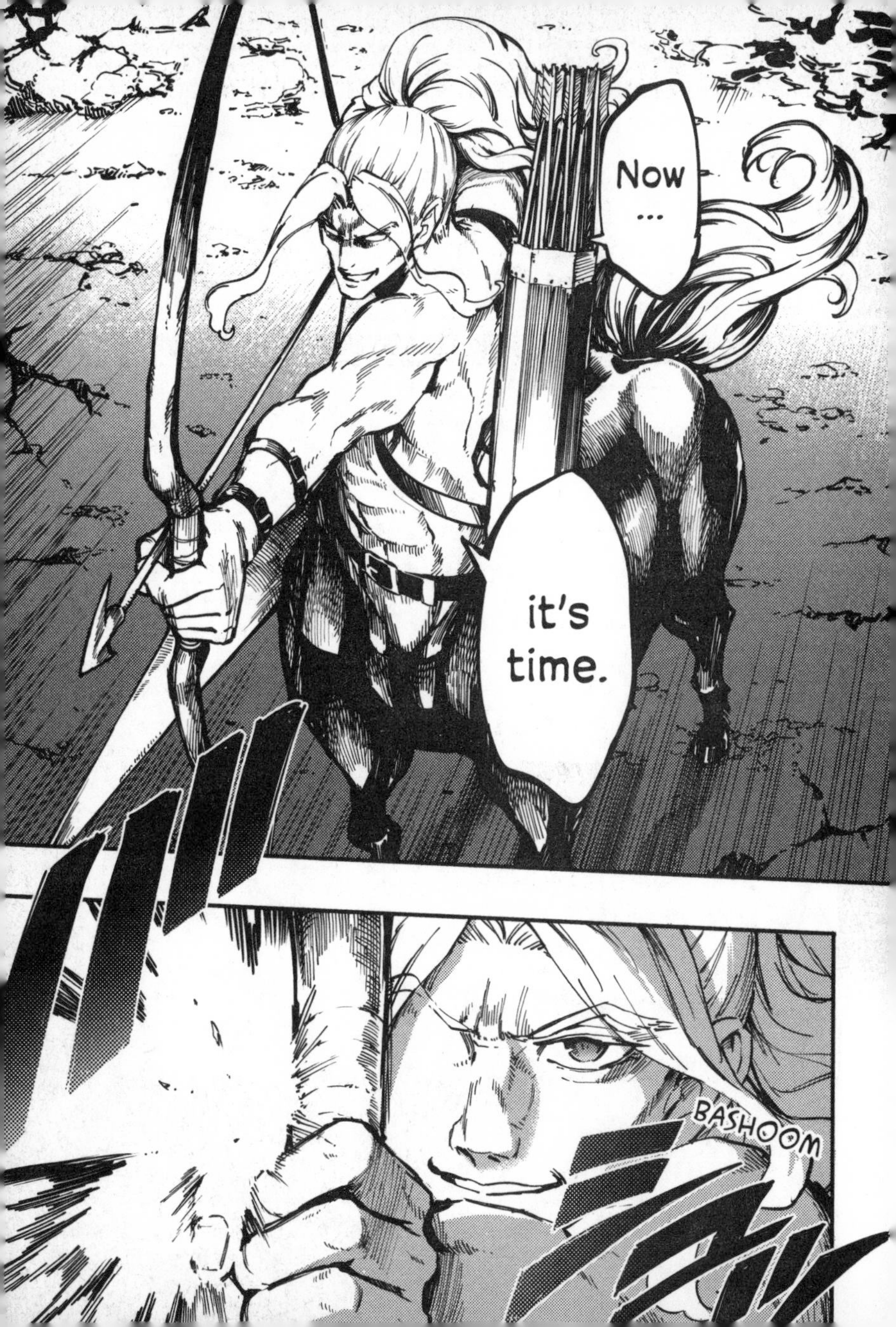
Now ...
it's time.
BASHOOM

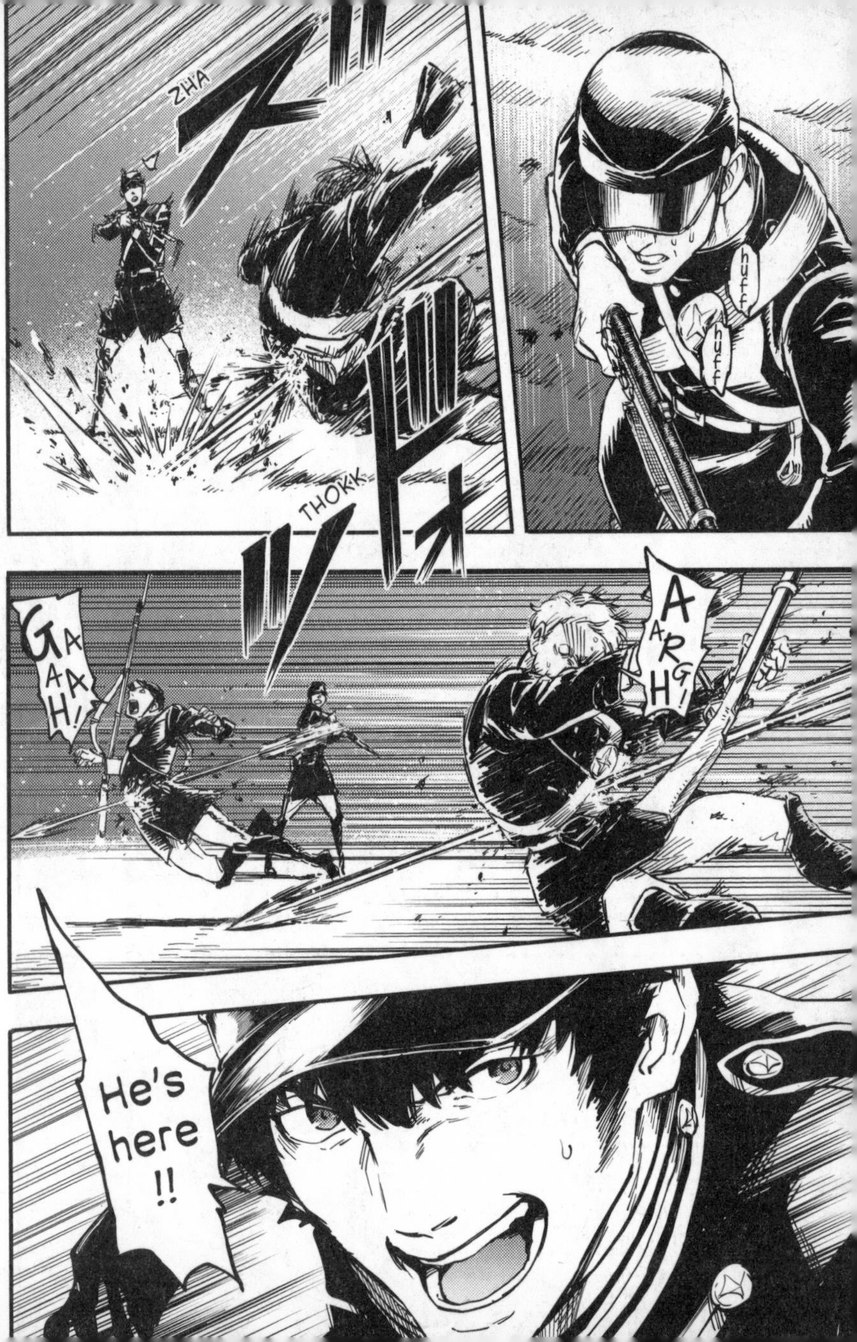
huff
huff
ZHA
THOKK
AARGH!
GAAAH!
He's here !!

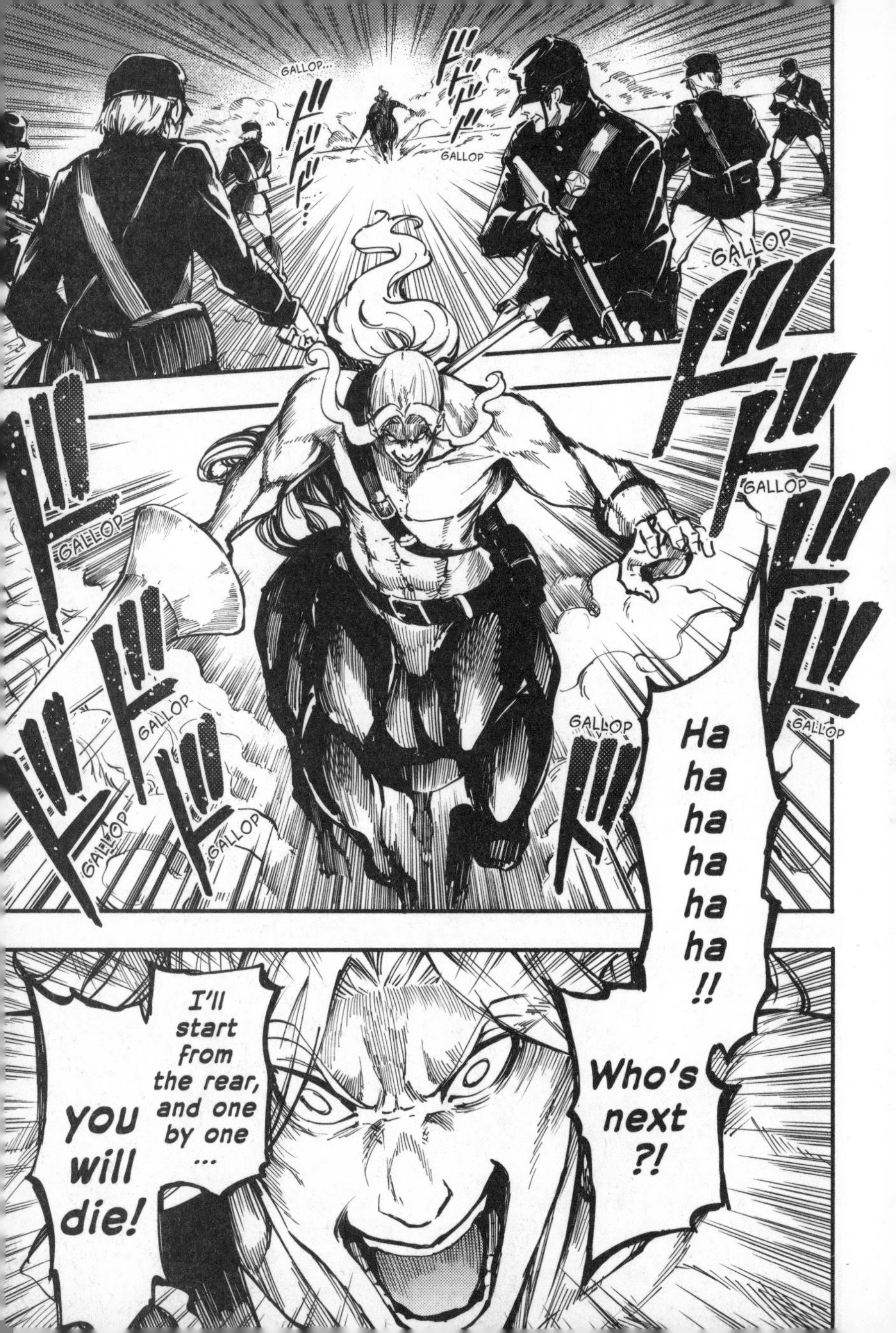
GALLOP
GALLOP
GALLOP...
GALLOP
GALLOP
GALLOP
GALLOP
GALLOP
GALLOP
GALLOP
Ha ha ha ha ha ha ha!!
Who's next?!
I'll start from the rear, and one by one ...
you will die!

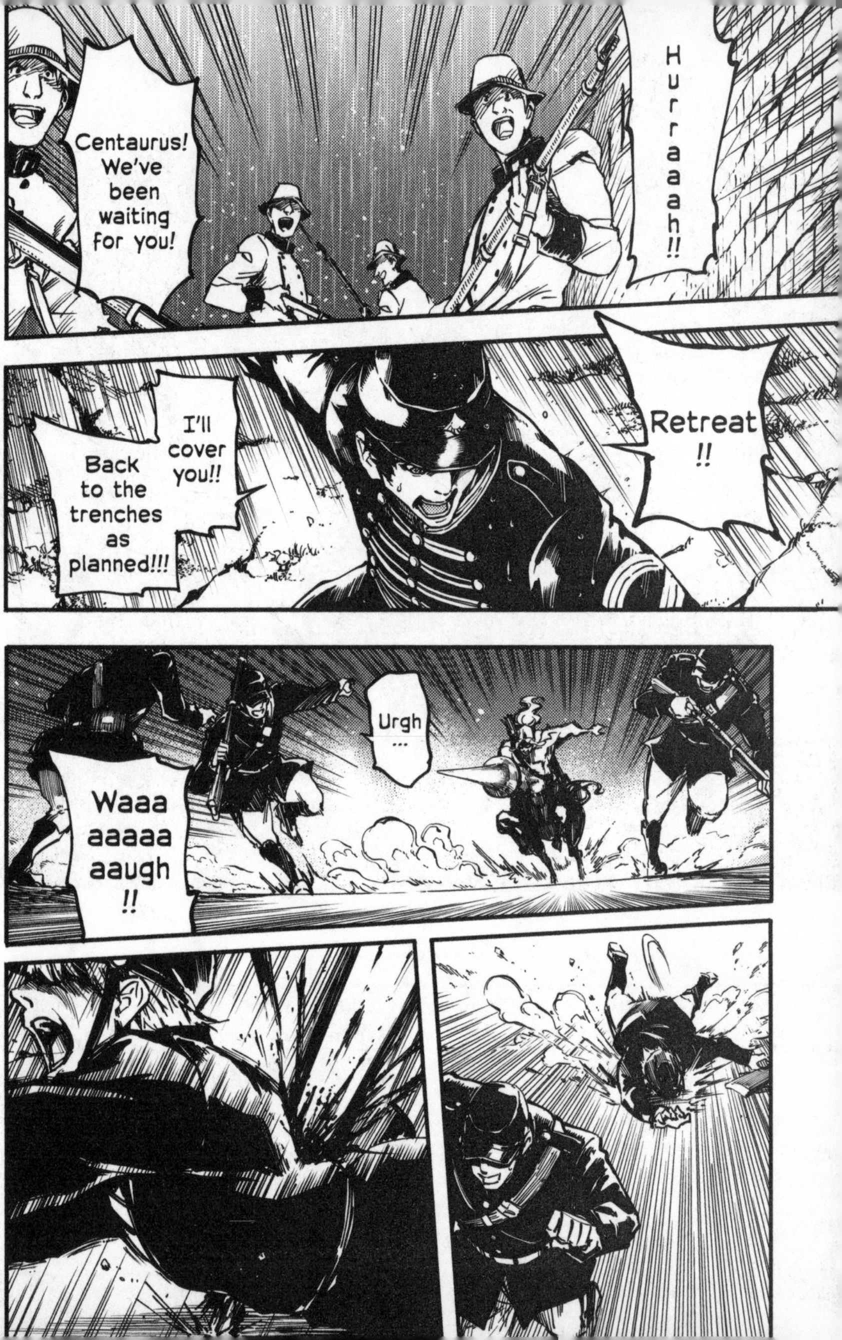
Hurraaah!!
Centaurus! We've been waiting for you!
Retreat!!
I'll cover you!!
Back to the trenches as planned!!!
Urgh...
Waaa aaaaa aaugh!!

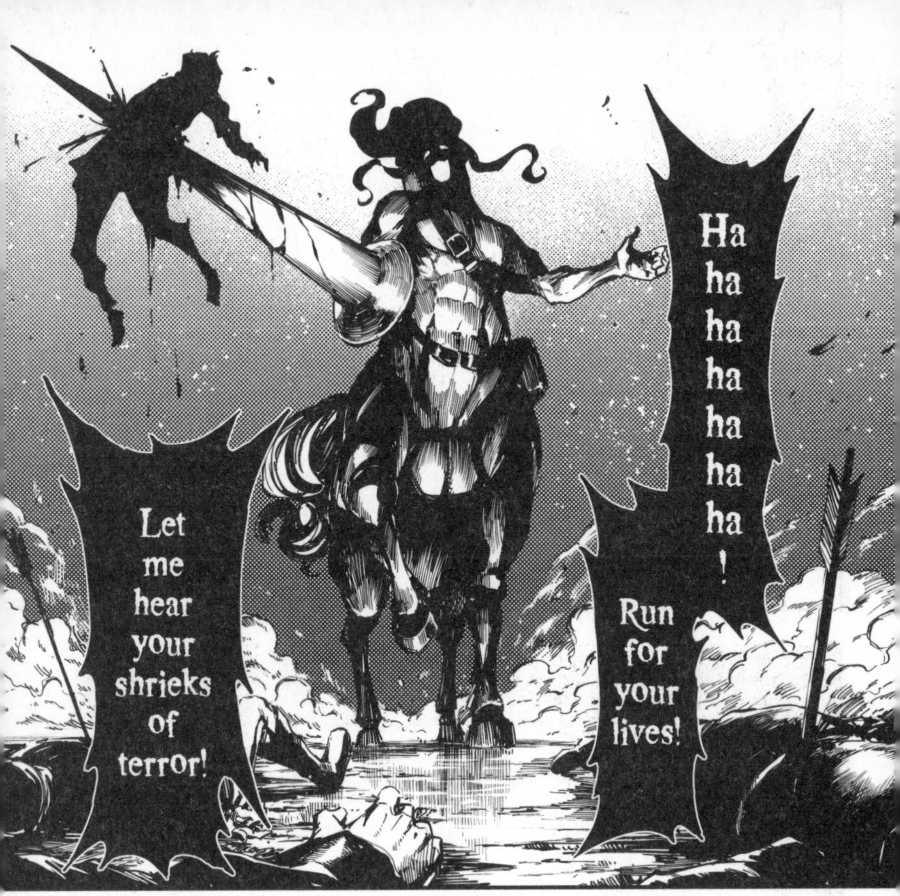

Ha ha ha ha ha ha ha!
Run for your lives!
Let me hear your shrieks of terror!

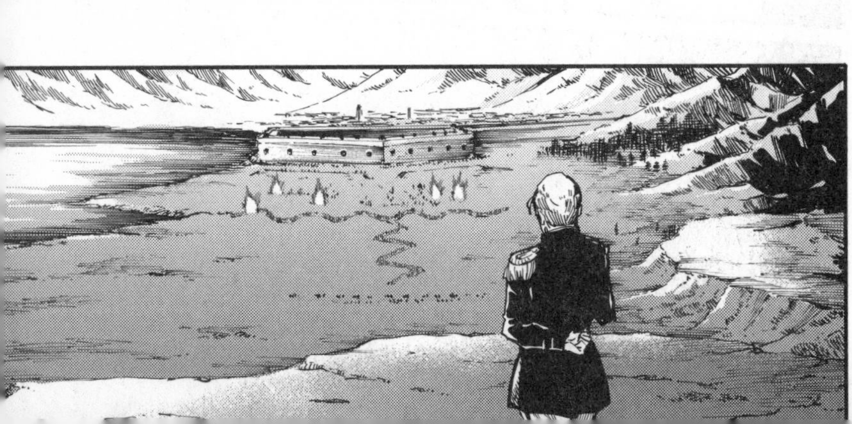

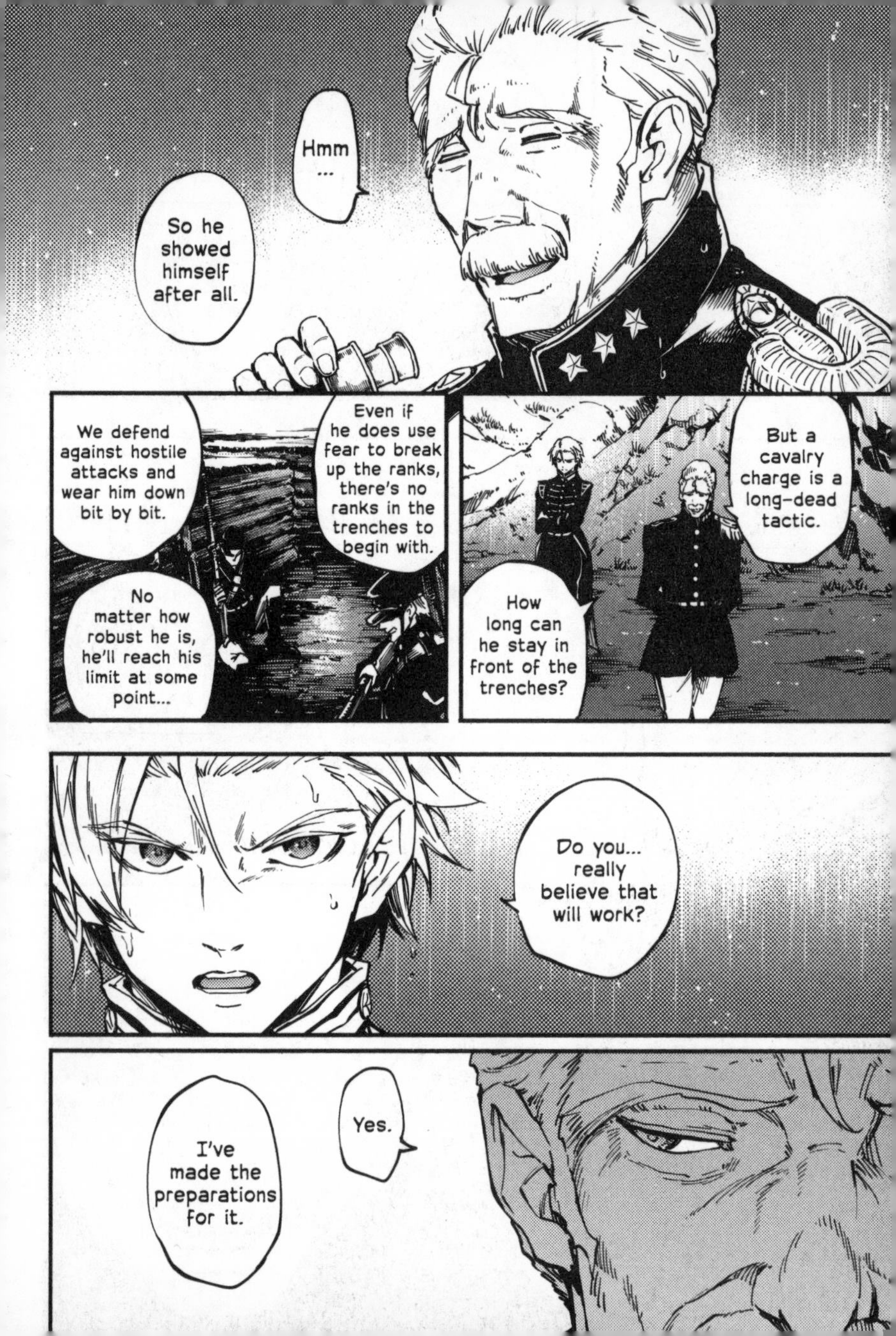
Hmm ...
So he showed himself after all.
But a cavalry charge is a long-dead tactic.
How long can he stay in front of the trenches?
Even if he does use fear to break up the ranks, there's no ranks in the trenches to begin with.
We defend against hostile attacks and wear him down bit by bit.
No matter how robust he is, he'll reach his limit at some point...
Do you... really believe that will work?
Yes.
I've made the preparations for it.

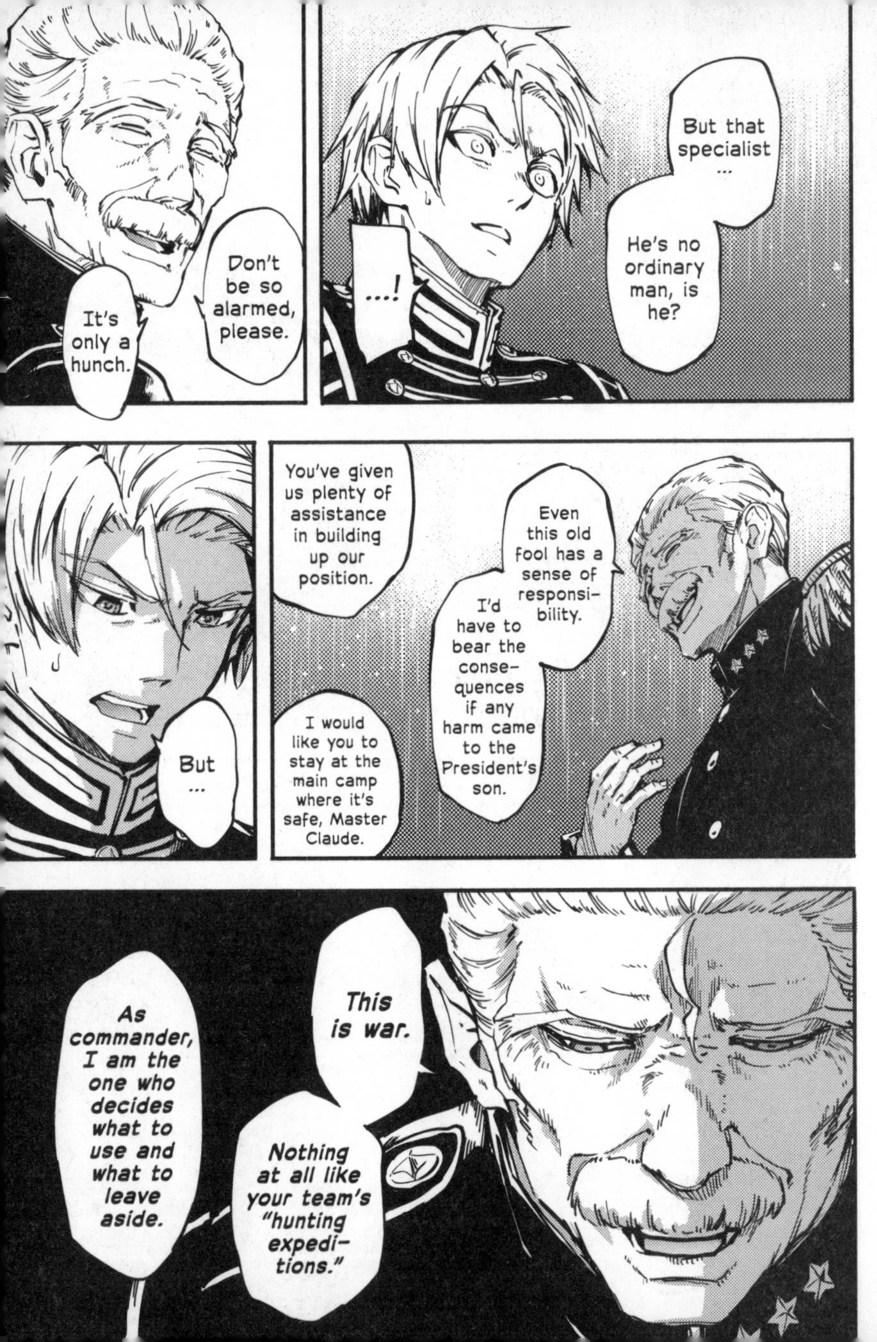
But that specialist ...
He's no ordinary man, is he?
...!
Don't be so alarmed, please.
It's only a hunch.
You've given us plenty of assistance in building up our position.
Even this old fool has a sense of responsibility.
I'd have to bear the consequences if any harm came to the President's son.
I would like you to stay at the main camp where it's safe, Master Claude.
But ...
This is war.
Nothing at all like your team's "hunting expeditions."
As commander, I am the one who decides what to use and what to leave aside.

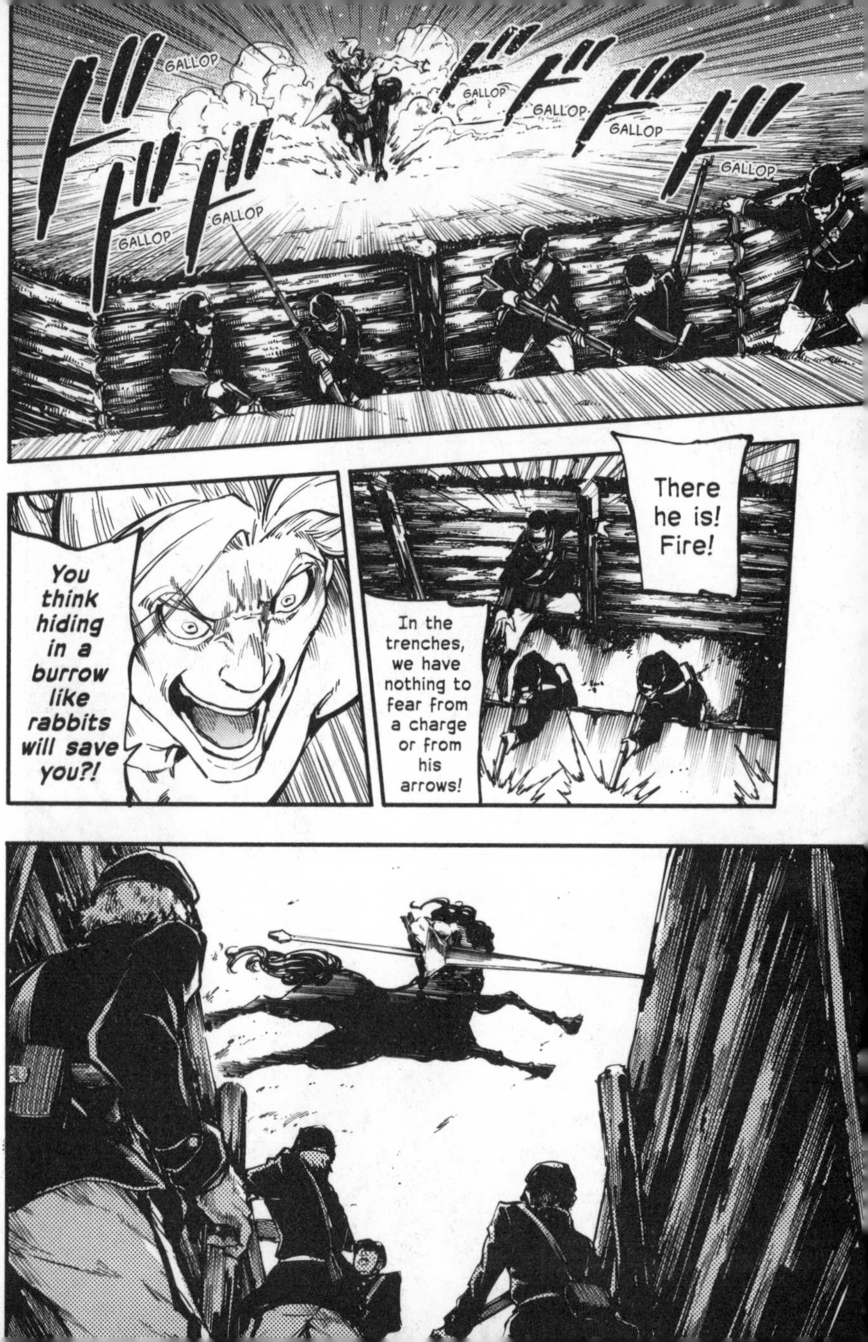

GALLOP
GALLOP
GALLOP
GALLOP
GALLOP
GALLOP
GALLOP
There he is! Fire!
In the trenches, we have nothing to fear from a charge or from his arrows!
You think hiding in a burrow like rabbits will save you?!

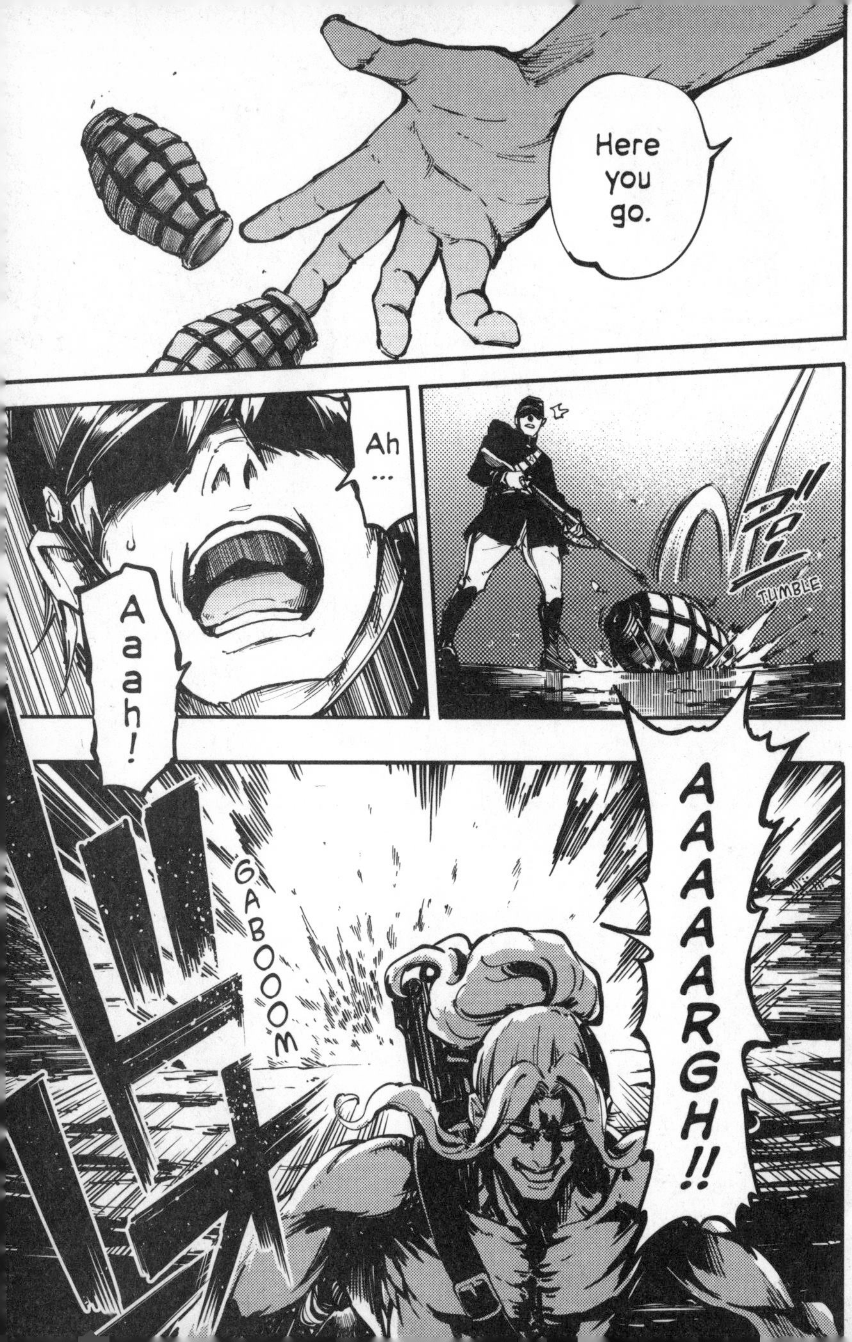
Here you go.
TUMBLE
Ah...
Aaah!
AAAAARGH!!
GABOOOOM

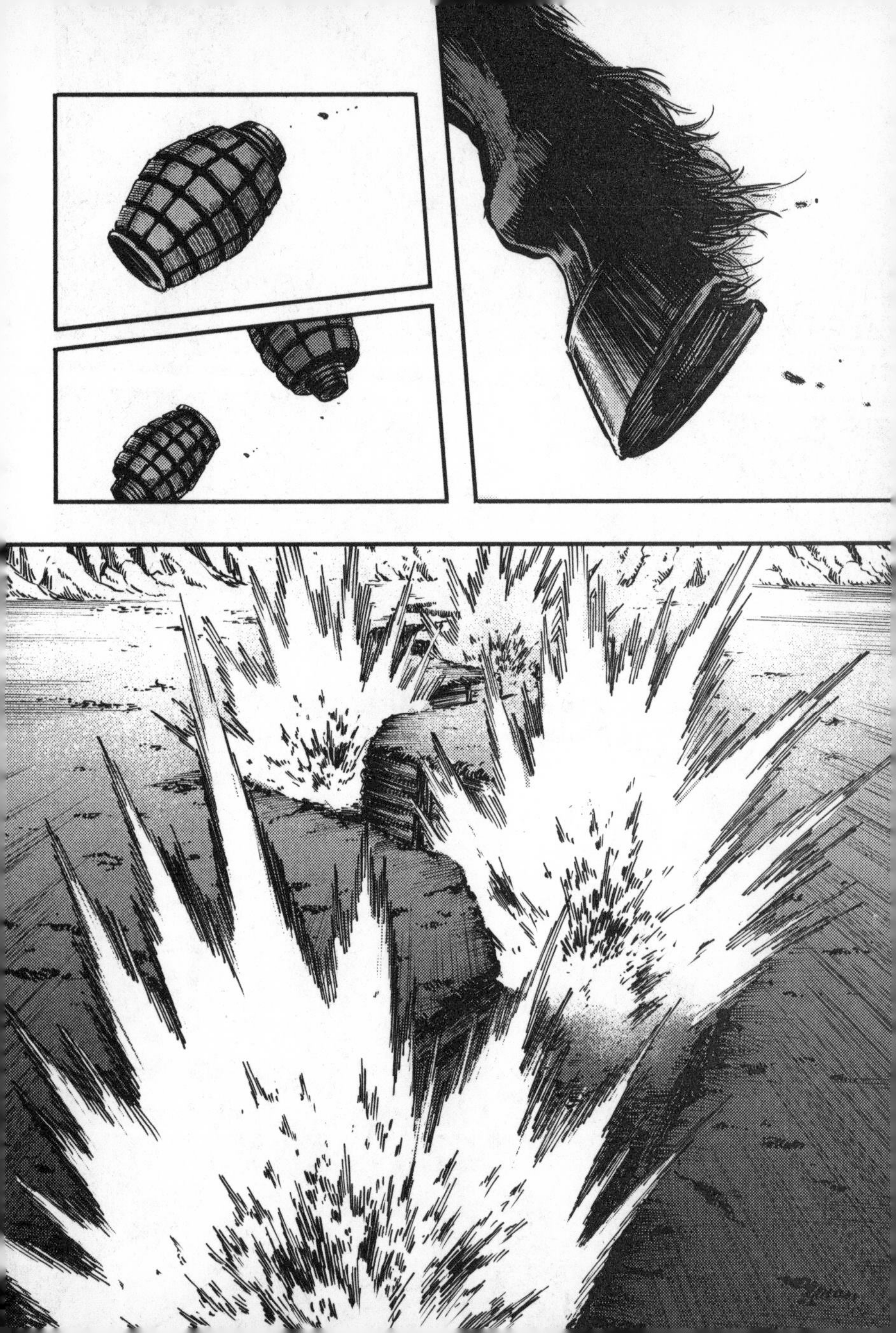

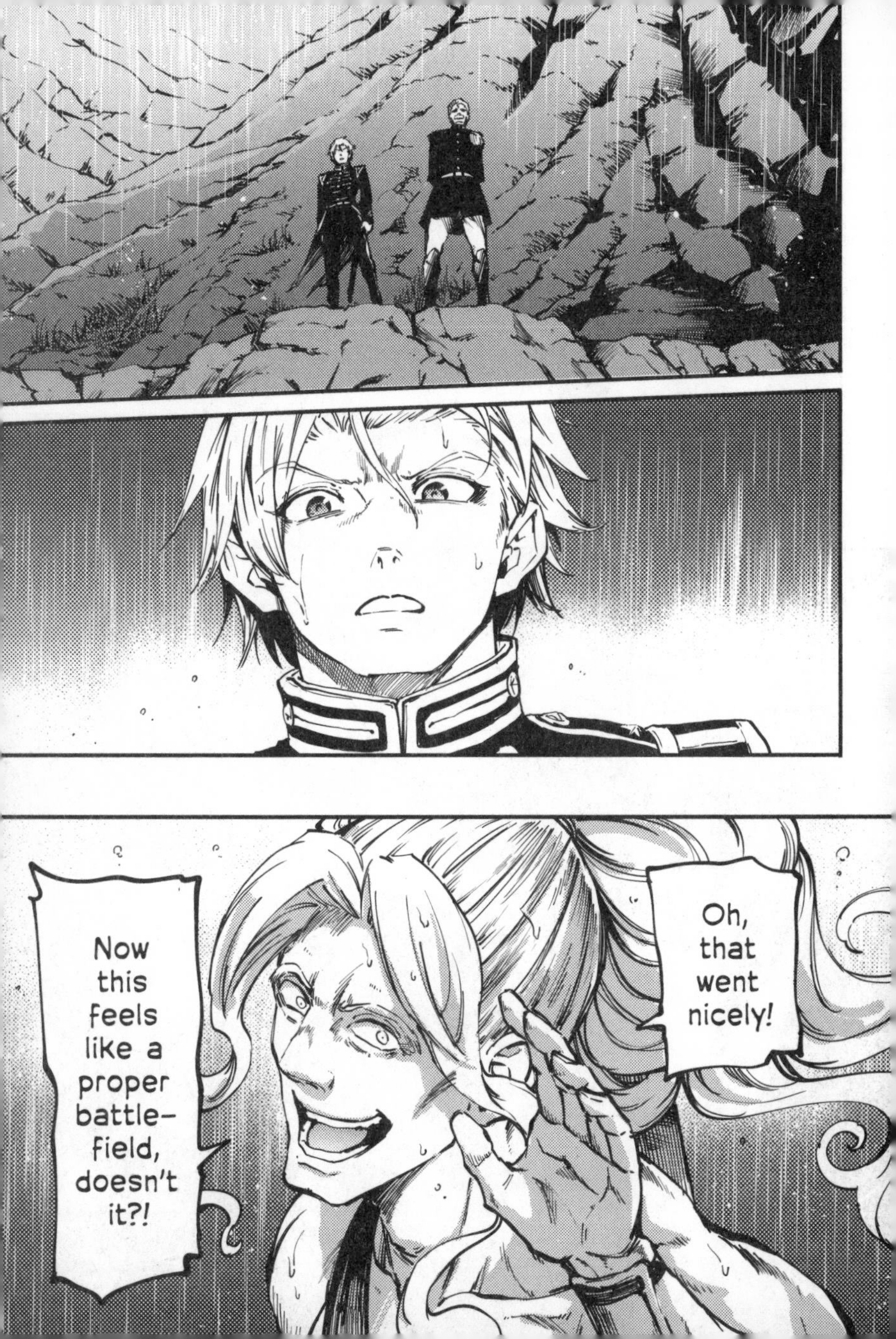
Oh, that went nicely!
Now this feels like a proper battle-field, doesn't it?!

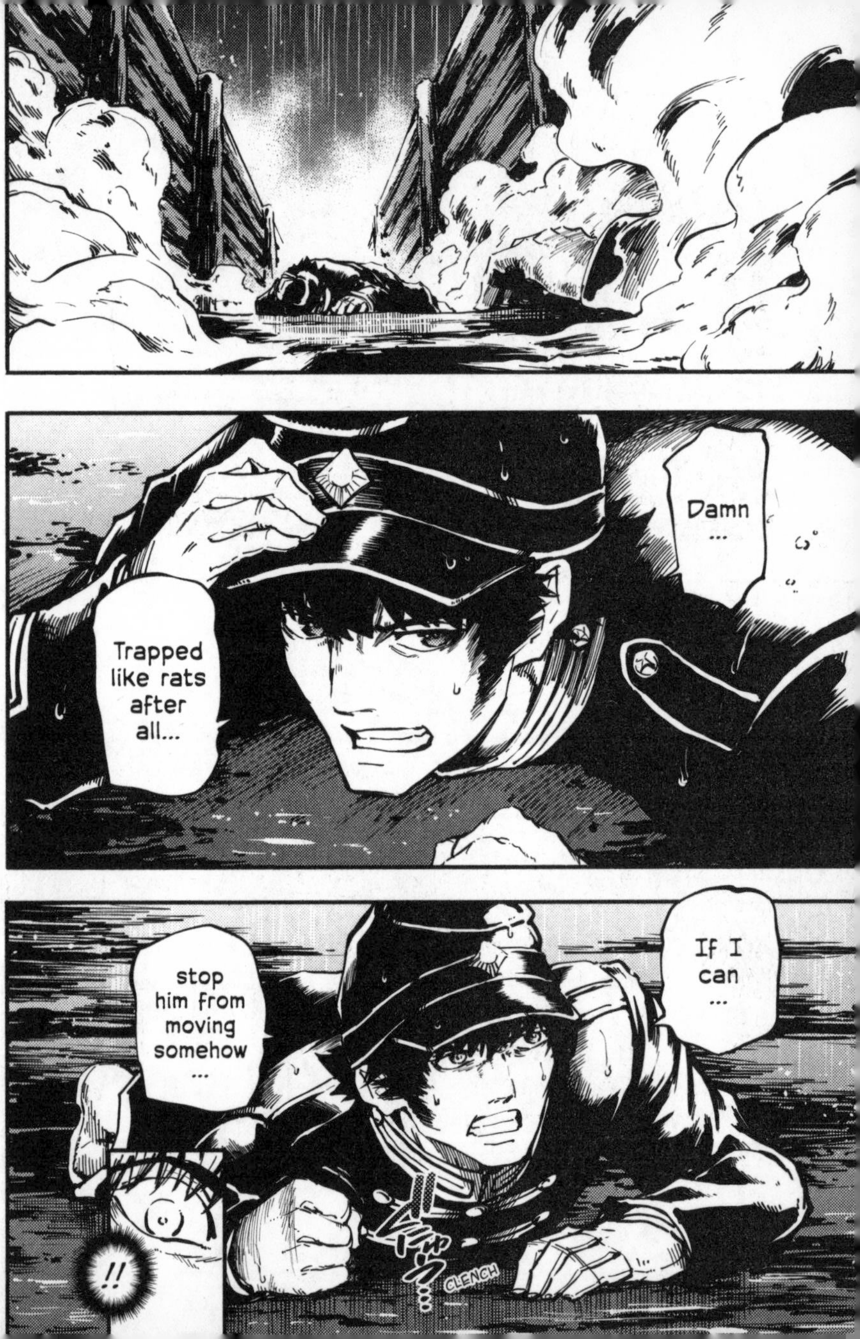
Damn ...
Trapped like rats after all...
If I can ...
stop him from moving somehow ...
CLENCH
!!

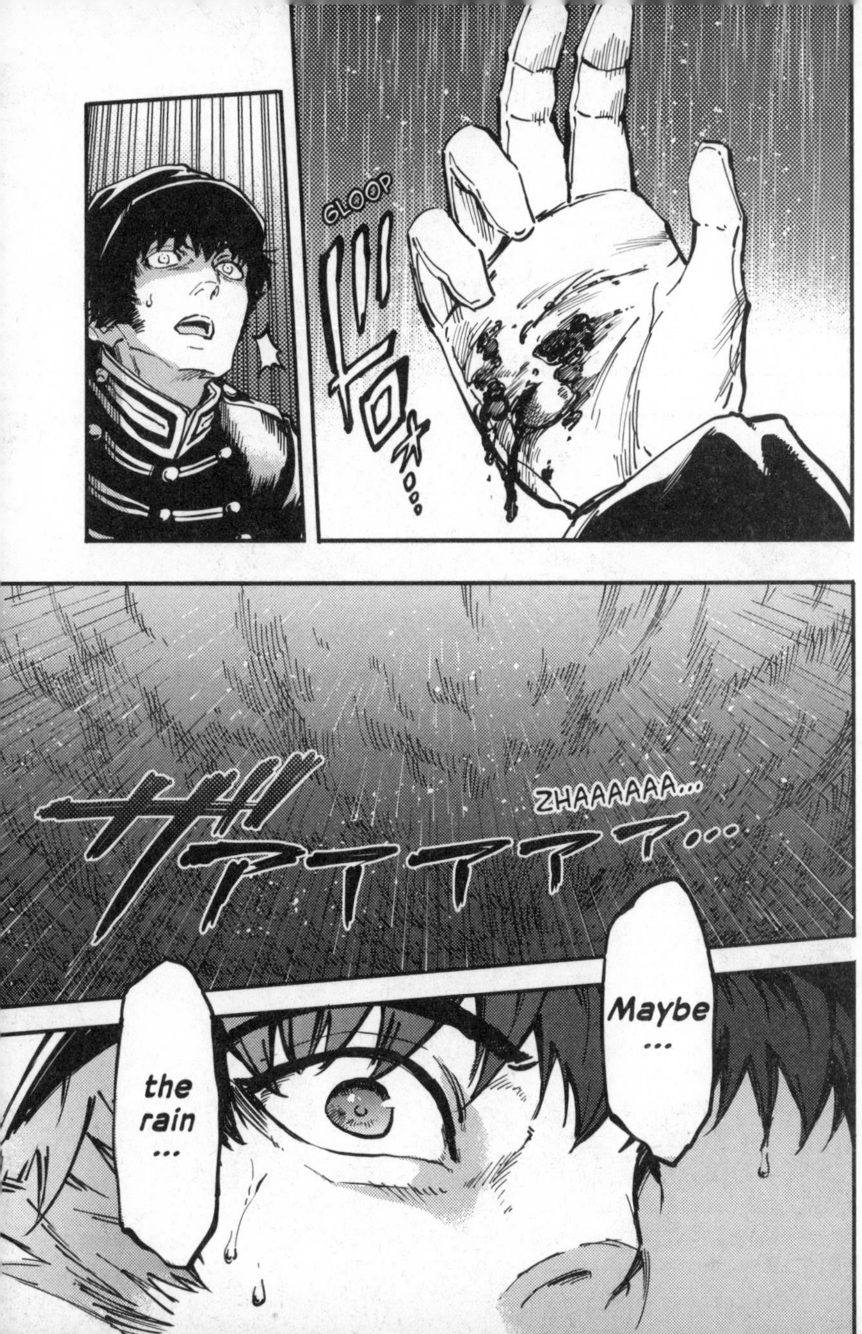
GLOOP
ドロォ…
ザアアアアア…
ZHAAAAAA…
Maybe …
the rain …

To the Abandoned
Sacred Beasts

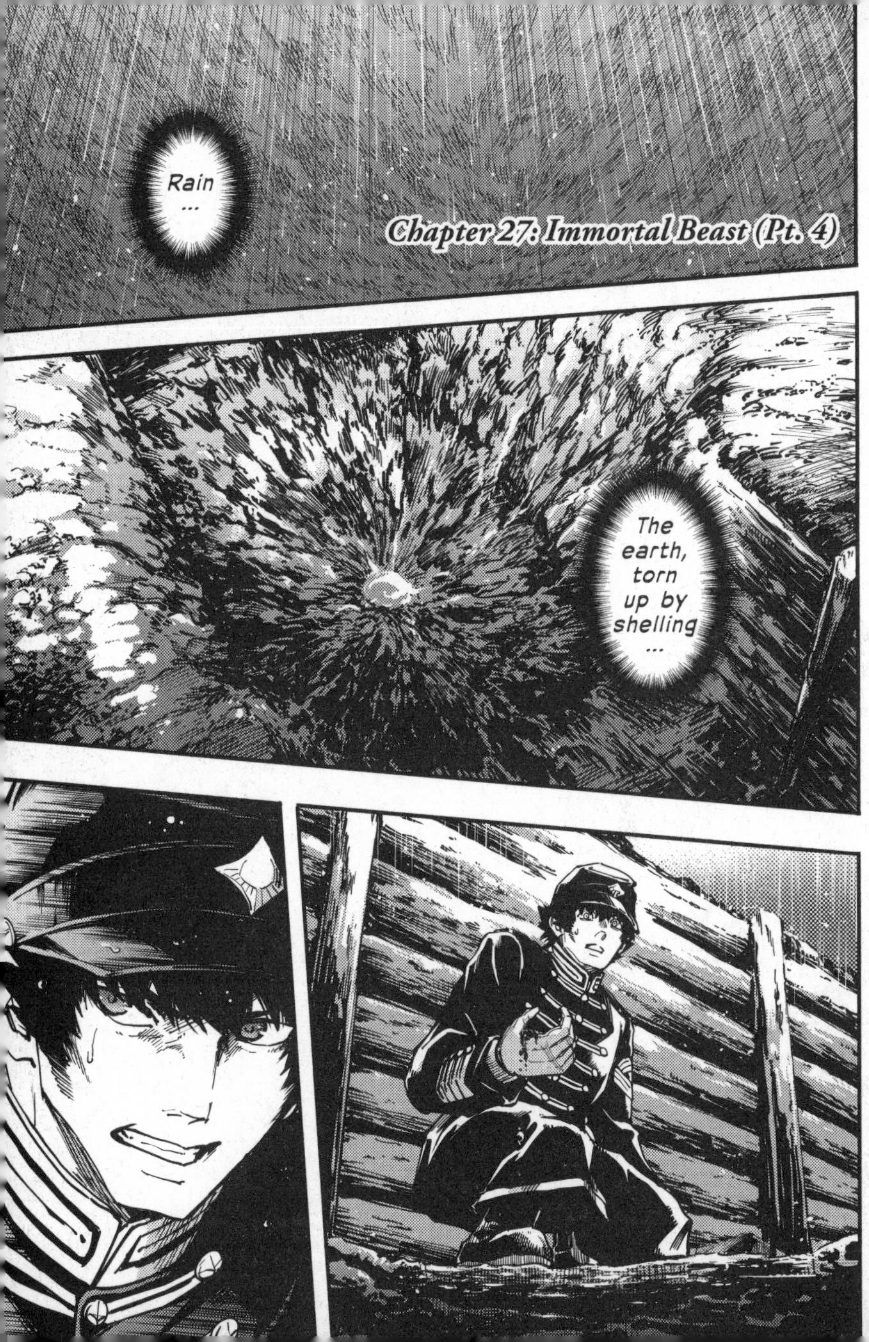
Rain ...
Chapter 27: Immortal Beast (Pt. 4)
The earth, torn up by shelling ...

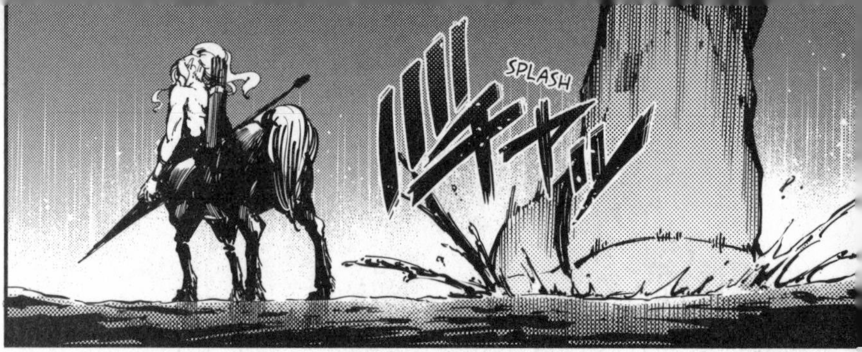
SPLASH
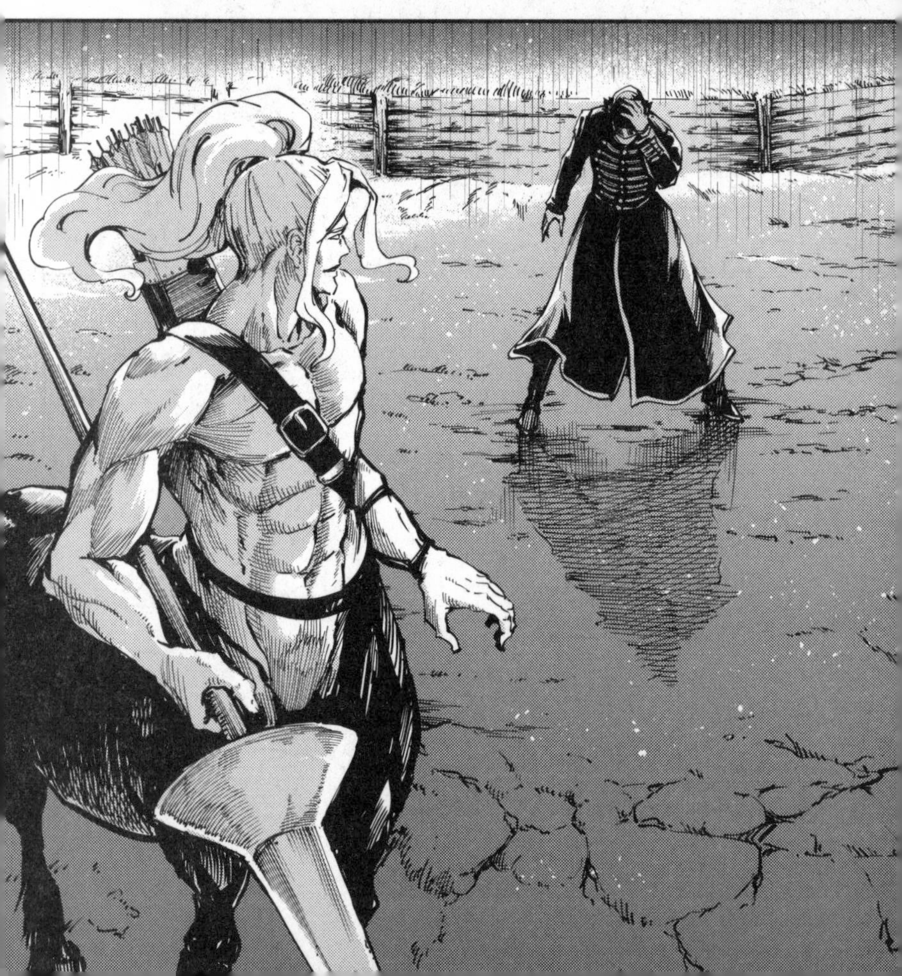

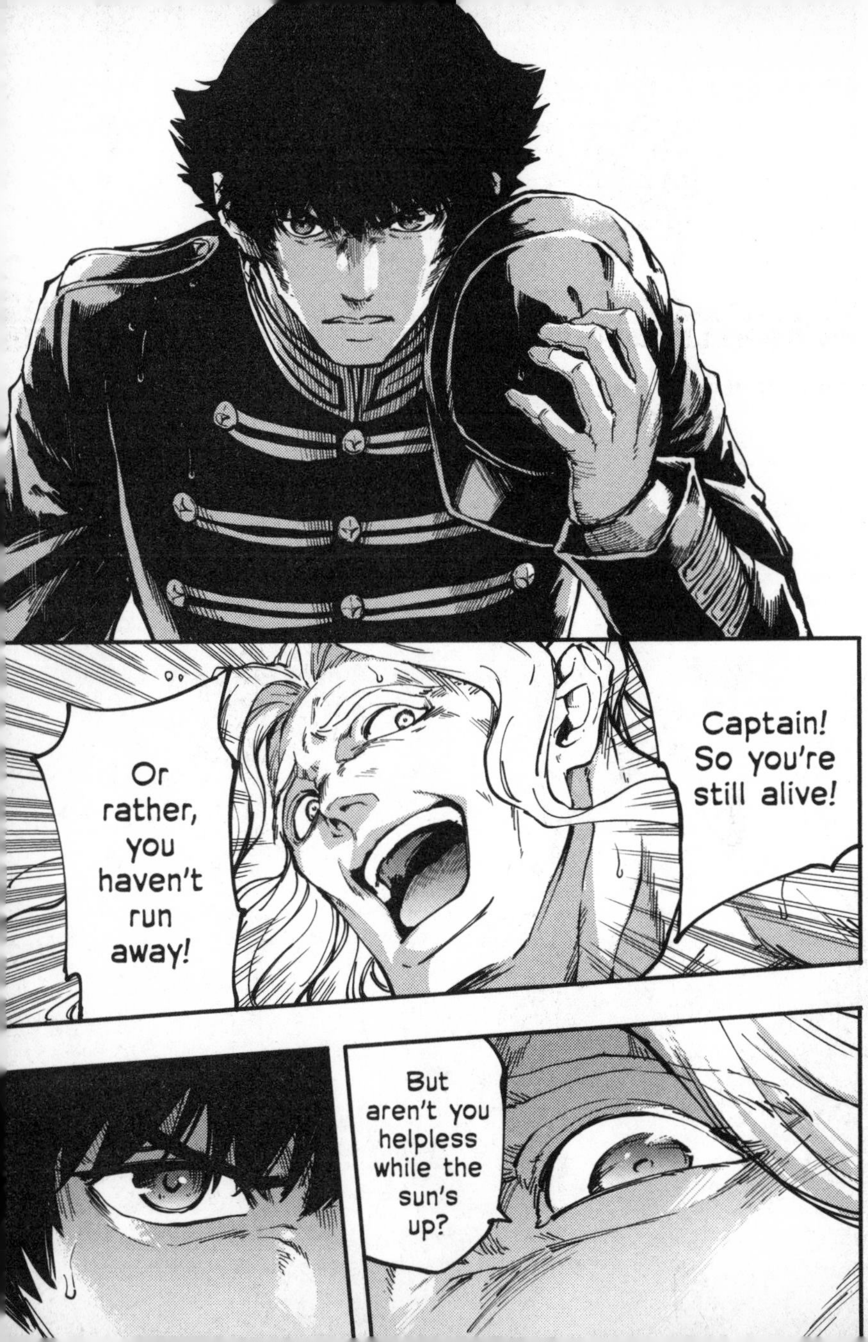
Captain! So you're still alive!
Or rather, you haven't run away!
But aren't you helpless while the sun's up?

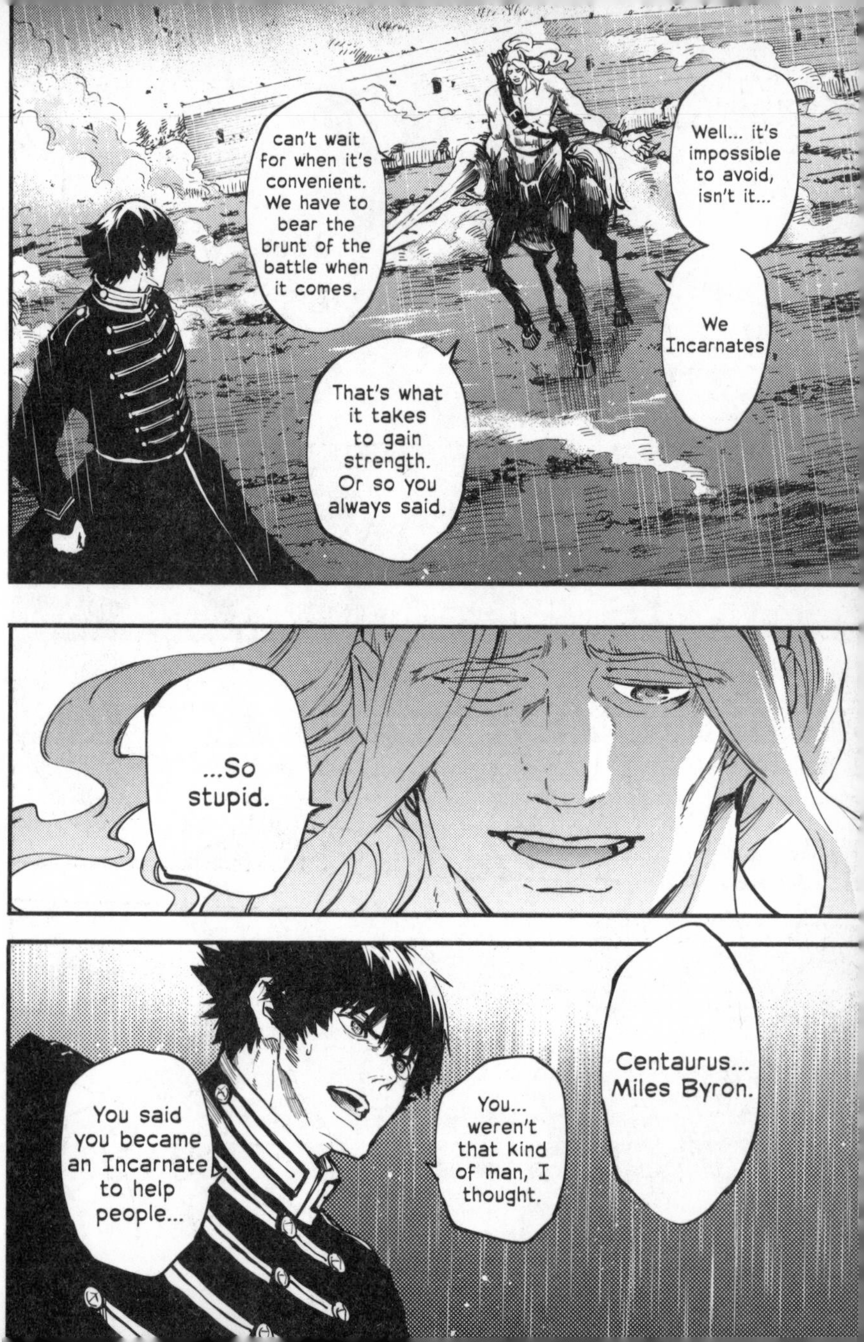
Well... it's impossible to avoid, isn't it...
We Incarnates
can't wait for when it's convenient. We have to bear the brunt of the battle when it comes.
That's what it takes to gain strength. Or so you always said.
...So stupid.
Centaurus... Miles Byron.
You... weren't that kind of man, I thought.
You said you became an Incarnate to help people...

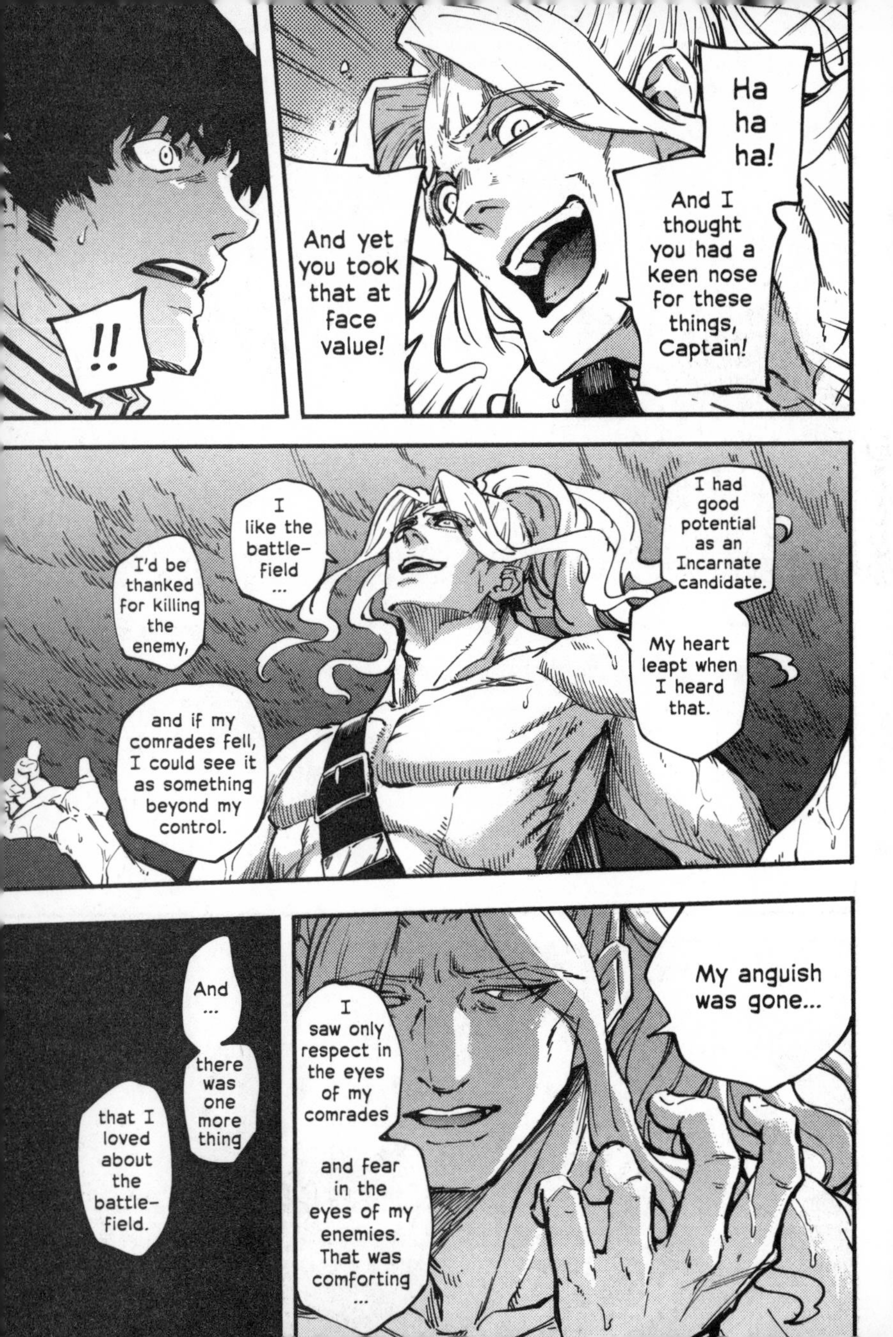
Ha ha ha!
And I thought you had a keen nose for these things, Captain!
And yet you took that at face value!
!!
I had good potential as an Incarnate candidate.
My heart leapt when I heard that.
I like the battlefield ...
I'd be thanked for killing the enemy,
and if my comrades fell, I could see it as something beyond my control.
My anguish was gone...
I saw only respect in the eyes of my comrades
and fear in the eyes of my enemies. That was comforting ...
And ...
there was one more thing
that I loved about the battlefield.

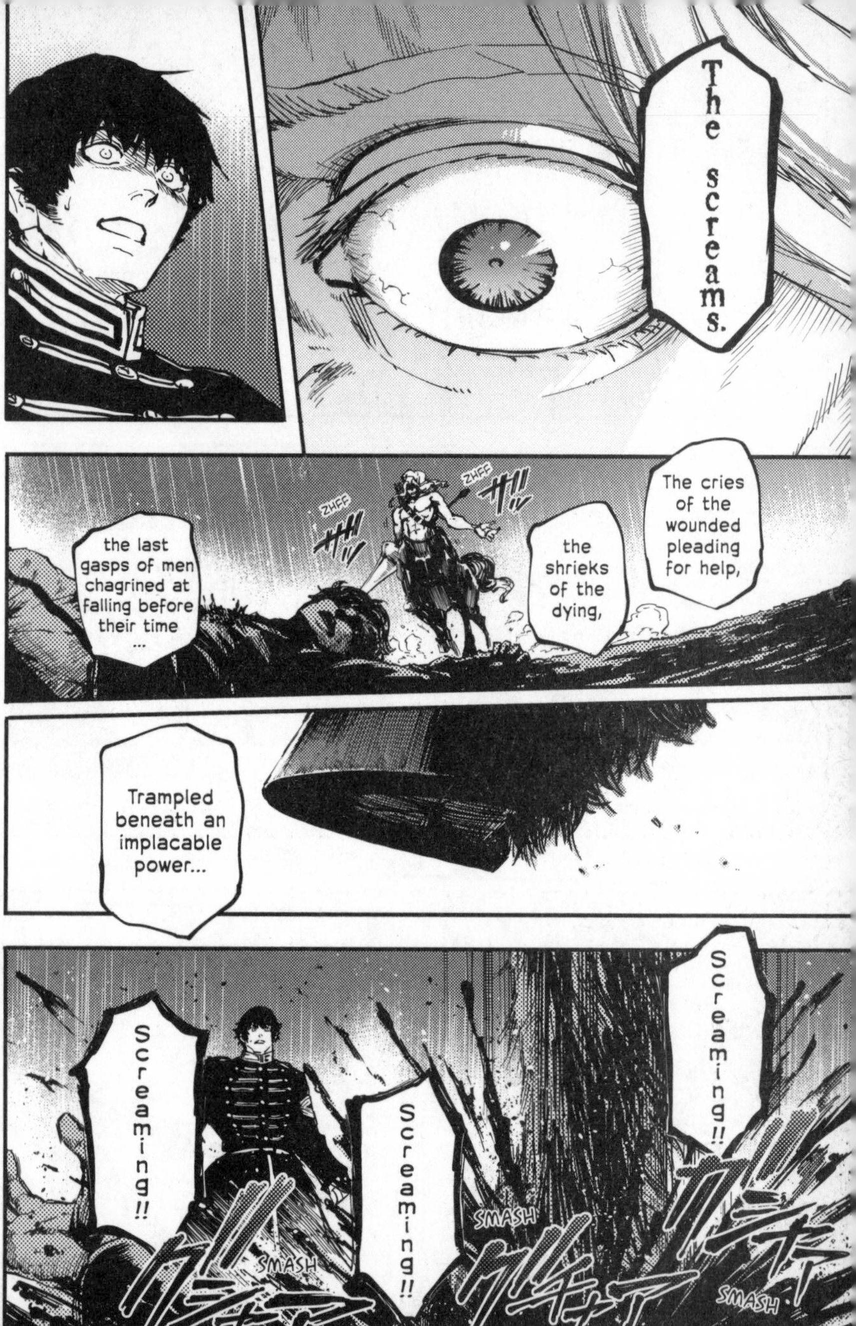
The screams.
The cries of the wounded pleading for help,
ZHFF
the shrieks of the dying,
ZHFF
the last gasps of men chagrined at falling before their time ...
Trampled beneath an implacable power...
Screaming!!
SMASH
Screaming!!
SMASH
Screaming!!
SMASH

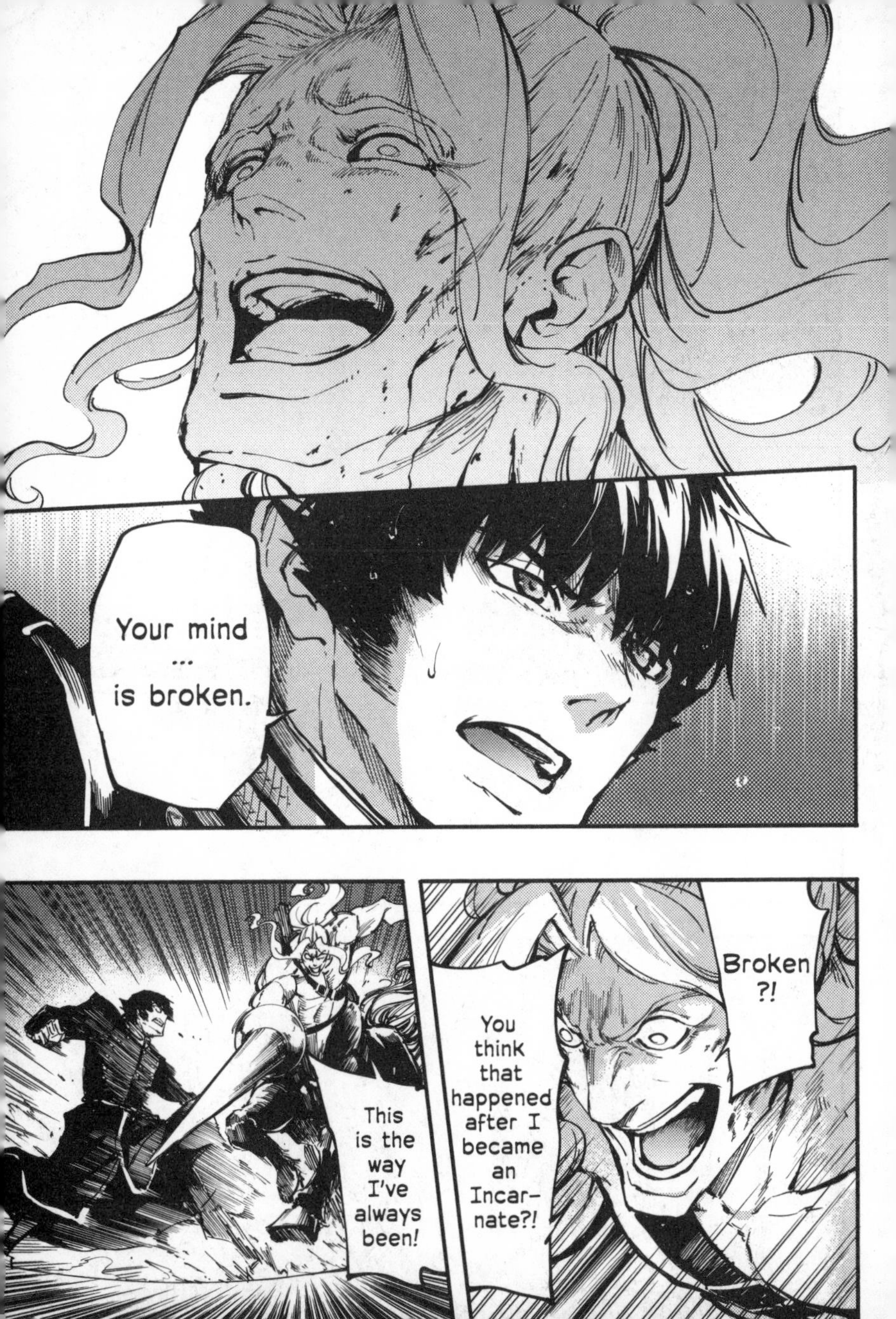
Your mind ... is broken.
Broken?!
You think that happened after I became an Incarnate?!
This is the way I've always been!

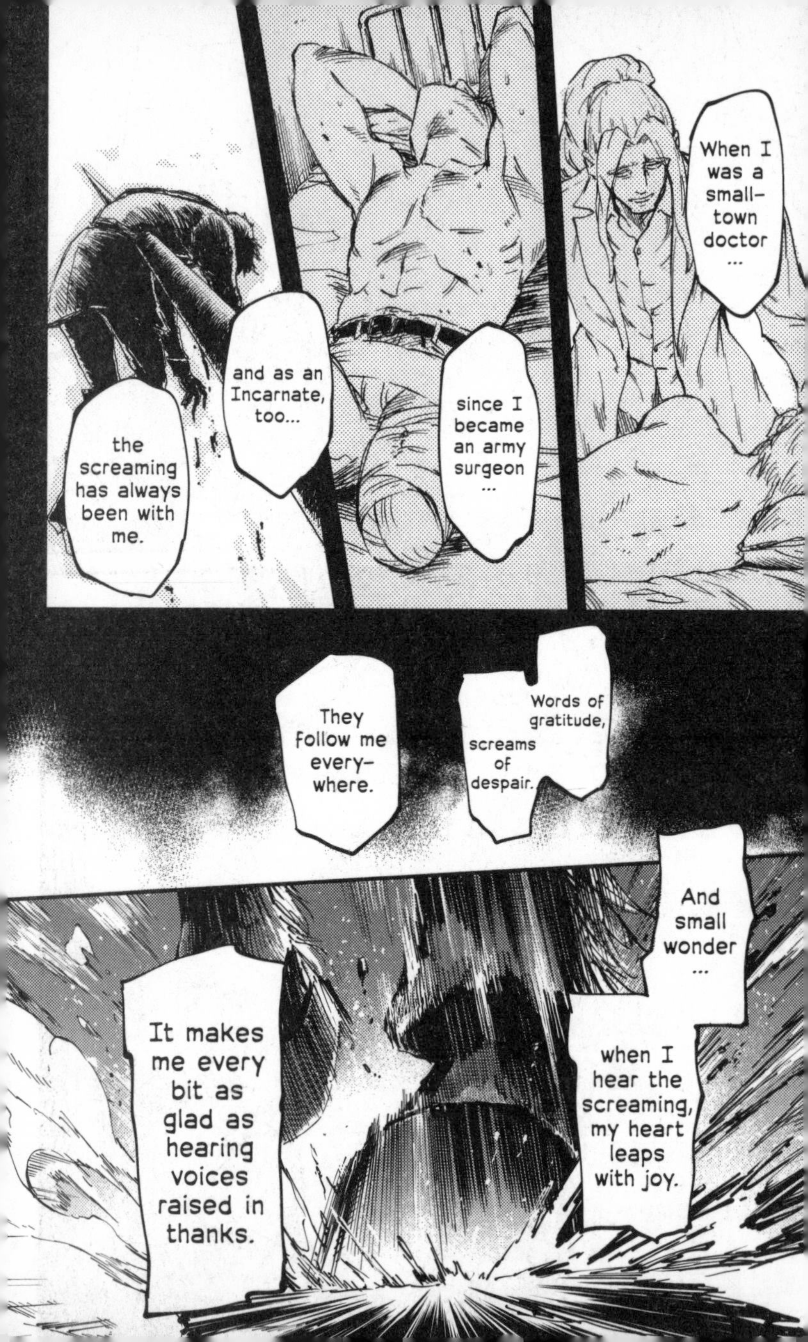
When I was a small-town doctor ...
since I became an army surgeon ...
and as an Incarnate, too...
the screaming has always been with me.
Words of gratitude, screams of despair.
They follow me every-where.
And small wonder ...
when I hear the screaming, my heart leaps with joy.
It makes me every bit as glad as hearing voices raised in thanks.

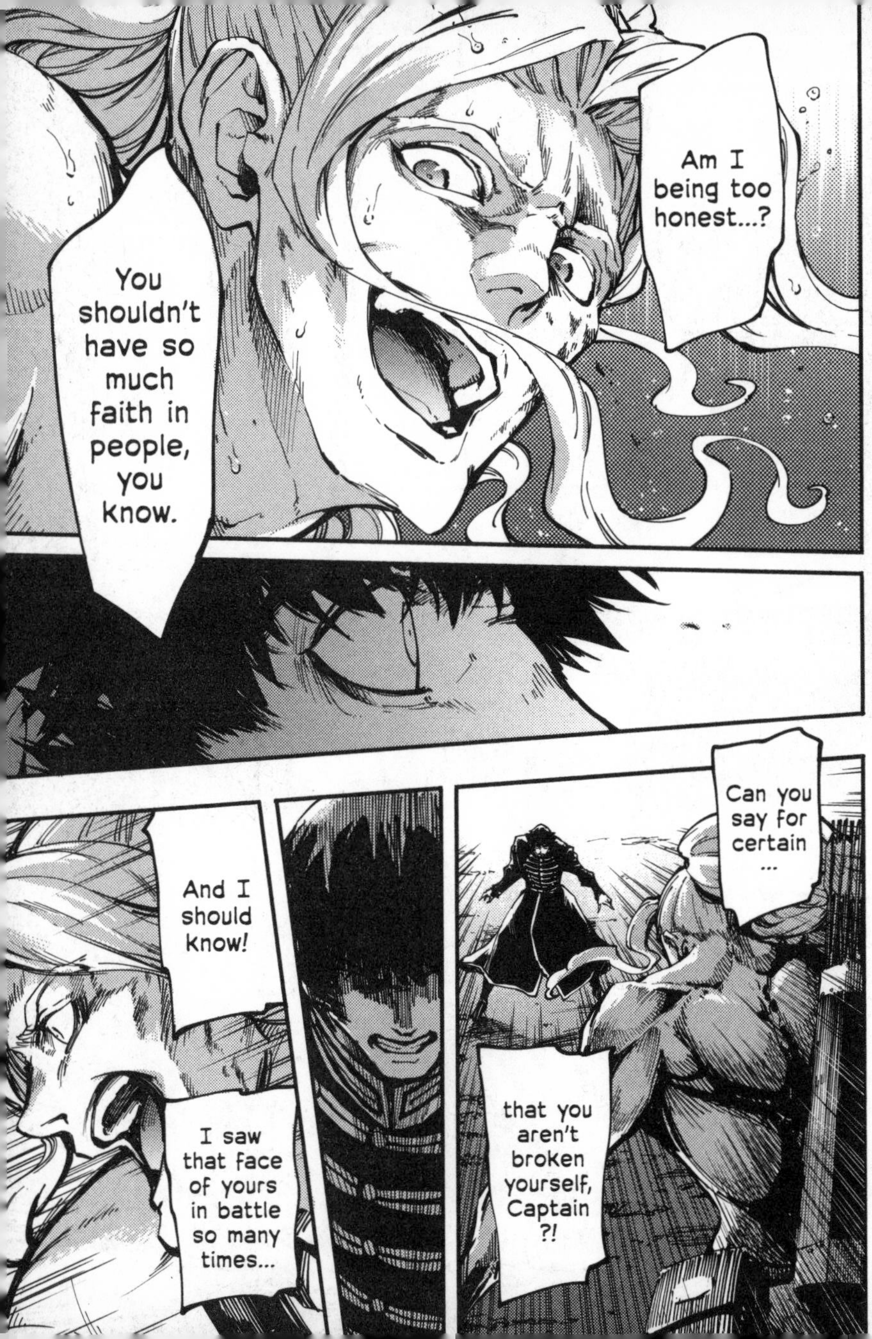
Am I being too honest...?
You shouldn't have so much faith in people, you know.
Can you say for certain ...
that you aren't broken yourself, Captain ?!
And I should know!
I saw that face of yours in battle so many times...

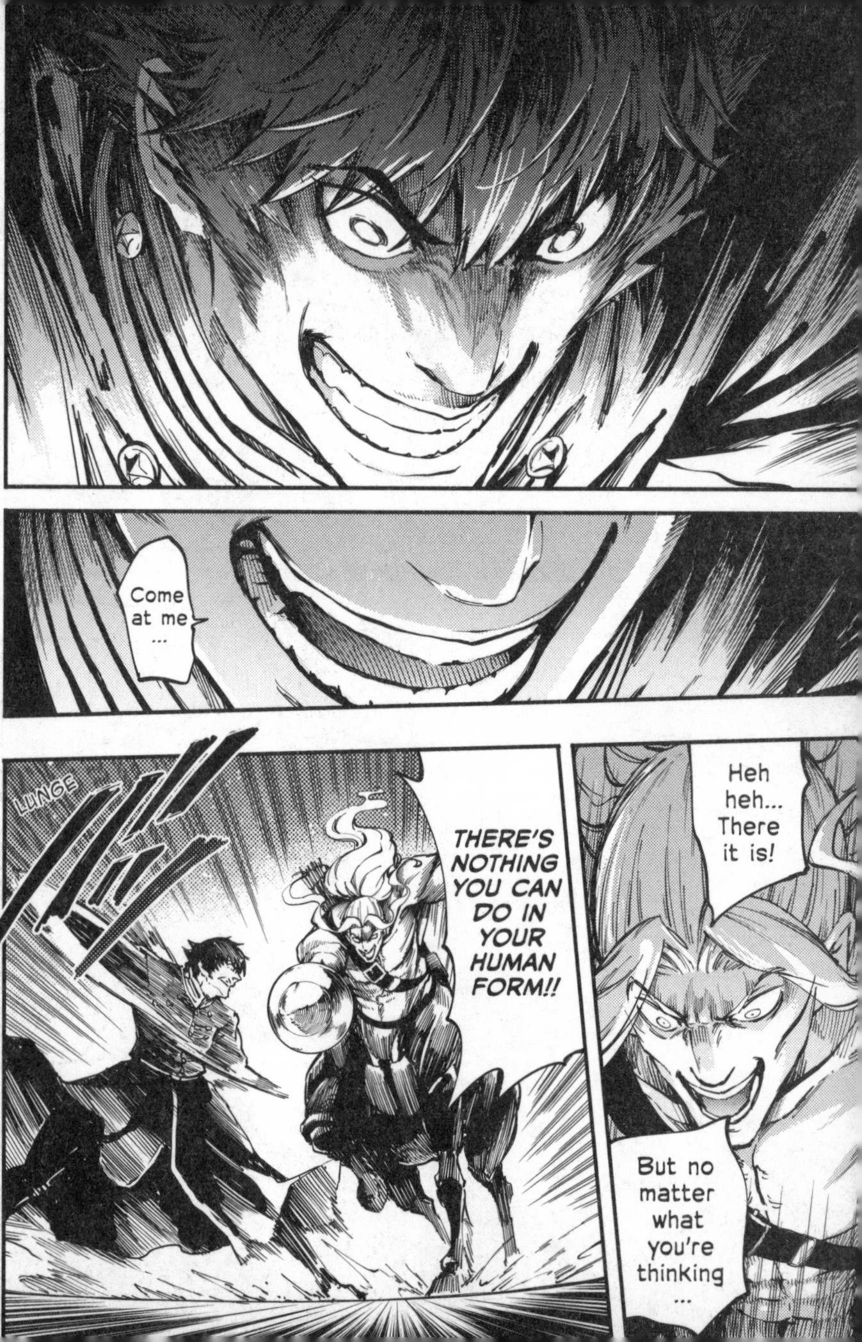
Come at me ...
Heh heh... There it is!
But no matter what you're thinking ...
THERE'S NOTHING YOU CAN DO IN YOUR HUMAN FORM!!
LUNGE

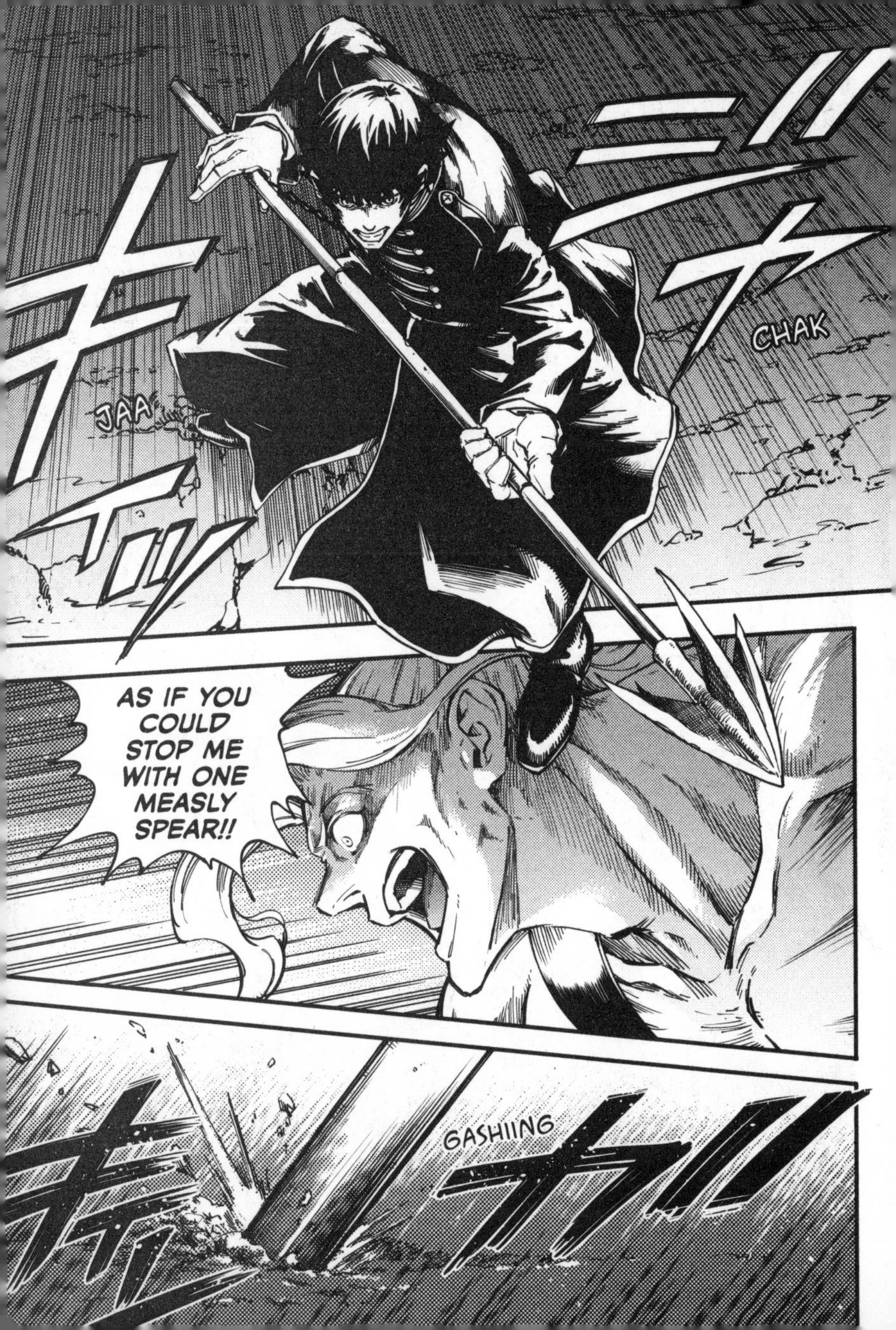
CHAK
JAA
AS IF YOU COULD STOP ME WITH ONE MEASLY SPEAR!!
GASHIING

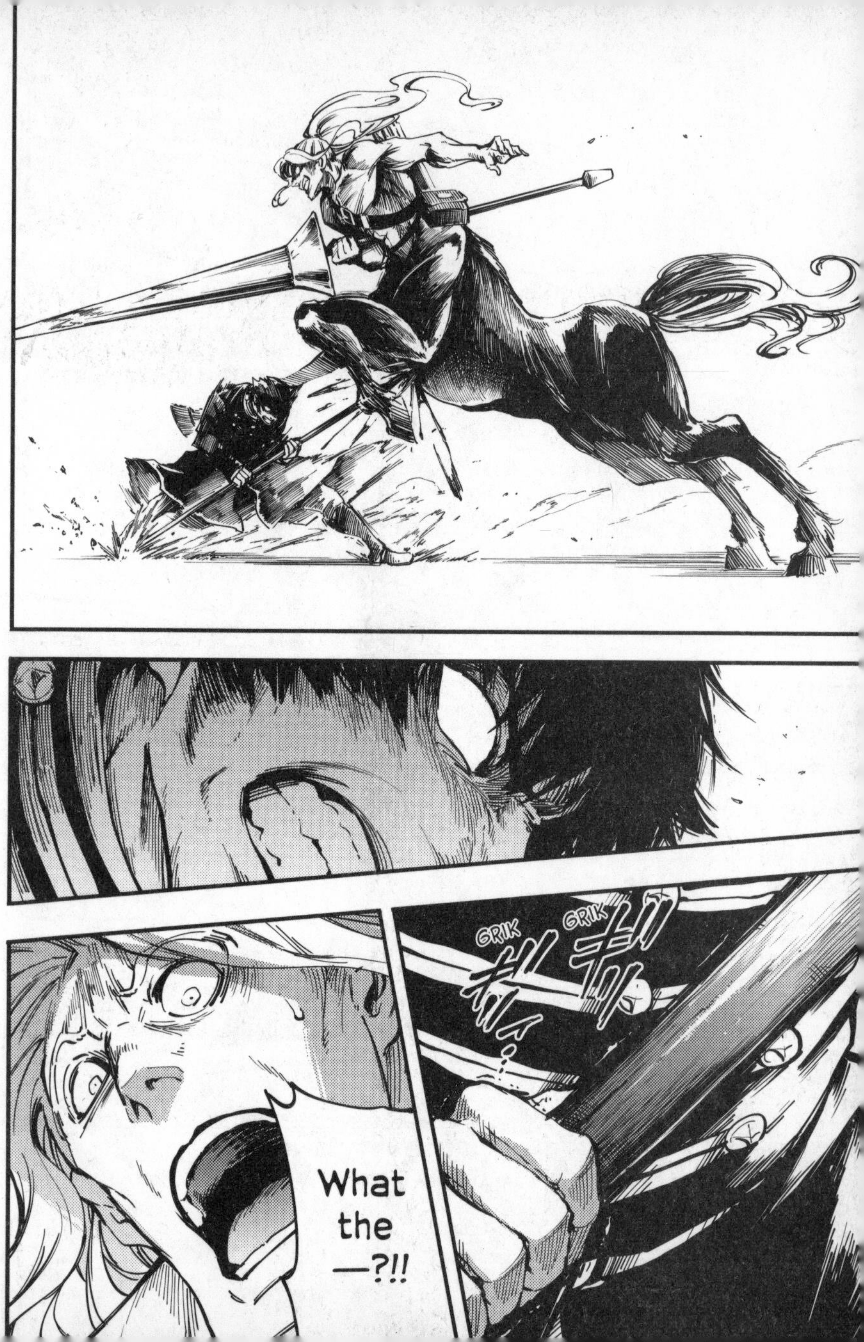
GRIK GRIK
What the —?!!

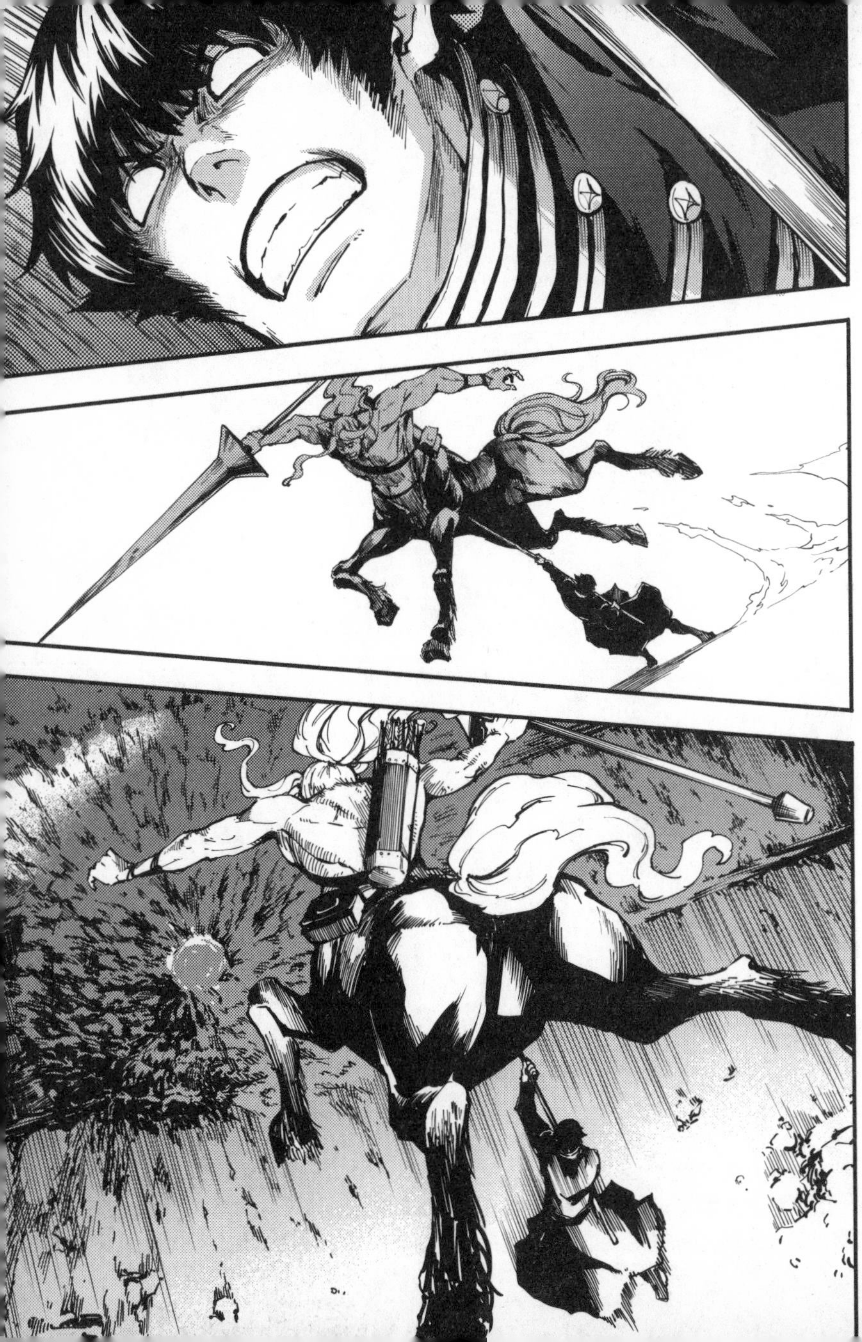

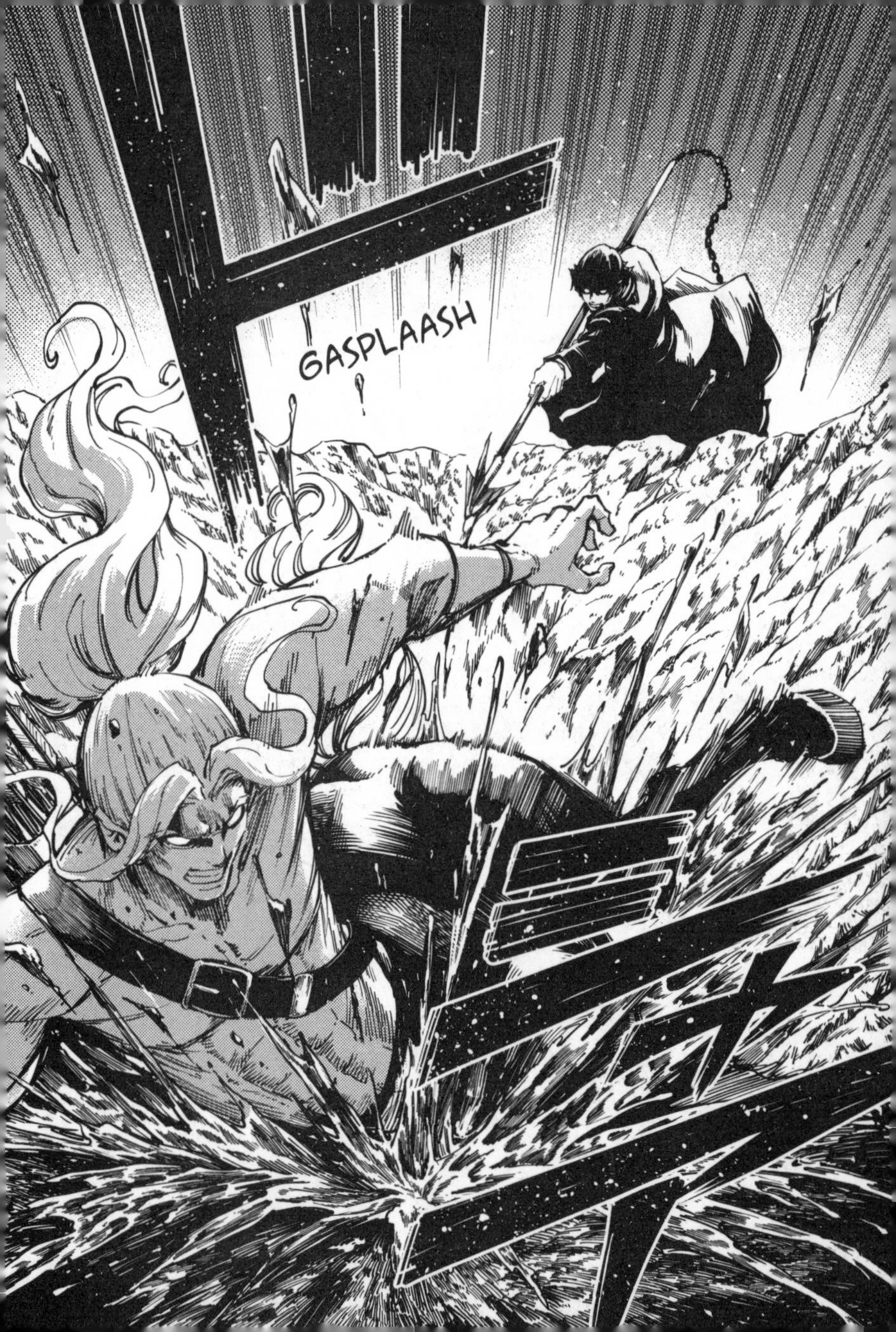
GASPLAASH

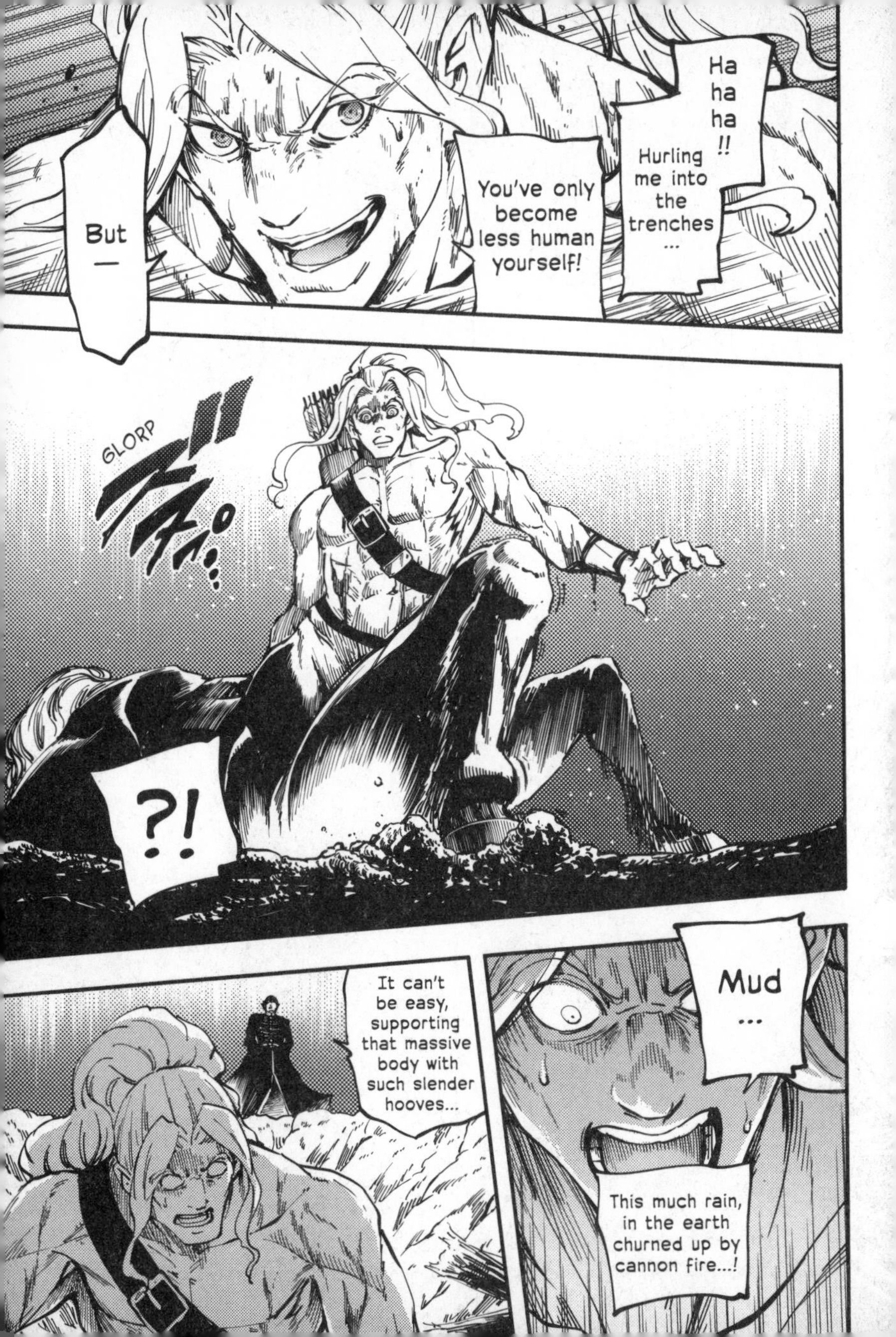
Ha ha ha!!
Hurling me into the trenches...
You've only become less human yourself!
But—
GLORP
?!
Mud...
This much rain, in the earth churned up by cannon fire...!
It can't be easy, supporting that massive body with such slender hooves...

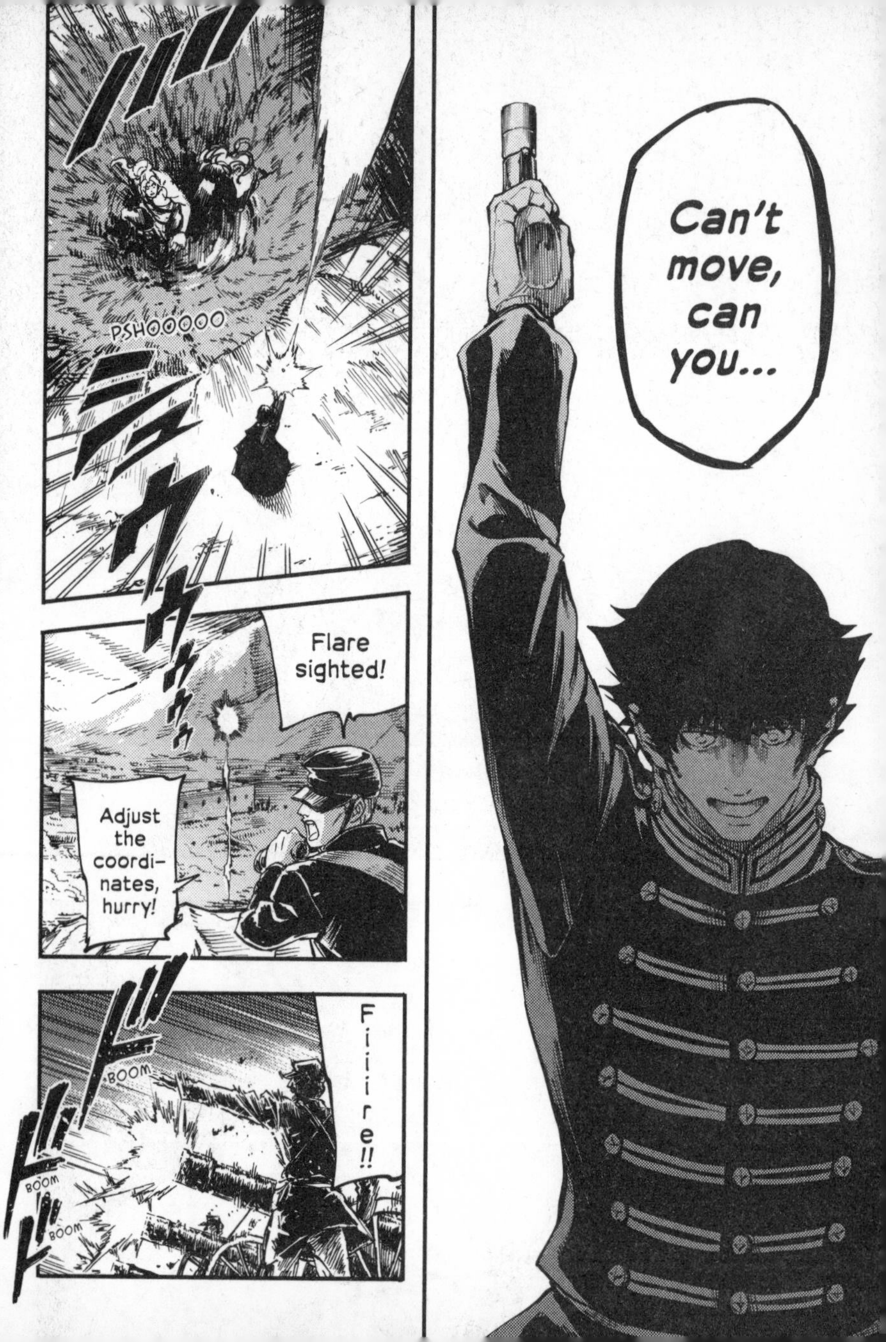
Can't move, can you...
PSHOOOOO
Flare sighted!
Adjust the coordi-nates, hurry!
Fiiire!!
BOOM
BOOM
BOOM

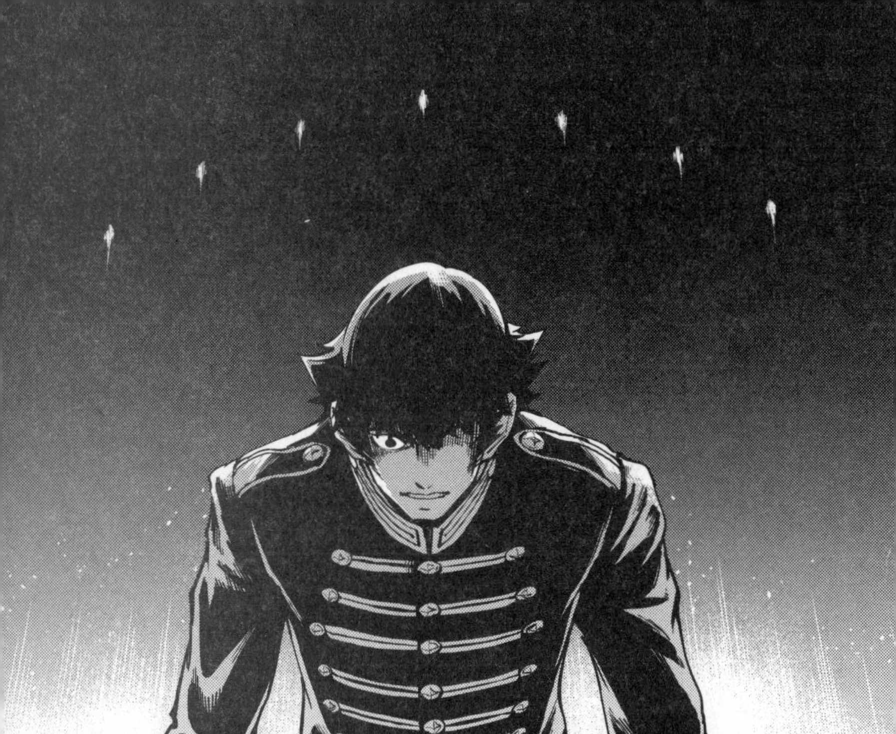
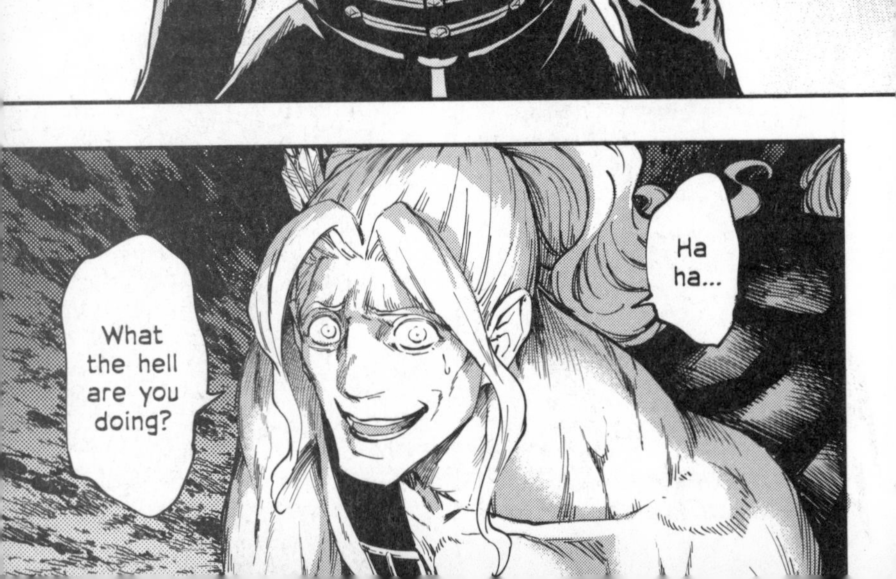
Ha ha...
What the hell are you doing?

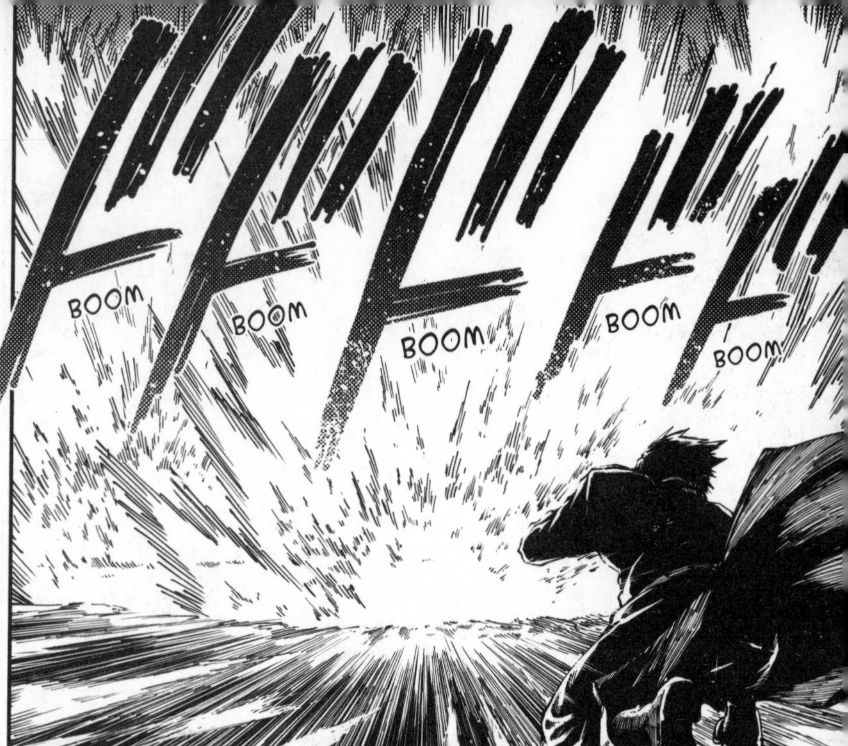
BOOM
BOOM
BOOM
BOOM
BOOM
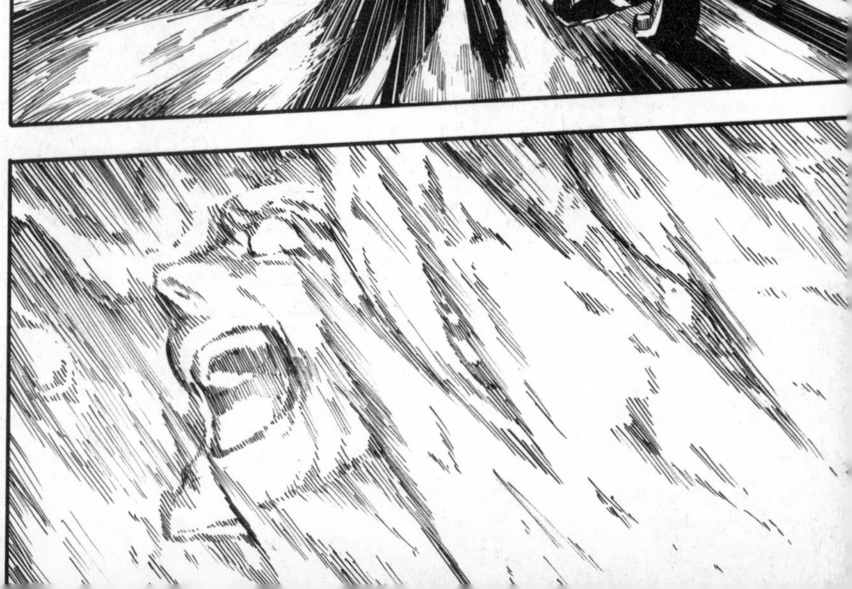

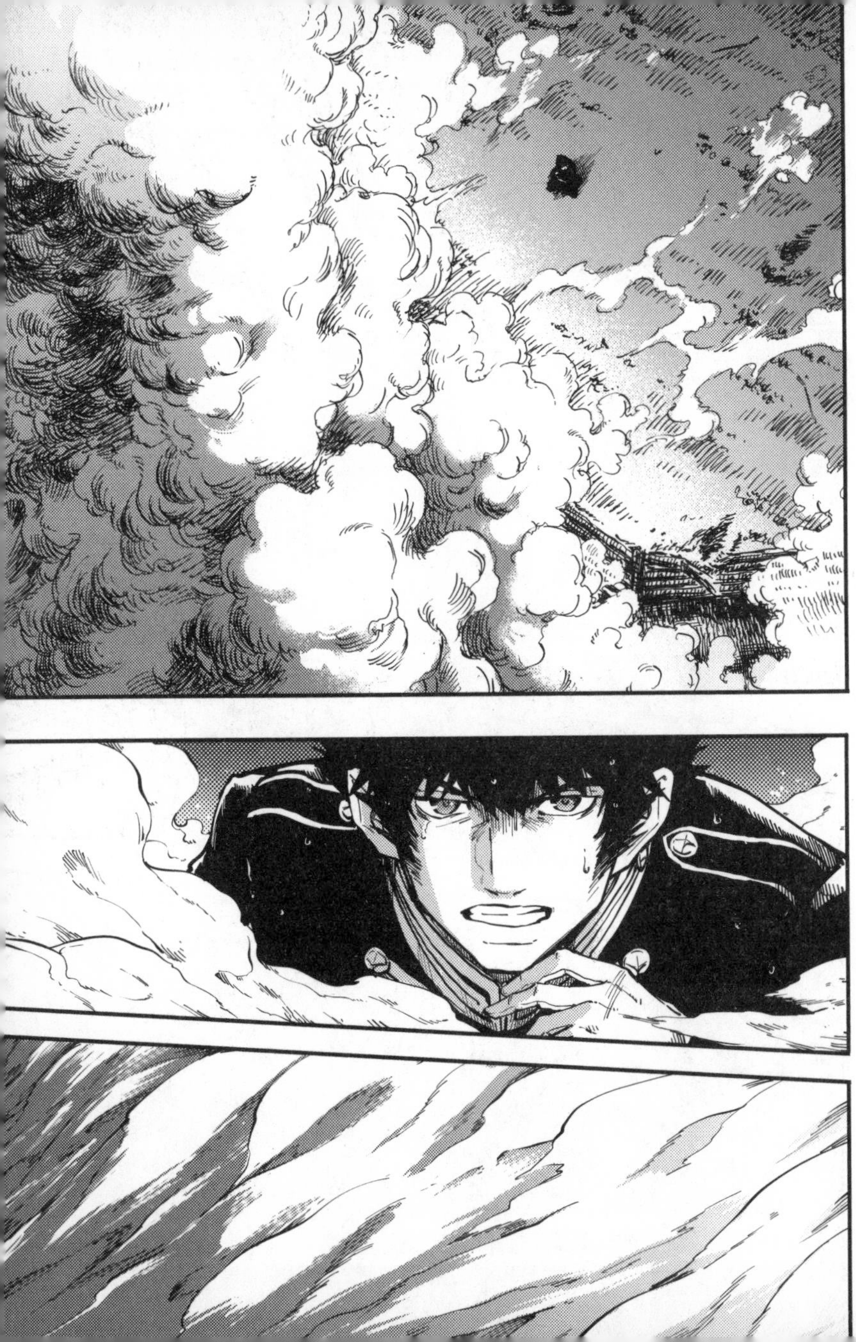

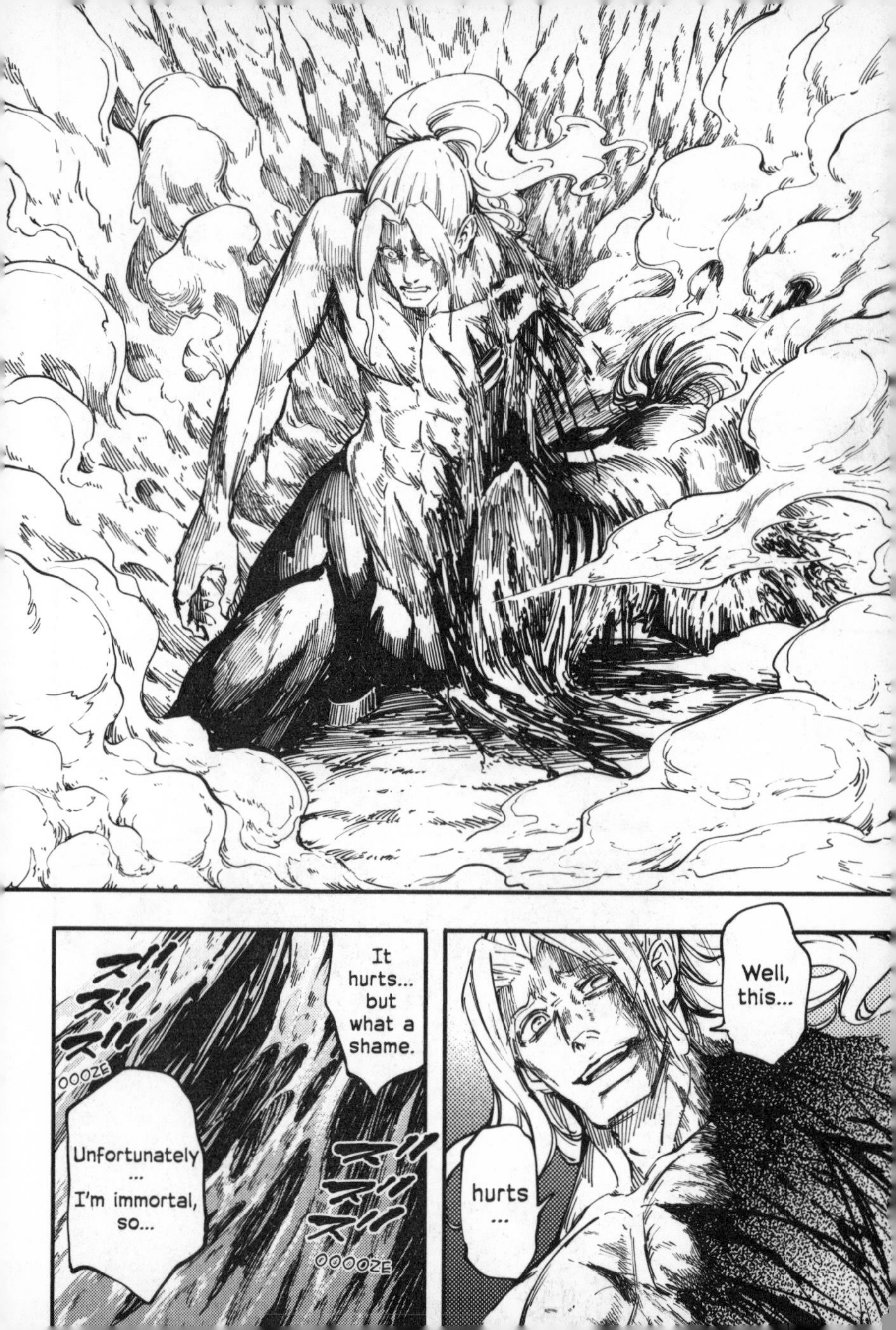
Well, this...
hurts ...
It hurts... but what a shame.
OOOZE
Unfortunately ... I'm immortal, so...
OOOOZE

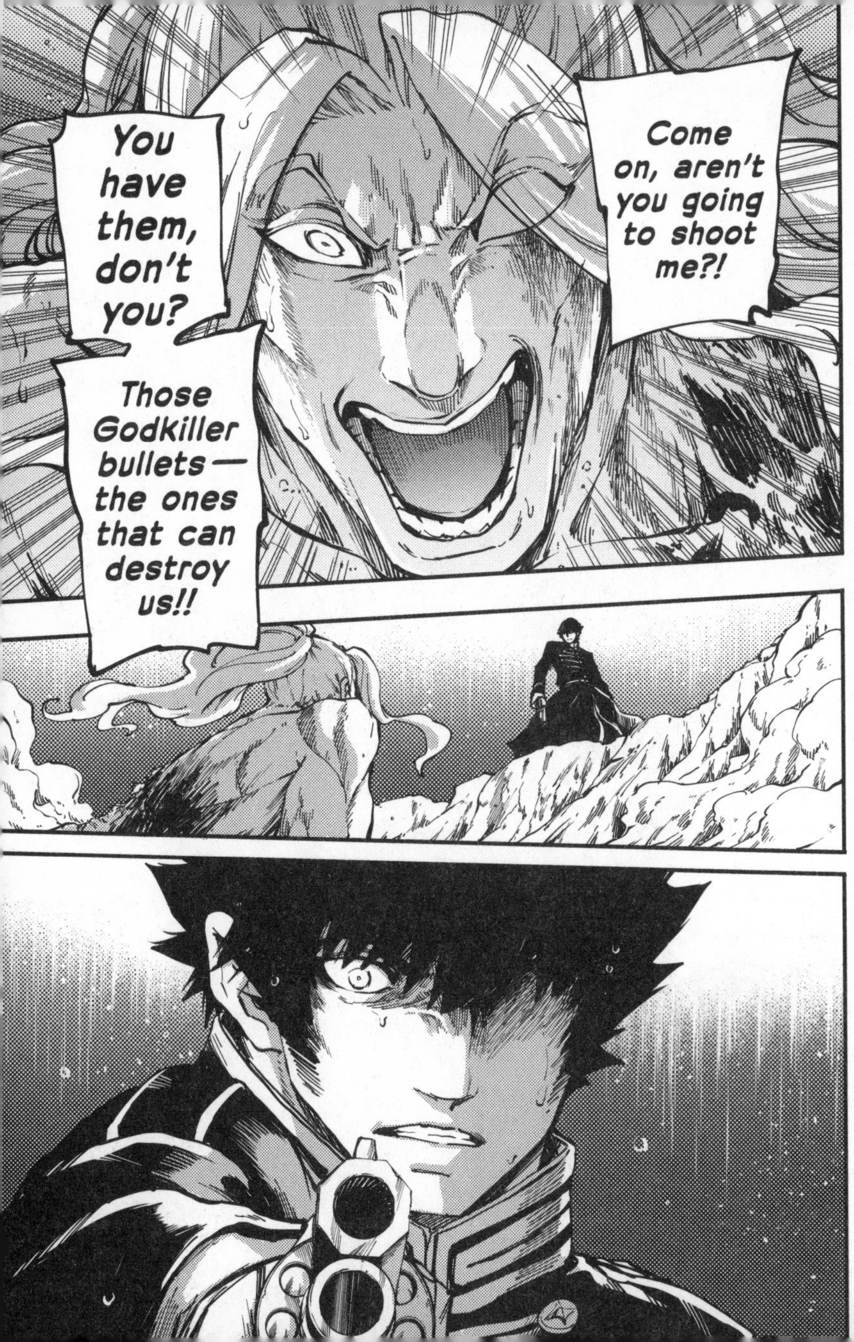
Come on, aren't you going to shoot me?!
You have them, don't you?
Those Godkiller bullets—the ones that can destroy us!!

To the Abandoned
Sacred Beasts

Chapter 28: Immortal Beast (Pt. 5)

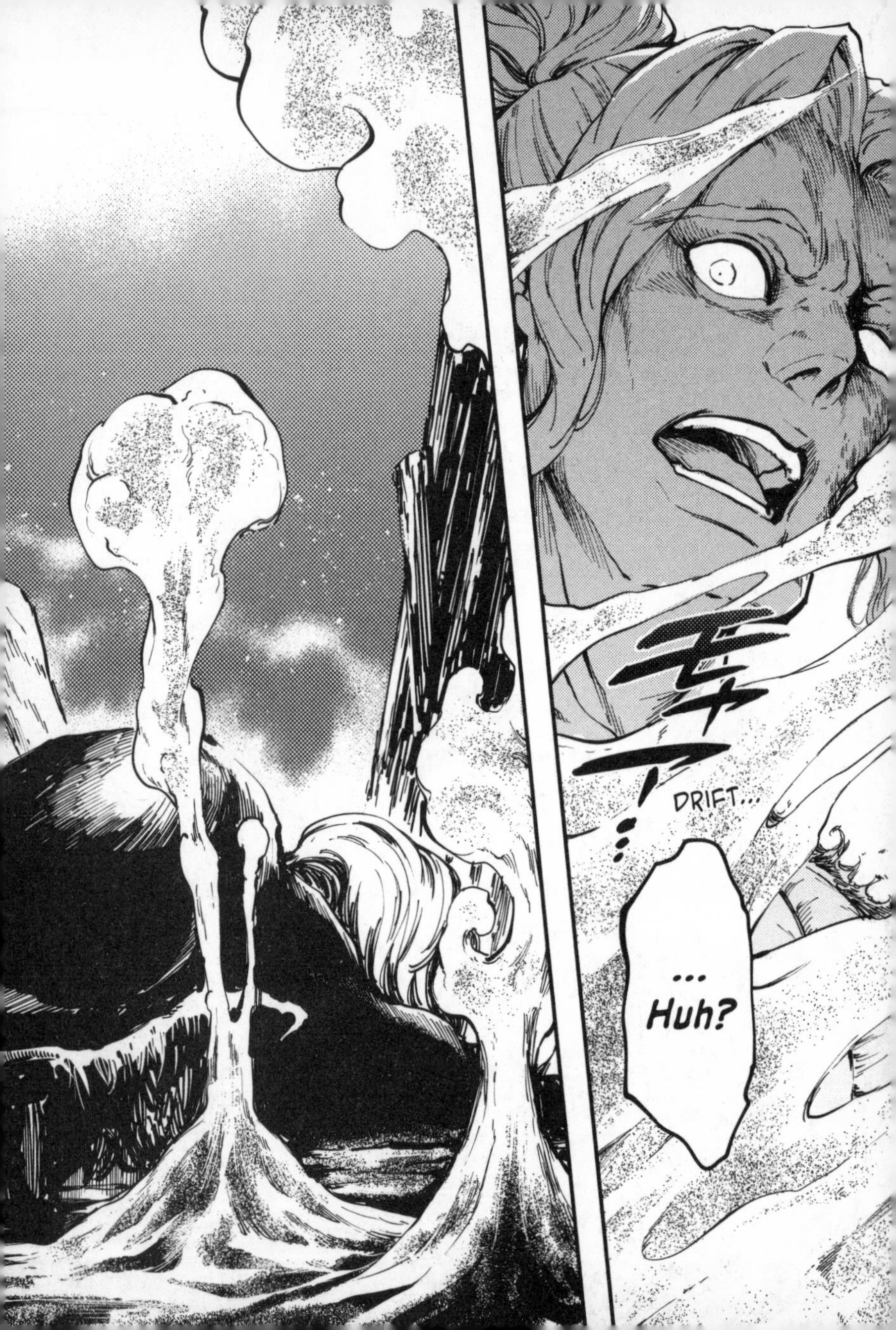
DRIFT...
... Huh?

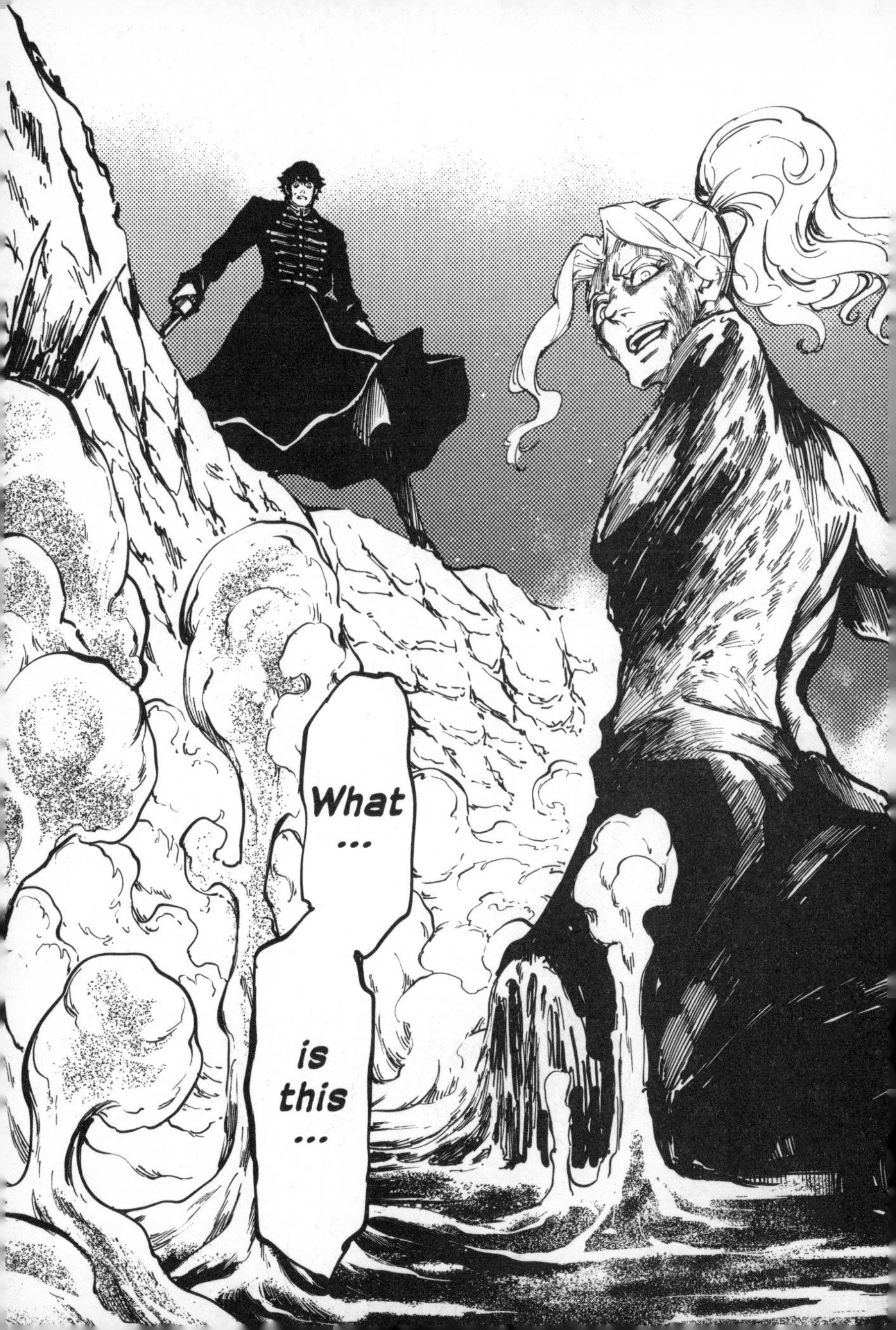
What ...
is this ...

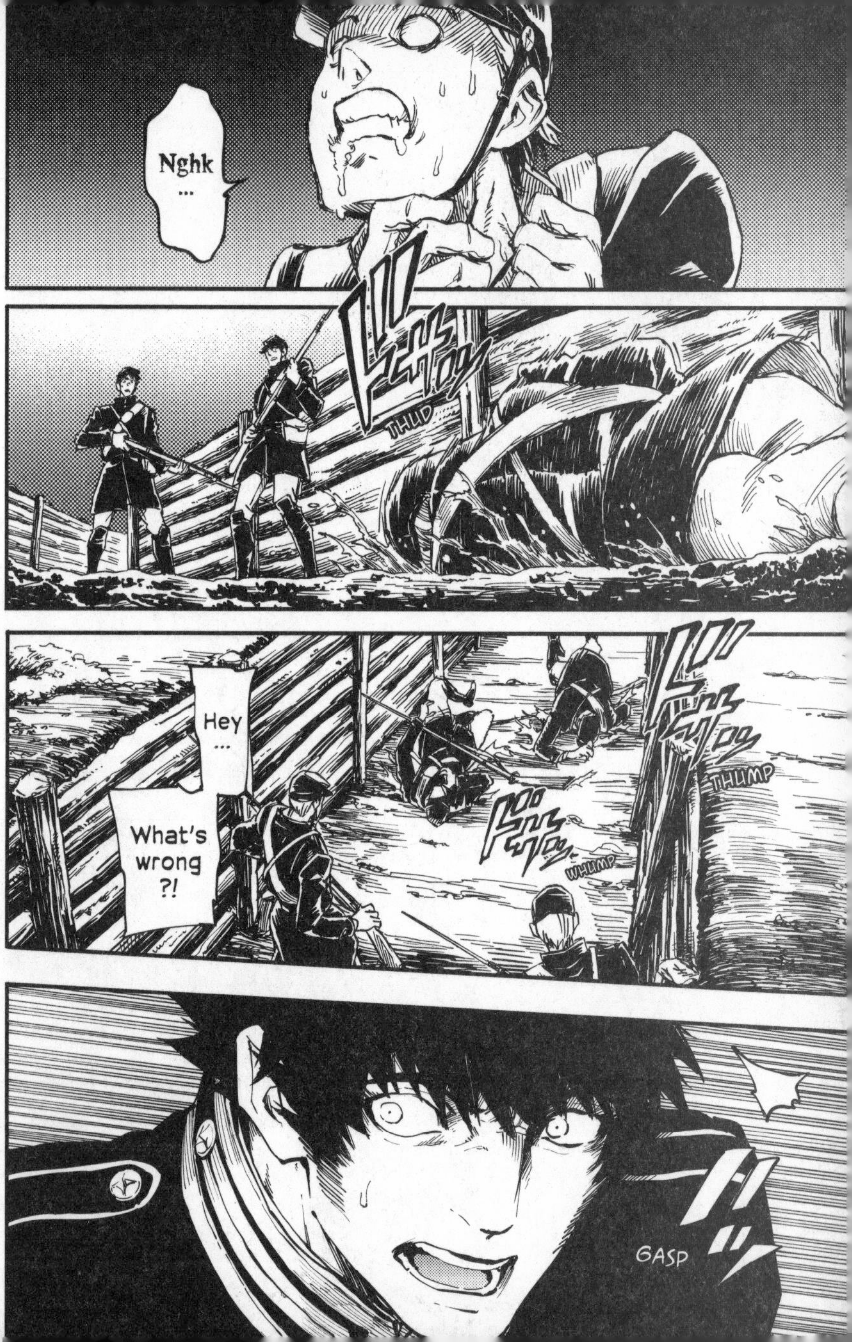
Nghk
...
THUD
THUMP
WHUMP
Hey
...
What's
wrong
?!
GASP

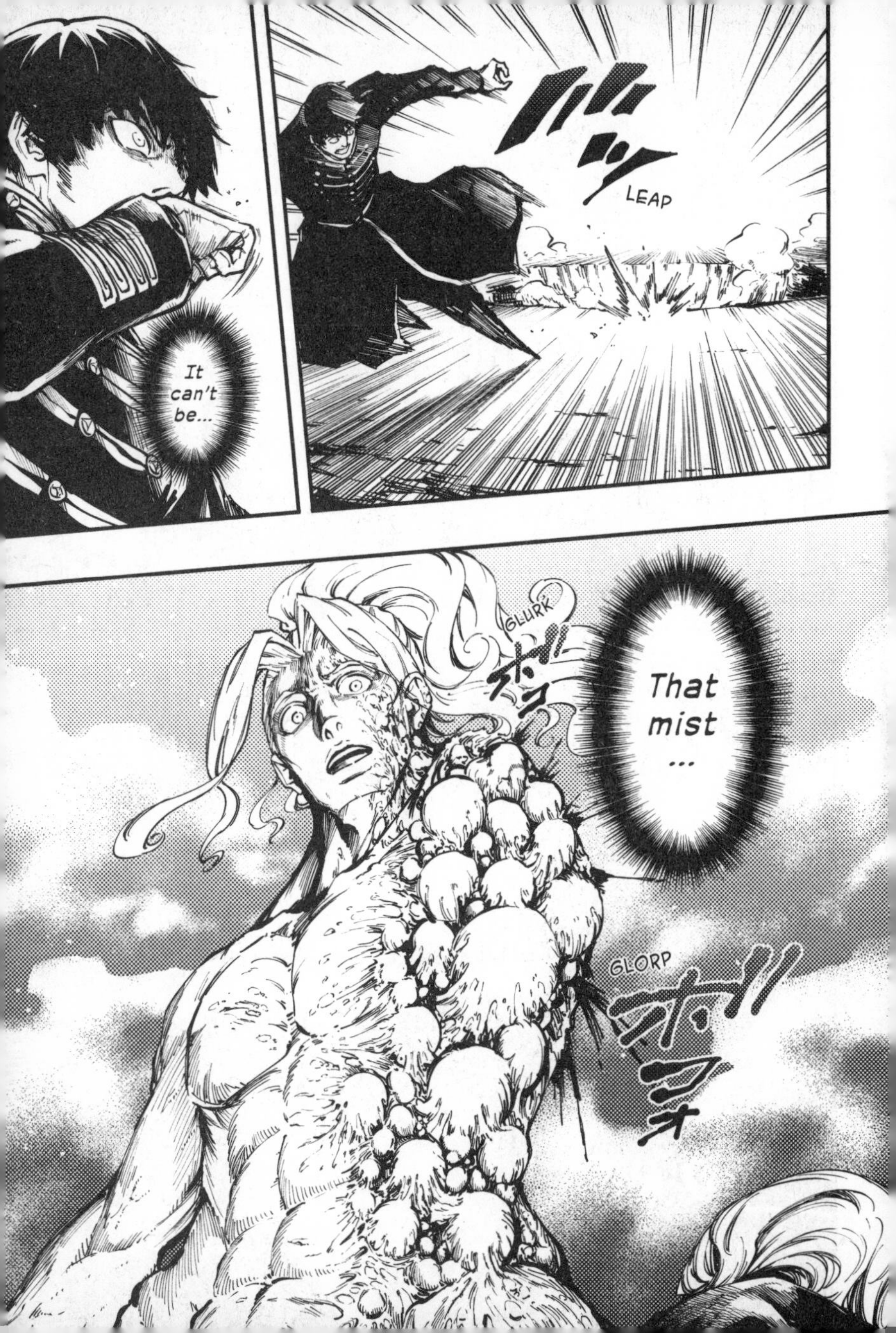

LEAP
It can't be...
That mist ...
GLURK
GLORP

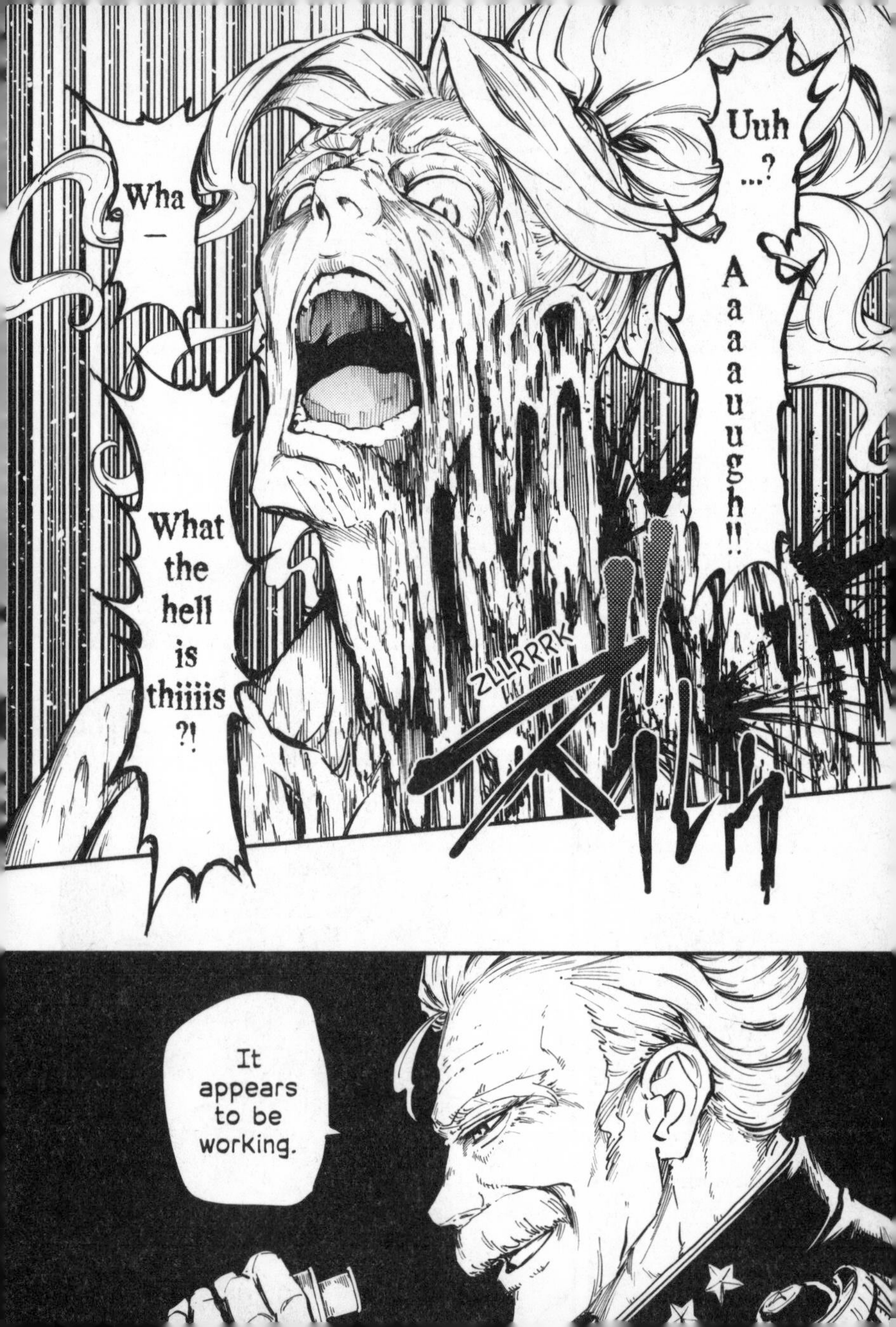

Uuh ...? Aaaaaugh!!
ZLLRRRK
Wha—
What the hell is thiiiis?!
It appears to be working.

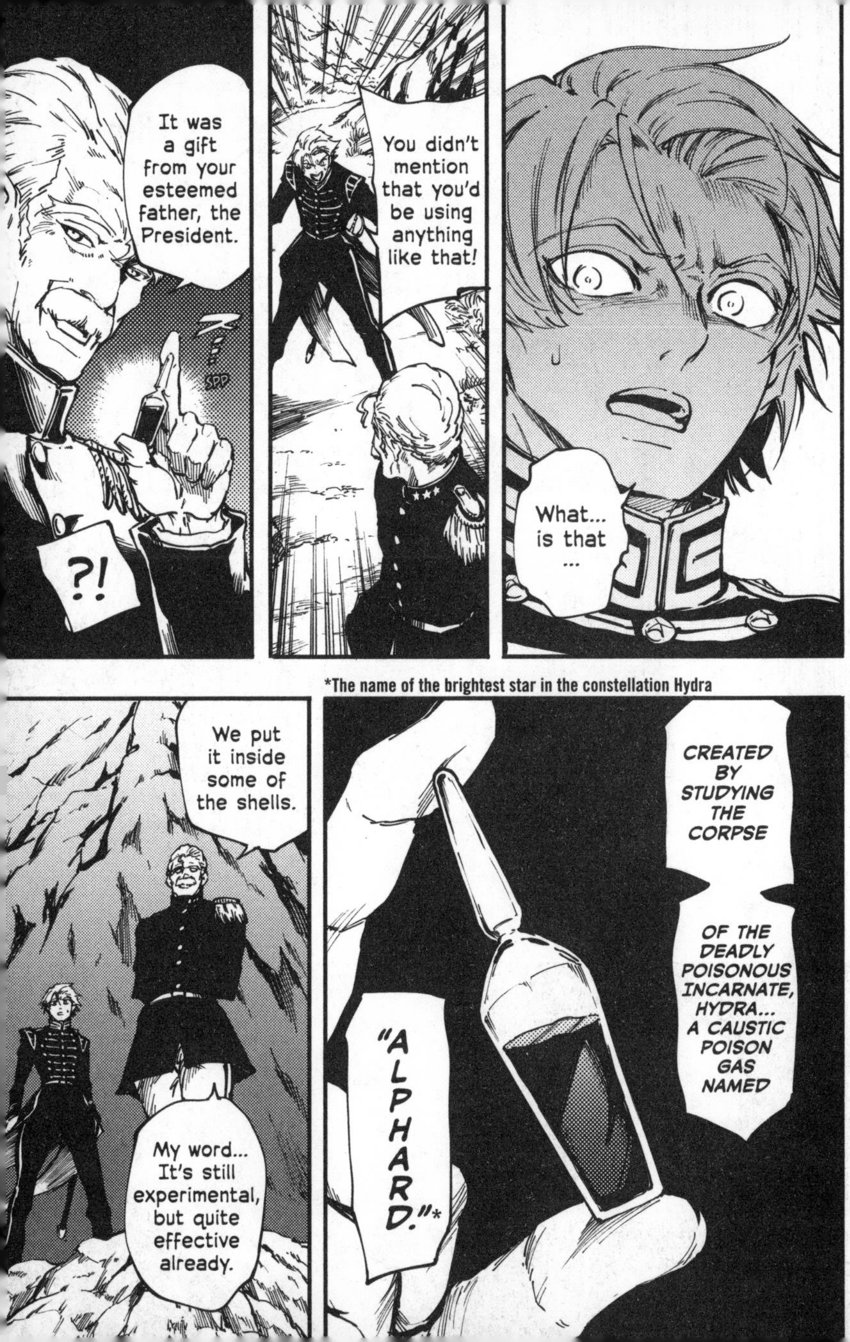
What... is that ...
You didn't mention that you'd be using anything like that!
It was a gift from your esteemed father, the President.
SPP
?!
CREATED BY STUDYING THE CORPSE
OF THE DEADLY POISONOUS INCARNATE, HYDRA... A CAUSTIC POISON GAS NAMED
"ALPHARD."*
We put it inside some of the shells.
My word... It's still experimental, but quite effective already.

*The name of the brightest star in the constellation Hydra

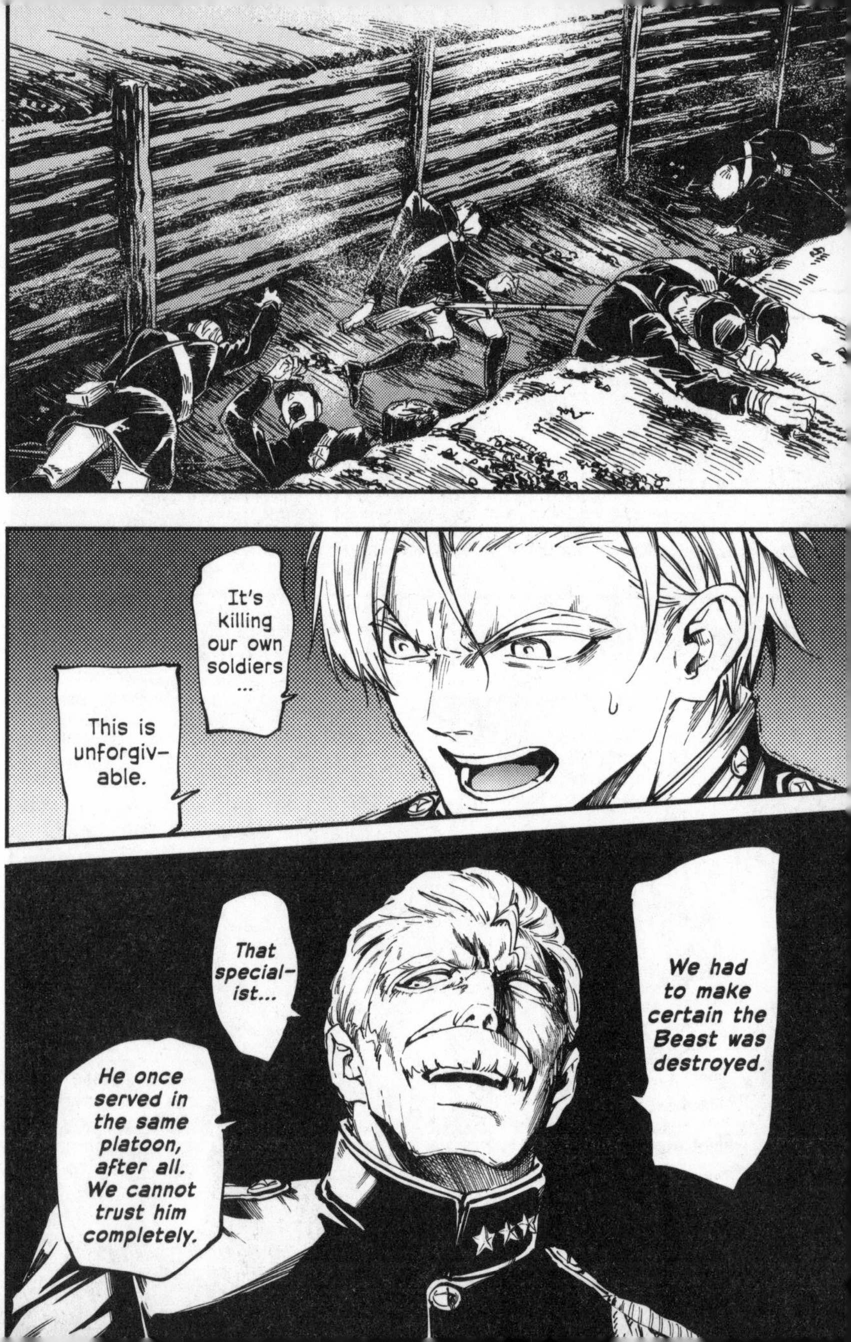

It's killing our own soldiers ...
This is unforgiv-able.
We had to make certain the Beast was destroyed.
That special-ist...
He once served in the same platoon, after all. We cannot trust him completely.

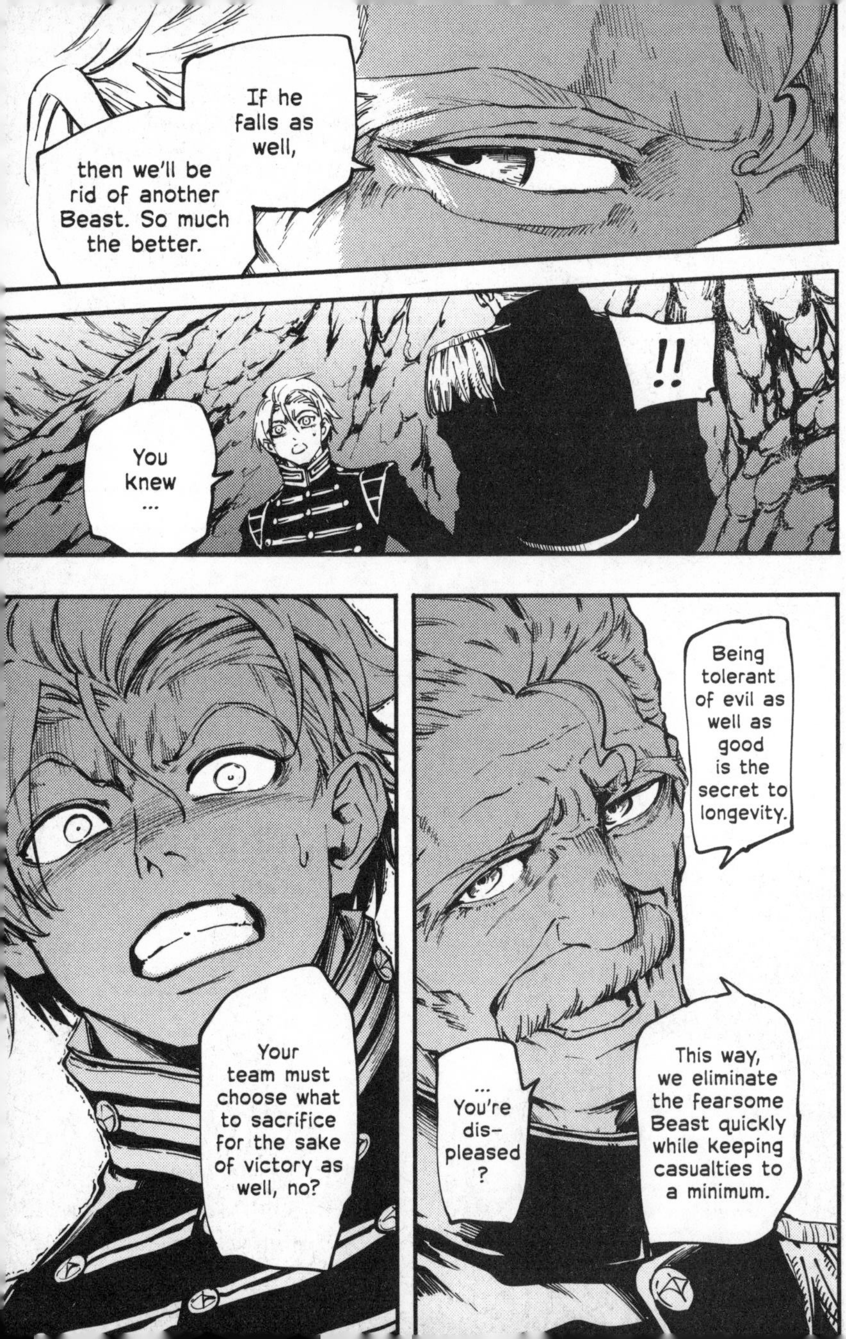
If he falls as well,
then we'll be rid of another Beast. So much the better.
!!
You knew ...
Being tolerant of evil as well as good is the secret to longevity.
This way, we eliminate the fearsome Beast quickly while keeping casualties to a minimum.
... You're dis-pleased ?
Your team must choose what to sacrifice for the sake of victory as well, no?

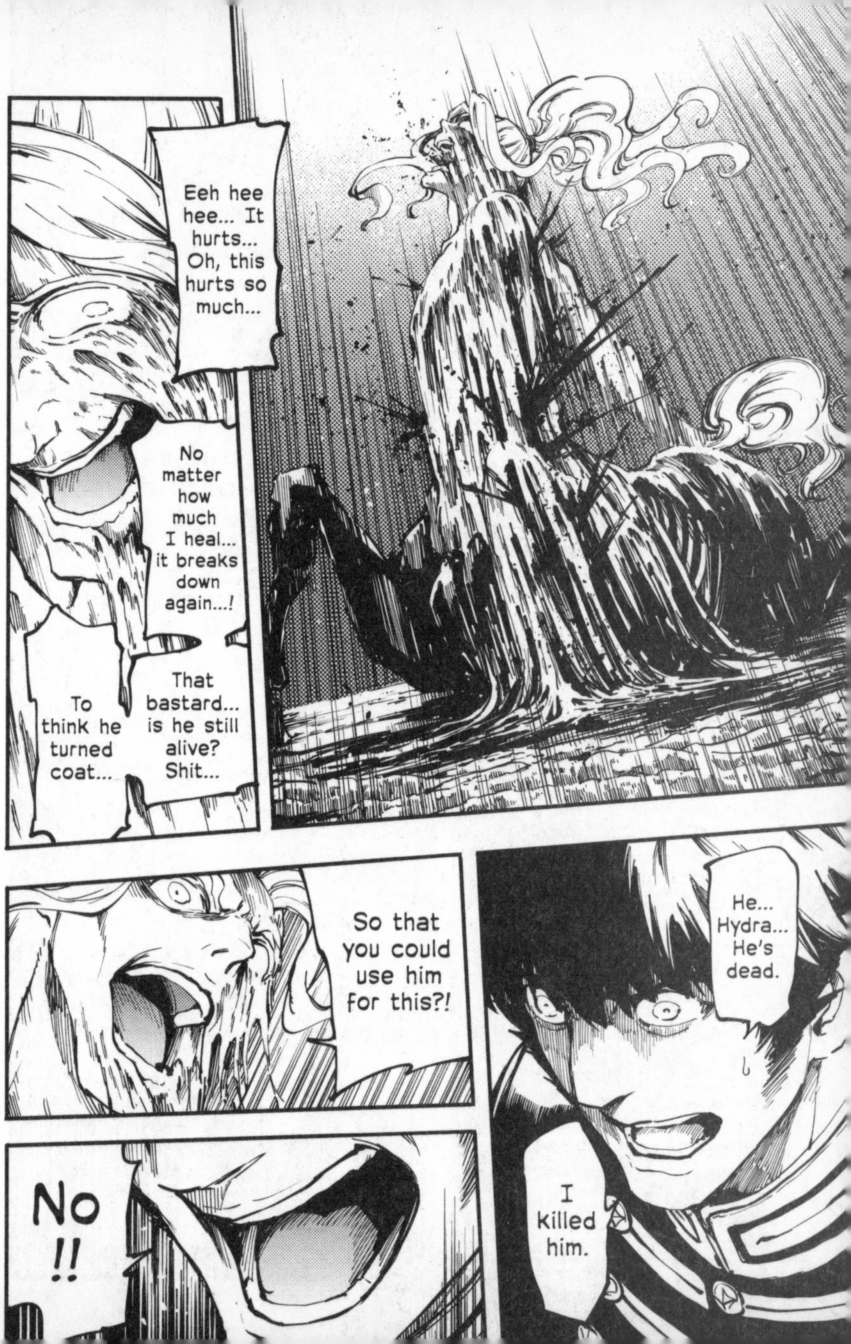
Eeh hee hee... It hurts... Oh, this hurts so much...
No matter how much I heal... it breaks down again...!
That bastard... is he still alive? Shit...
To think he turned coat...
He... Hydra... He's dead.
I killed him.
So that you could use him for this?!
No !!

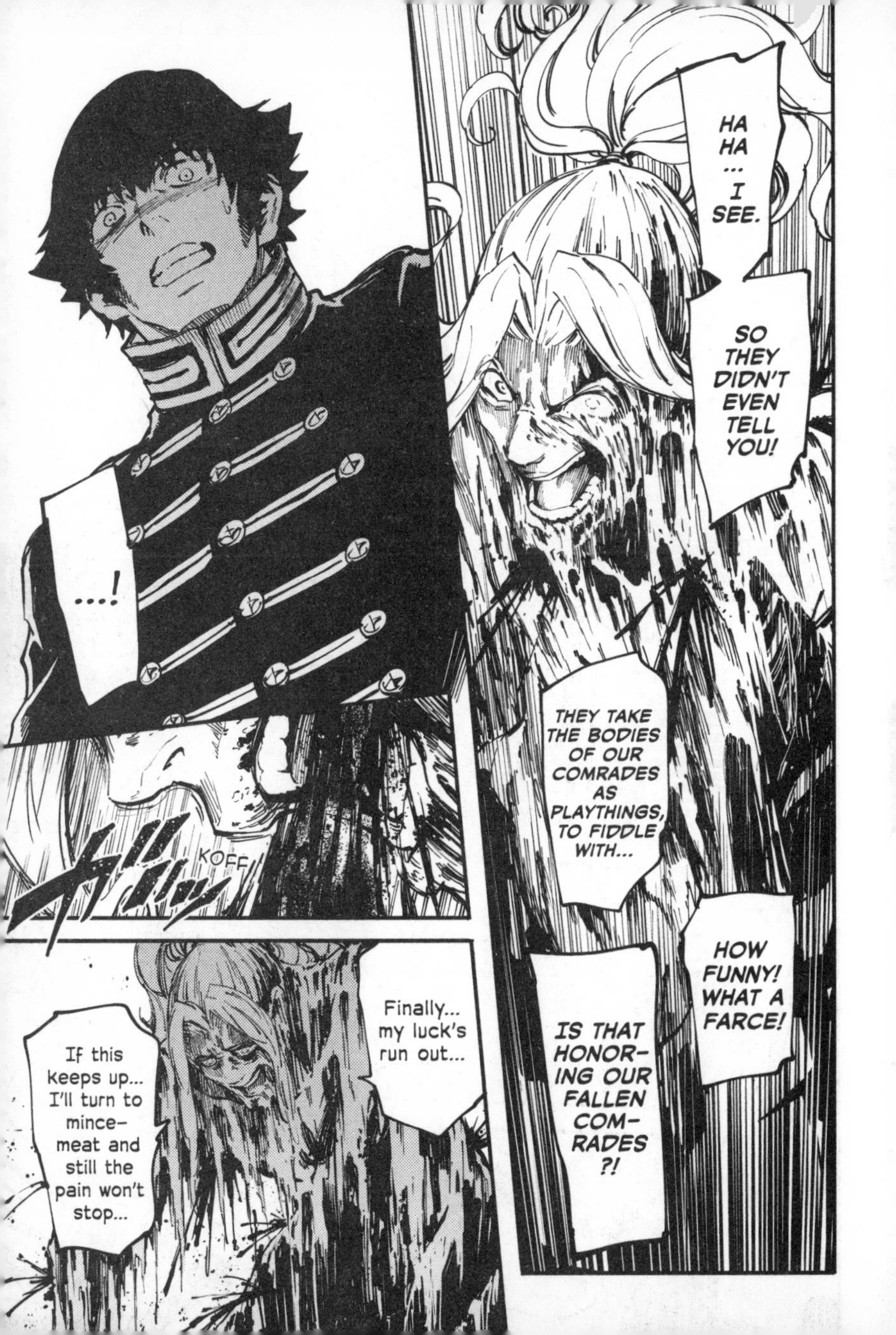
HA HA ... I SEE.
SO THEY DIDN'T EVEN TELL YOU!
THEY TAKE THE BODIES OF OUR COMRADES AS PLAYTHINGS, TO FIDDLE WITH...
HOW FUNNY! WHAT A FARCE!
IS THAT HONOR-ING OUR FALLEN COM-RADES ?!
...!
KOFF
Finally... my luck's run out...
If this keeps up... I'll turn to mince-meat and still the pain won't stop...

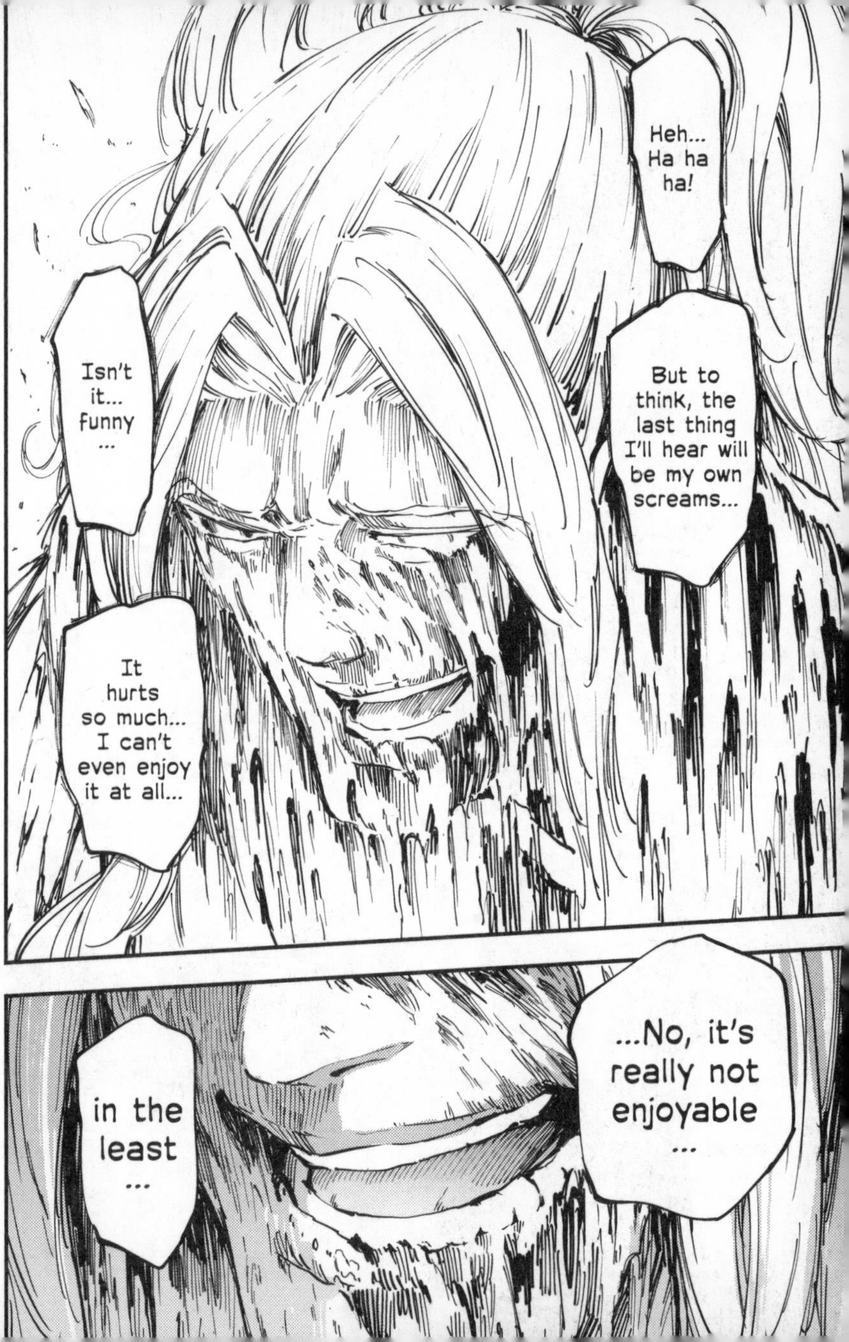
Heh... Ha ha ha!
But to think, the last thing I'll hear will be my own screams...
Isn't it... funny ...
It hurts so much... I can't even enjoy it at all...
...No, it's really not enjoyable ...
in the least ...

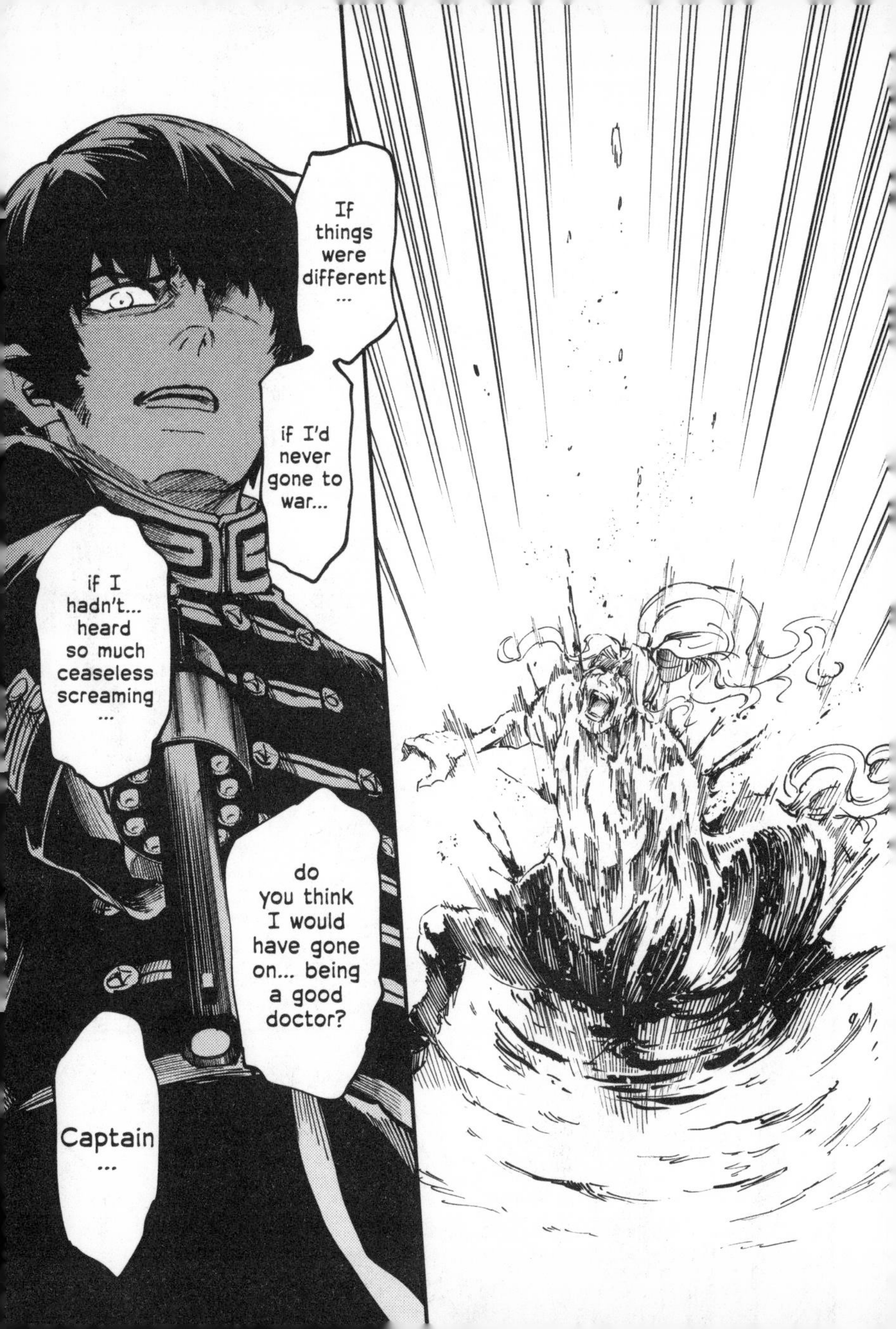
If things were different...
if I'd never gone to war...
if I hadn't... heard so much ceaseless screaming...
do you think I would have gone on... being a good doctor?
Captain...

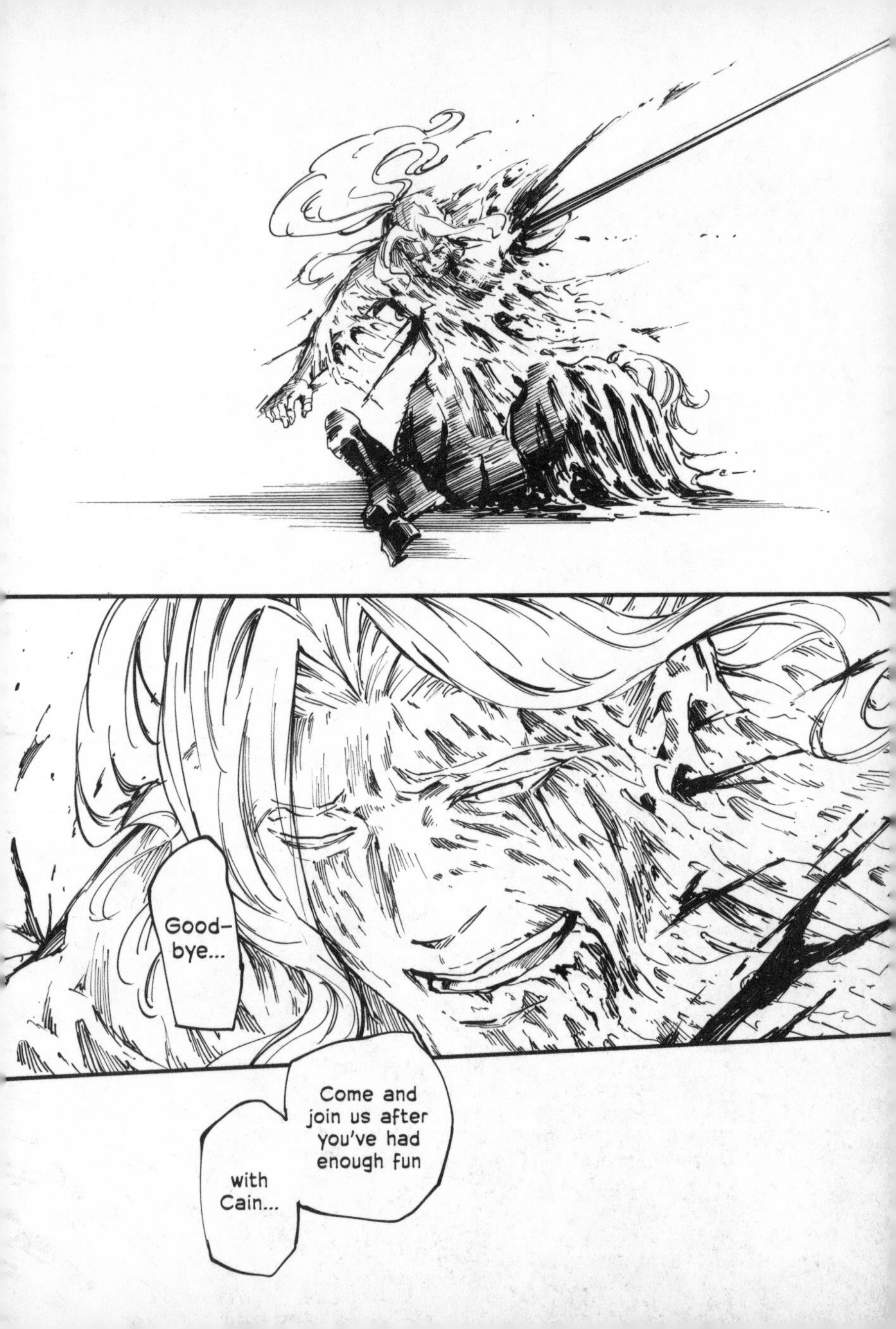
Good-bye...
Come and join us after you've had enough fun
with Cain...

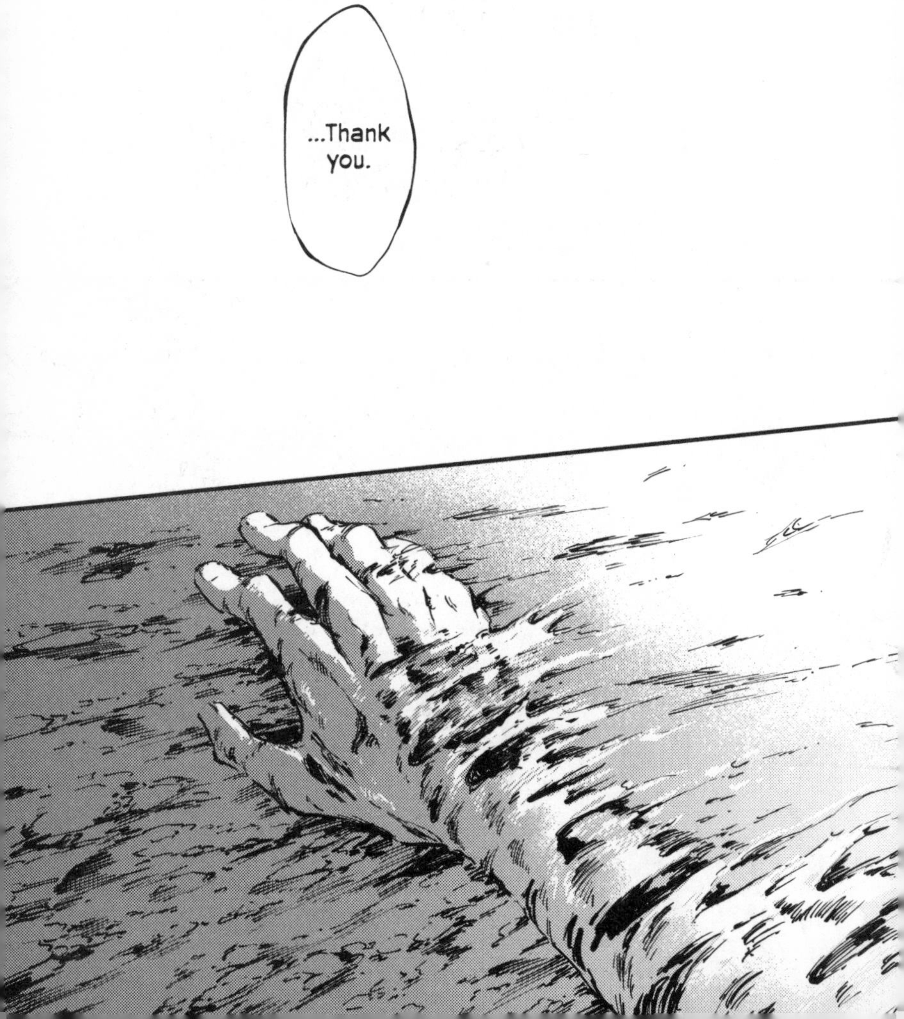
...Thank you.

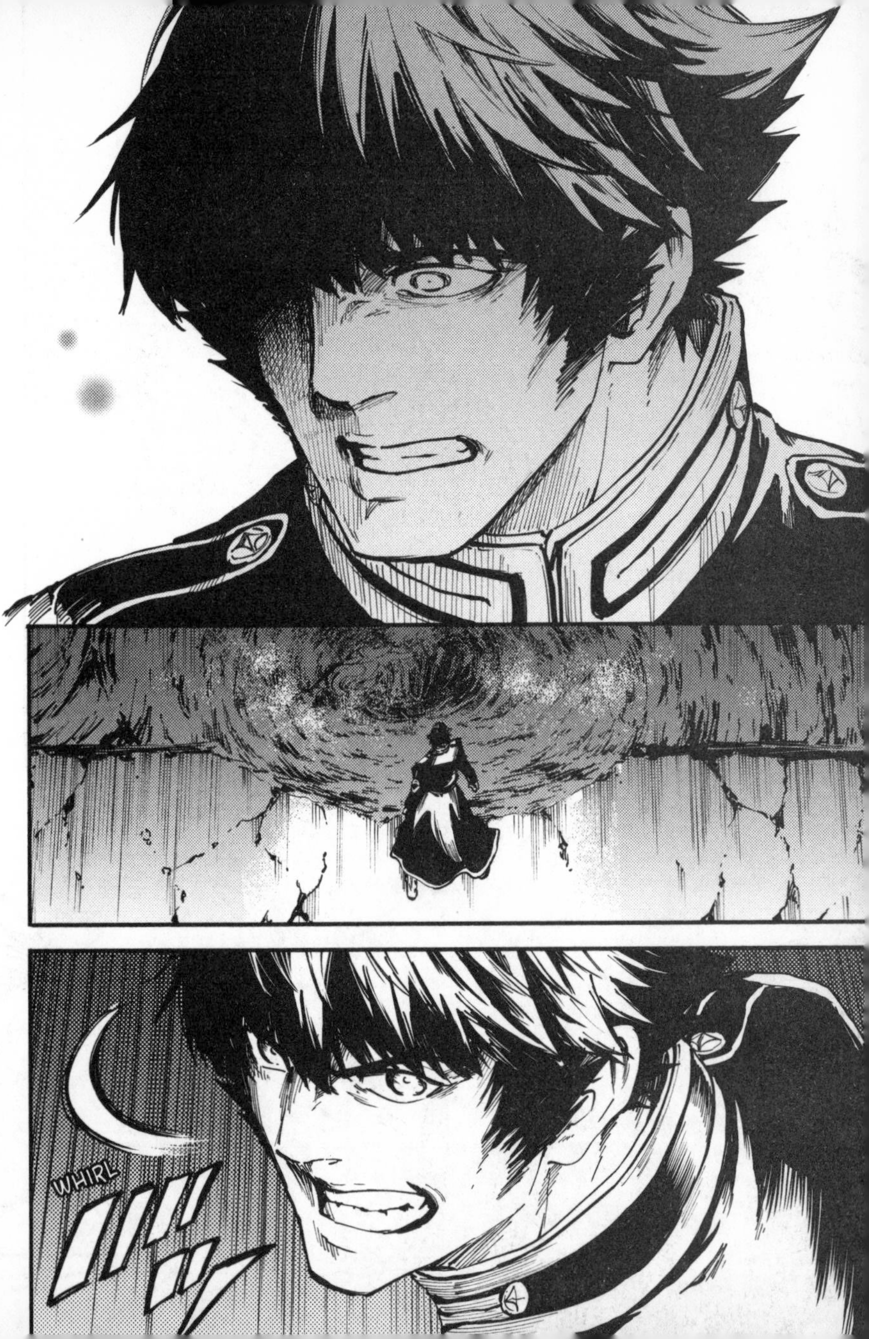
WHIRL

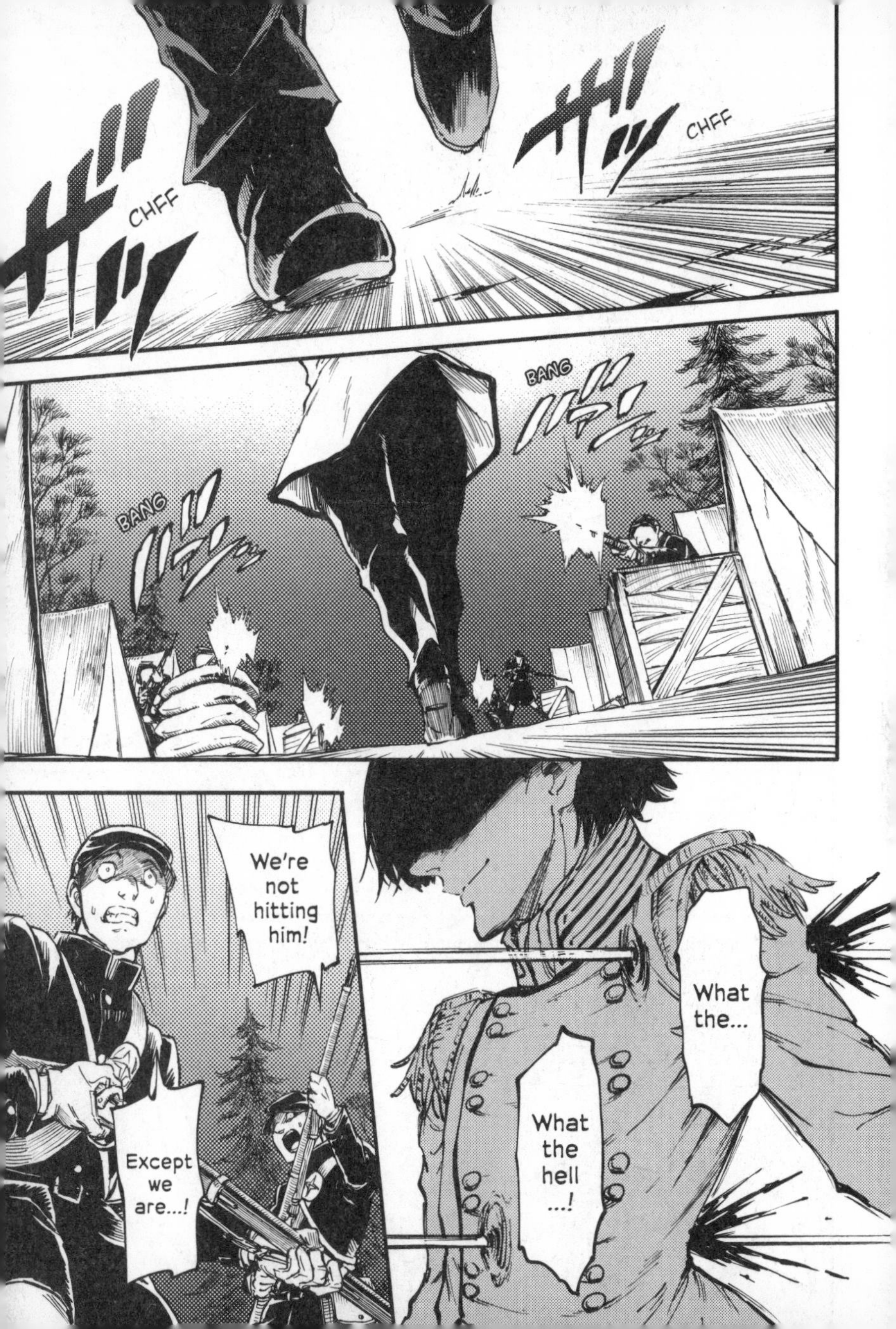
CHFF
CHFF
BANG
BANG
What the...
What the hell ...!
We're not hitting him!
Except we are...!

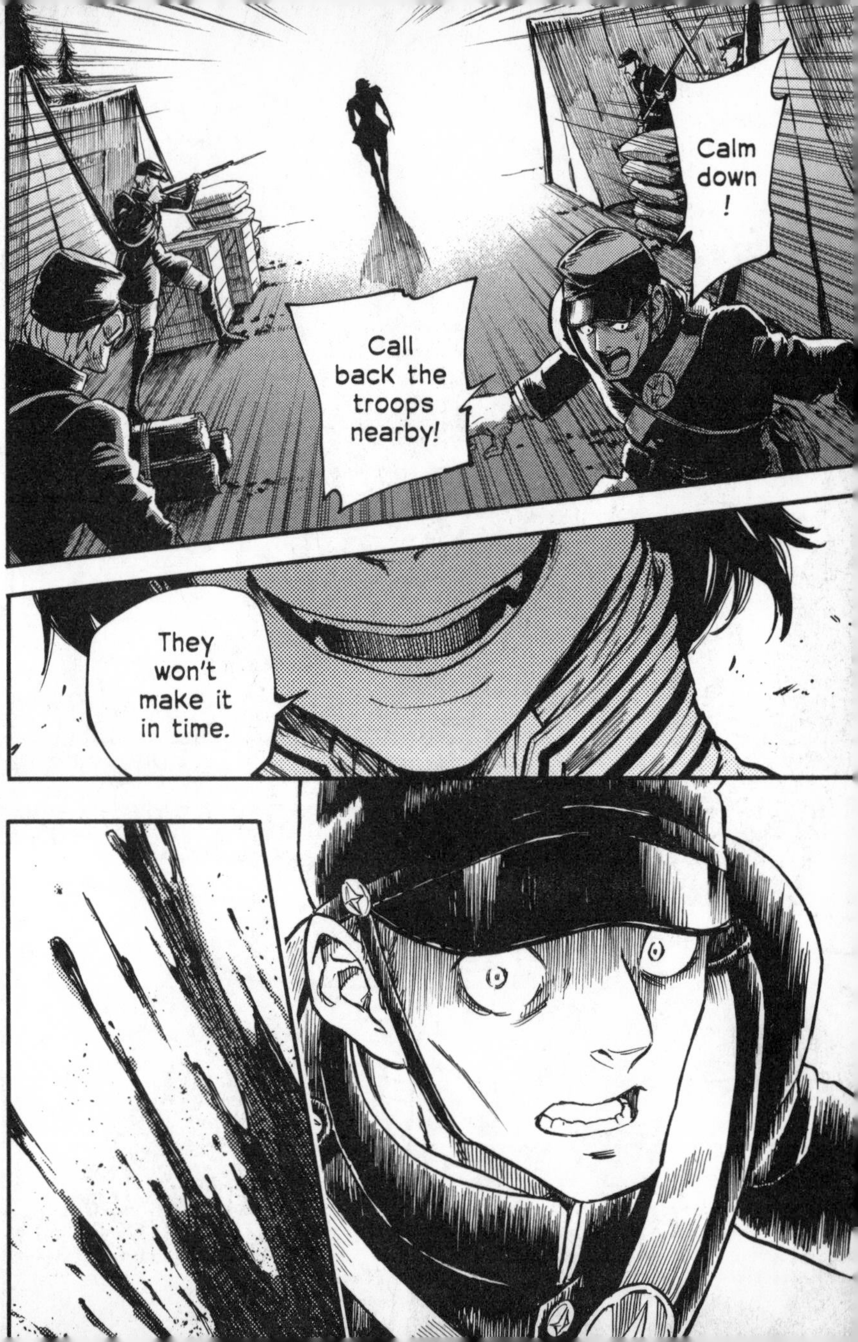
Calm down!
Call back the troops nearby!
They won't make it in time.

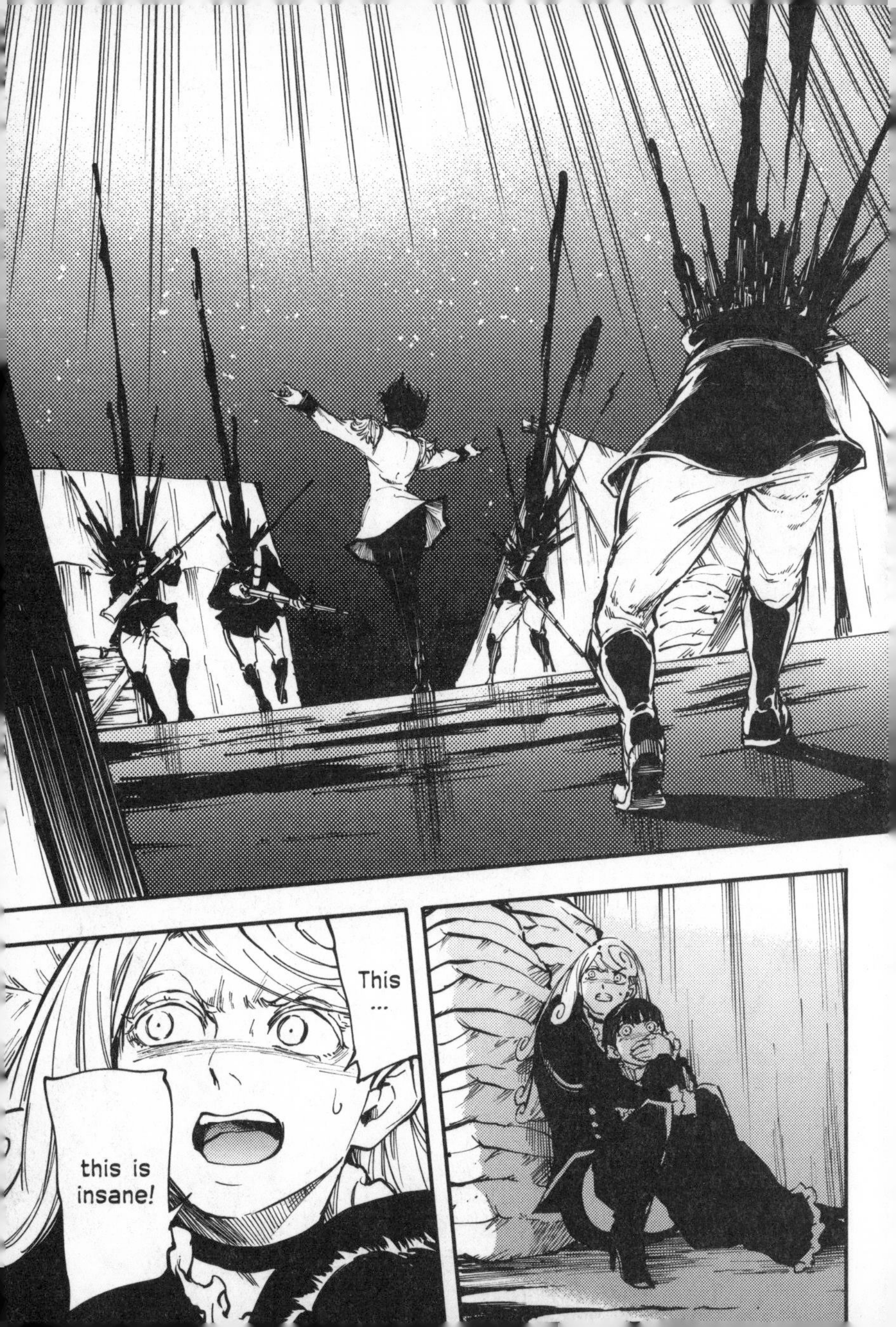
This ...
this is insane!

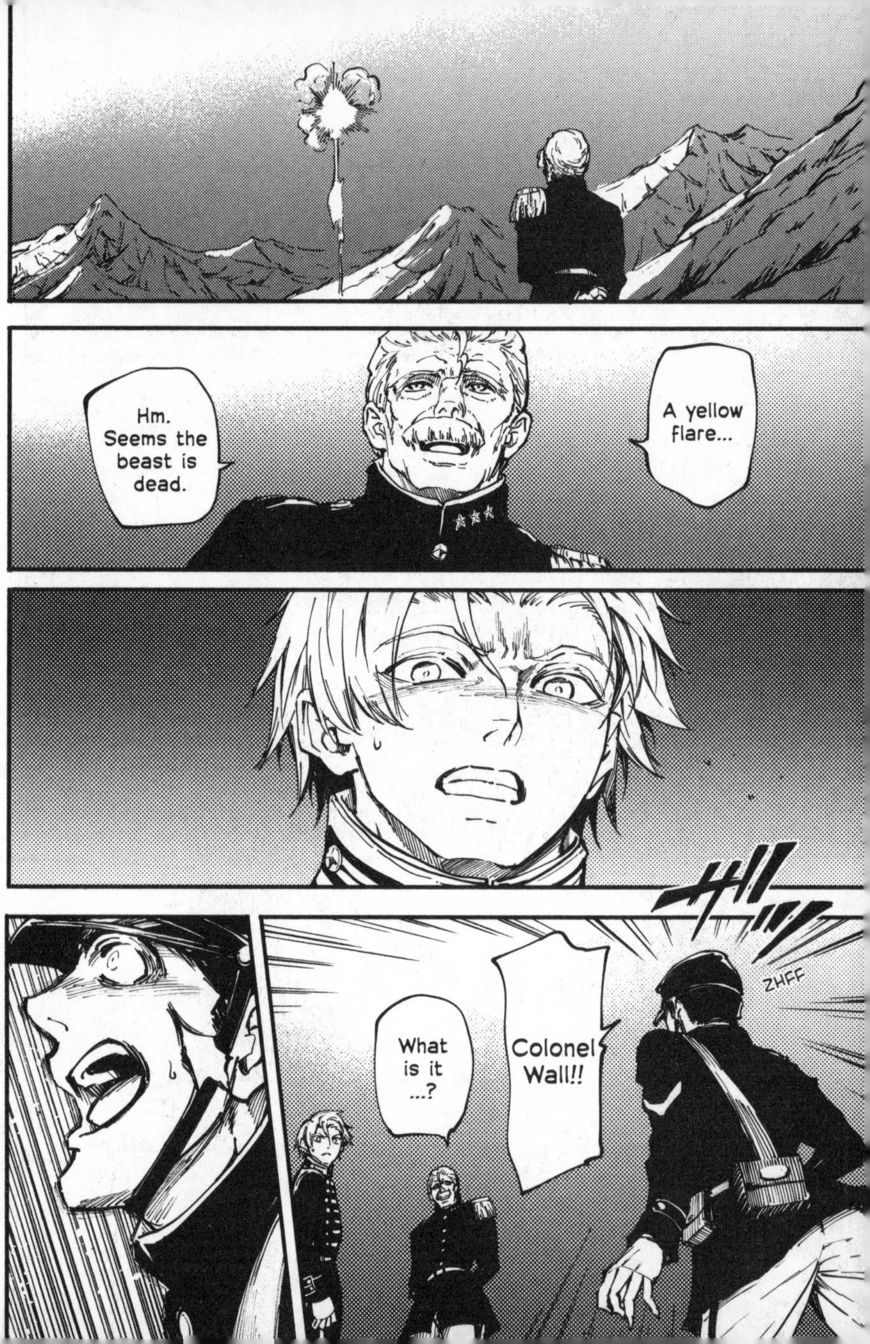
A yellow flare...
Hm. Seems the beast is dead.
ZHFF
Colonel Wall!!
What is it ...?

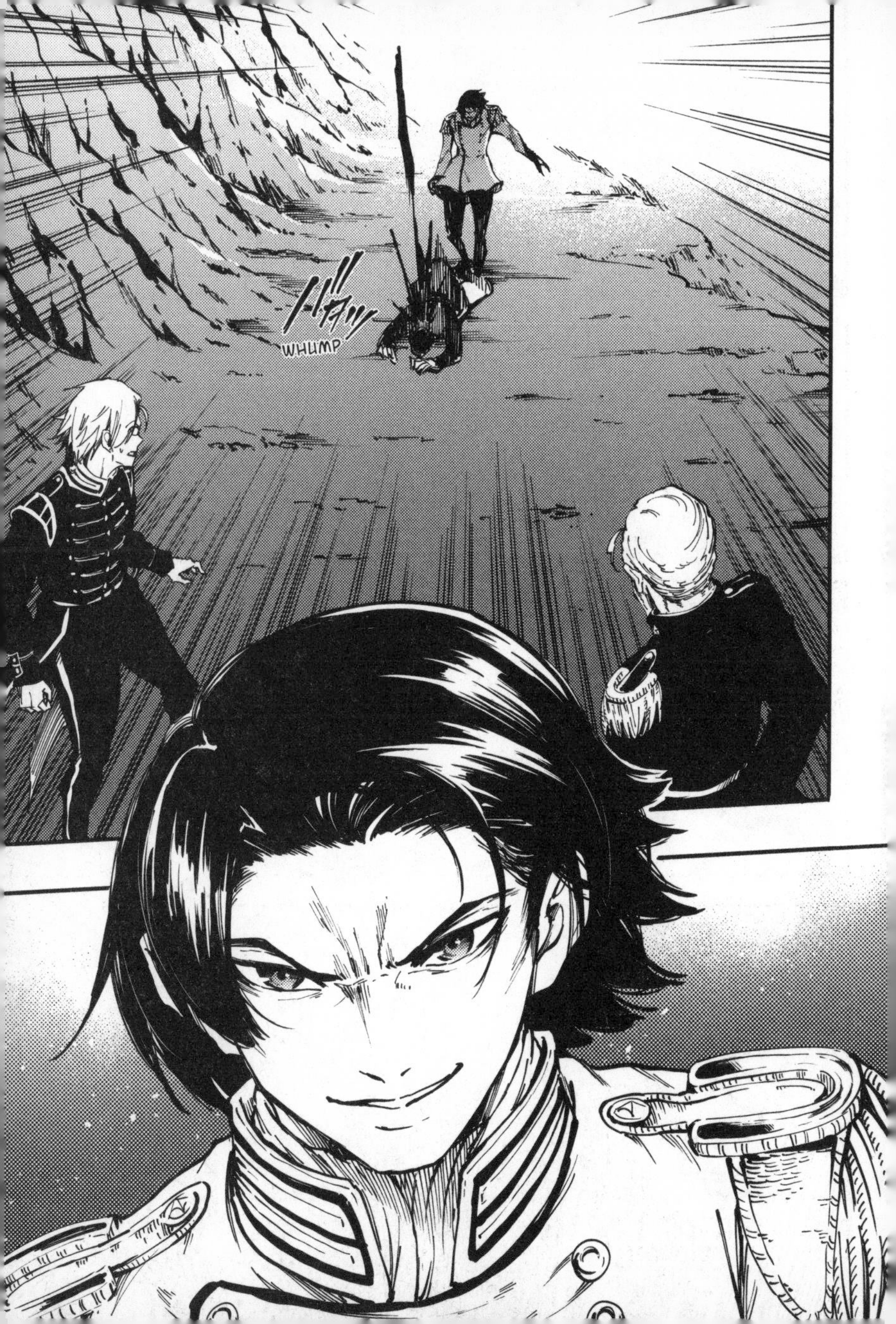

バダッ
WHUMP

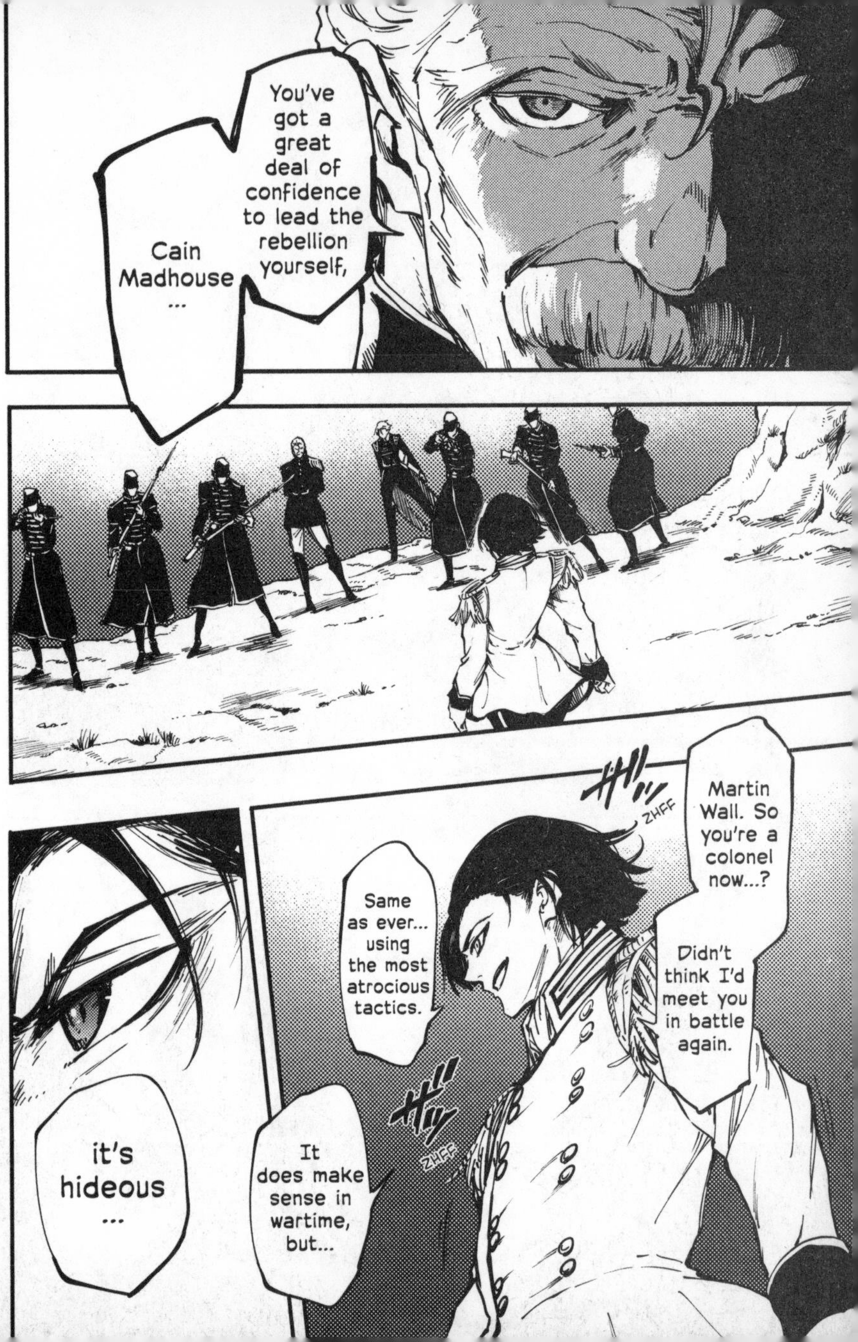
You've got a great deal of confidence to lead the rebellion yourself,
Cain Madhouse ...
ZHFF
Martin Wall. So you're a colonel now...?
Didn't think I'd meet you in battle again.
Same as ever... using the most atrocious tactics.
ZHFF
It does make sense in wartime, but...
it's hideous ...

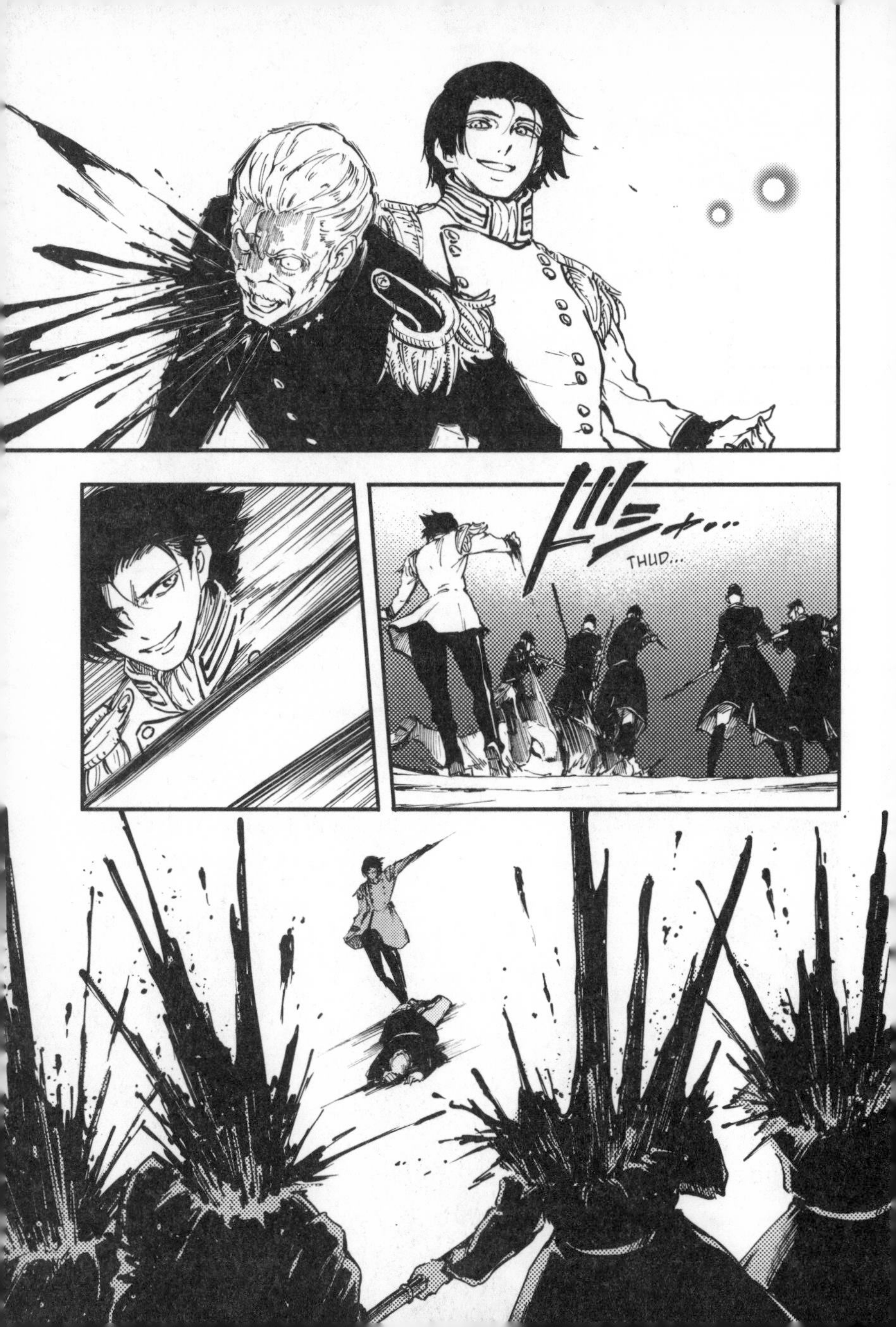
THUD...

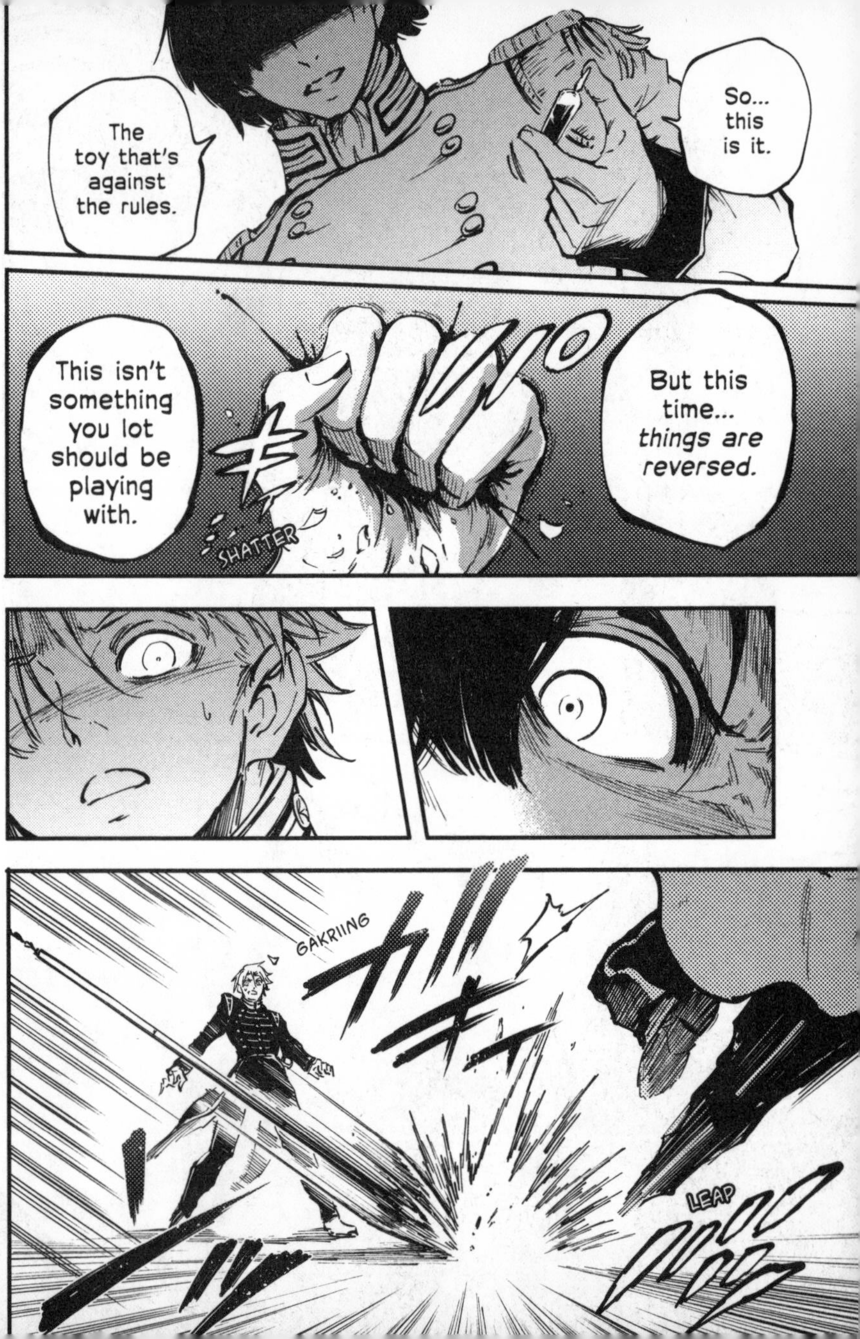
So... this is it.
The toy that's against the rules.
But this time... *things are* reversed.
This isn't something you lot should be playing with.
SHATTER
LEAP
GAKRIING

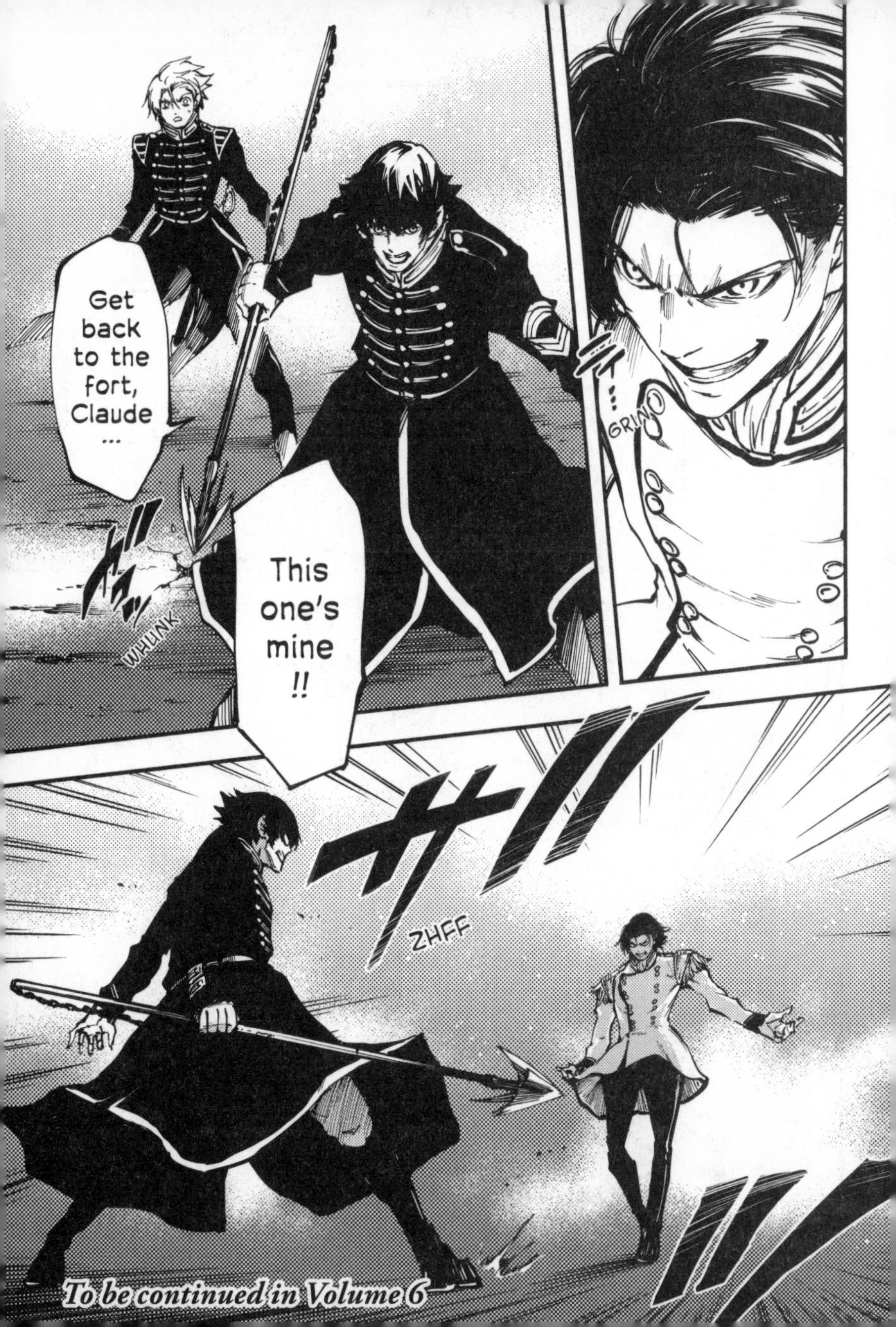
GRIN
Get back to the fort, Claude ...
This one's mine !!
WHUNK
ZHFF
To be continued in Volume 6

SACRED BEASTS PLUS #04

Hank !!
Ha ha ha!
WHAT IS WRONG
WITH THE MEN IN THIS WORLD ?!
Ignoring the charms of adult women!!
WELL ?!
JOLT
Where did this come from...

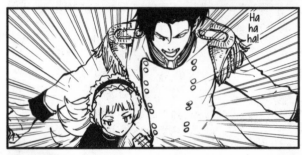

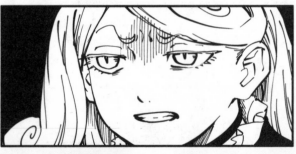

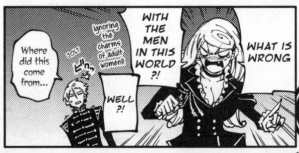

SACRED BEASTS PLUS

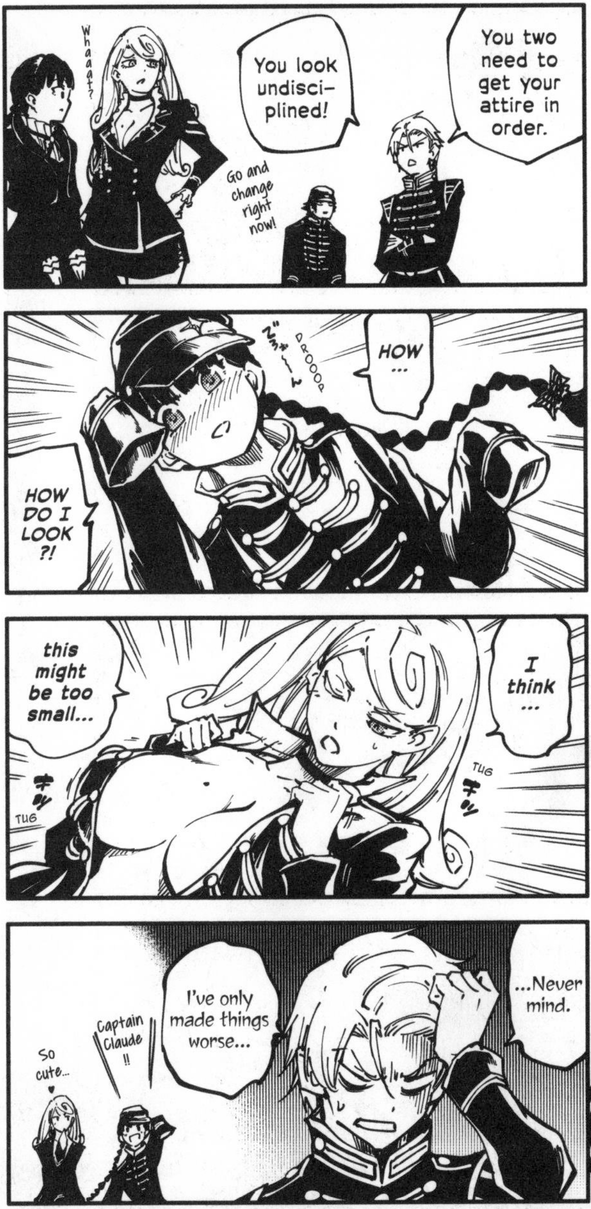
You two need to get your attire in order.
You look undisci-plined!
Go and change right now!
Whaaat?
HOW ...
DROOOP
HOW DO I LOOK ?!
I think ...
TUG
this might be too small...
TUG
...Never mind.
I've only made things worse...
Captain Claude !!
So cute... ♥

#05

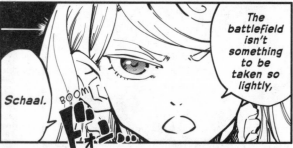

SACRED BEASTS PLUS #06

MY MIND'S MADE UP!
I'M GOING TO HELP OUT IN THE FIELD HOSPITAL!
I learned how to care for people in the orphanage!
Hold on.
The battlefield isn't something to be taken so lightly,
BOOM
Schaal.
!!
GLOOM...
I'm sorry. You're right...
I wouldn't be of any use...
WHEN THERE'S A GIRL WORKING IN THE FIELD HOSPITAL
MORE MEN END UP "INJURED"!!
I wasn't even in battle and I got shot!!
My head hurts!!
Oh, I fell over!
I dunno, I might be dying!!
UNDER-ESTIMATE SOLDIERS AND YOU'LL GET IN TROUBLE!
They all lie, every last one!!

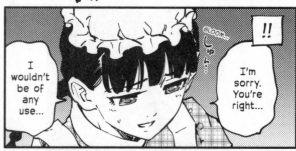

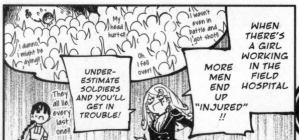

SACRED BEASTS PLUS

#07

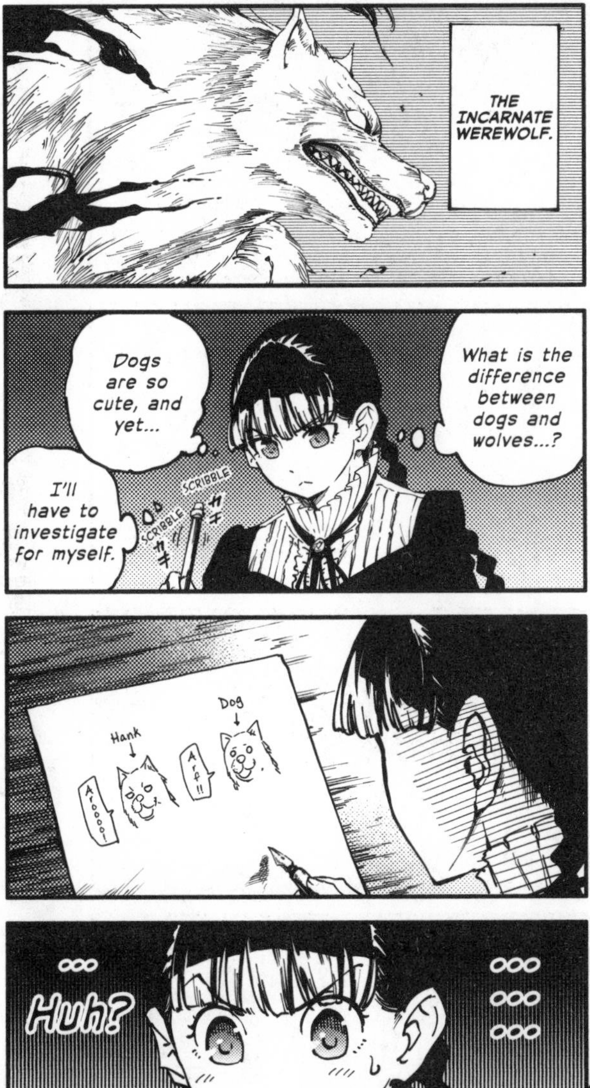
THE INCARNATE WEREWOLF.
What is the difference between dogs and wolves...?
Dogs are so cute, and yet...
SCRIBBLE
SCRIBBLE
I'll have to investigate for myself.
Dog
Arf!!
Hank
Arooooo!
Huh?

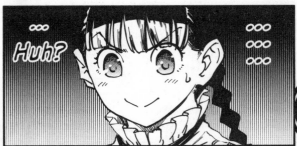

SACRED BEASTS PLUS #08

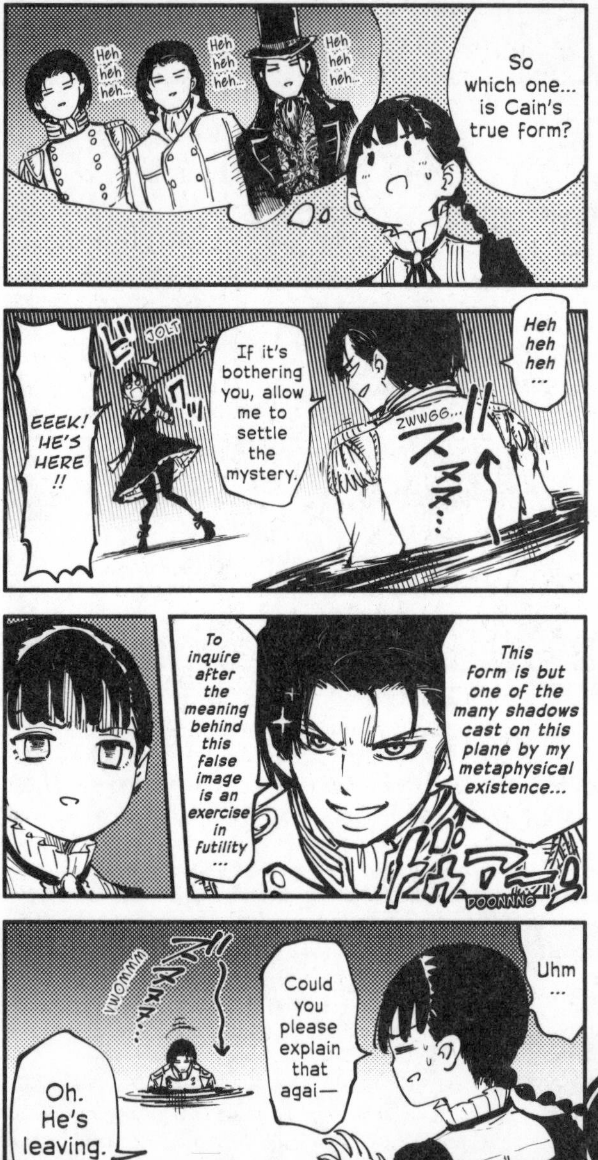
So which one... is Cain's true form?
Heh heh heh...
Heh heh heh...
Heh heh heh...
Heh heh heh ...
ZWWGG...
If it's bothering you, allow me to settle the mystery.
JOLT
EEEK! HE'S HERE !!
This form is but one of the many shadows cast on this plane by my metaphysical existence...
To inquire after the meaning behind this false image is an exercise in futility ...
DOONNNG
Uhm ...
Could you please explain that agai—
VWOMMM
Oh. He's leaving.

Sacred Beasts Encyclopedia Entries

file no. 24 | *Incarnate Centaurus*

Height: 13 ft.

The archer: Half man, half horse

An Incarnate that combines the assault force of a cavalryman and the ability to snipe from a distance. His upper body is human; his lower body, that of a horse. While the upper body appears human, in scale it matches the enormous equine portion below, giving those who face Centaurus in battle the uneasy sense that something is amiss, along with a subconscious sense of awe.

The strength of the horse's body allows it to charge and retreat at high speed. Ordinarily, the battlefield is ruled by numbers and a charge by a single soldier would be futile; however, Centaurus is able to disrupt enemy ranks with its massive size, speed, and striking appearance. He prioritizes those who would face him bravely, those who try to raise their voices to rally their comrades, and those who are the slowest to run away, impaling men upon his lance and brandishing their corpses. This is done to instill fear in the enemy; fear gives way to terror and confusion, disrupting even the most cohesive ranks and making the Centaur's charges all the more effective.

With his robust male upper body, he wields an archaic weapon splendidly—the bow. The arrows he uses have far larger arrowheads and thicker shafts than is traditional, pinning enemy soldiers to the ground and turning the battlefield to a scene of medieval torture. His mobility allows him to move freely across the battlefield and fire from the most tactical locations. One might say that there is no reason for Centaurus to insist on using a bow; his strength would be better exploited with a gun. However, using a gun inexplicably causes a substantial deterioration in his aim. Even after sufficient training in firearms, his ability never improved beyond that of an average human. This was a disappointing result for an Incarnate that was expected to have superior brawn and focus, but irrefutable: Guns simply do not suit Centaurus. On occasion, Incarnates can exhibit perplexing peculiarities that emerge as flaws in the field.

The reason for this remains utterly unclear. The factors that determine the physical forms of Incarnates are also a mystery, serving as a reminder that the creation of Incarnates is a technology that cannot be completely controlled.

Centaurus's skin has neither scales nor a shell, and his equine coat is not at all tough. This lack of physical defense marks his sole vulnerability in the tactic of charging into the enemy ranks. His regenerative ability and vitality are higher than average, but not outstanding, and pale in comparison to those of Nidhogg or Behemoth. While various means of compensating for this weakness were explored, including equipping him with armor and deploying him in teams with other Incarnates, these all impeded Centaurus's chief strength—speed—and were never used in the field. With his solitary, swift charges and the unparalleled precision of his phantom-like sniping, the Centaurus ruled the battlefield in the time of the Civil War.

file no. 25 | *Bold Creek*

The old town, originally founded as a foothold from which to develop the western region, was rebuilt as a military stronghold for New Patria.

Bold Creek,
Capital of the Frontier

An abandoned outpost from the age of expansion

In the age of expansion, Before the Civil War, people ventured forth from the capital of Newfort, crossing the great mountain range to head west.

Bold Creek was a town built to serve as the first foothold for settlers after crossing the mountain range. Built on the flatland beside a river fed by meltwater from the mountain range, it served as a large trading area for the frontiersmen. They let their dreams run wild on the uncultivated, unexplored lands, but enthusiasm waned as it became known that barren wastelands lay beyond, and then the Civil War left those dreams unfulfilled. Those who remained after the war struggled with the inconvenience of travel to the mountain-locked capital and the duty to support the people stranded in the west. The railroads to the west were laid far to the south of Bold Creek, and few people crossed the mountains to visit. Only fugitive outlaws who couldn't remain in the capital or those with questionable pasts would brave the dangerous journey. Now, this place is nothing but an out-of-the-way town hoping for a resurgence of the western frontier boom.

Sacred Beasts Encyclopedia Entries

Bold Creek Fort: A hastily-built but durable stronghold

A fortress constructed on filled-in farmlands that stretched out between the town and the mountain range.

Built from bricks, earth and wood, it is somewhat old-fashioned, but this was more than enough to stop the attacks of the Northern army weakened by the Civil War and stretched thin by having to send some forces to defend the capital. The simple construction allowed for completion in an astonishingly short time (with the help of Incarnates). By the time the Northern army had crossed the Great Mountain range and caught wind of the construction, the fort was already nearly finished,

and succeeded in delaying their first strike. It was even equipped with gun platforms on the walls (though not many), and with battle-hardened former Southern soldiers at the core of its forces, morale was high, enhancing the defensive capabilities of the fort beyond its scale. In front of the fortress is an earthwork fortification that overlooks the mountain range, allowing for soldiers to prevent simple approaches by the enemy. It is unclear if the absence of trenches is due to a tactical choice not to impede the mobility of Centaurus, or because they lacked the technique to dig them.

file no. 26 | *Trenches*

Graves to dodge the rain of death

Ditches dug into the ground as a defense against gunfire in several battlefields toward the end of the Civil War.

Trenches are made by digging into the ground as deep as a man's height, then adding fortifications to prevent collapse, platforms for shooting, drainage gutters, and scaffolding to ease running through the mud. Technological advances, including rifles, led to significant improvements in the accuracy and range of guns. As a result, traditional line infantry became depleted as they advanced toward enemy territory and became less effective. As the war dragged on, artillery technology also improved; facing off against lighter cannon with longer ranges, advancing en masse only increased casualties when strikes landed, making soldiers easy pickings for the enemy. The strategy of advancing slowly, hidden in the trenches to avoid enemy fire, then charging at the end, became more widespread. Although trenches worked as shelter from enemy fire, it was a miserable environment. Not only would rain soak into everything, but in lowlands, water would often seep up from underneath—it was constantly damp. In prolonged battles, it was not uncommon for diseases to spread, devastating armies from within.

file no. 27 | *Bayonet*

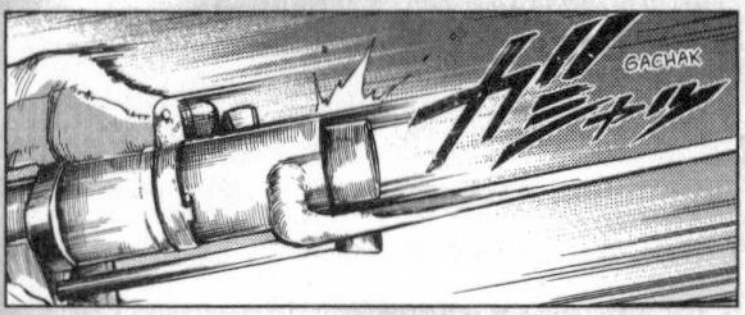
GACHAK

A last-resort blade

A weapon attached to the end of a gun for use in close combat.

Fitted on the end of a long rifle, it is used primarily to stab, like a spear, and is useless outside of close-range combat. Rifles were supposed to mark the end of infantry charges, and they, along with bayonets, should have become obsolete. However, with the trenches dug to avoid rifle fire, bayonets became relevant once again. Charges after advancing via the trenches and close combat against enemies that surged into the trenches became common. Close combat weapons such as sabers and knives were disfavored due to their weight and the vulnerable openings created when switching to them, and were not often used. Sabers held by commanding officers, as symbols of authority, were an exception. By the final days of the Civil War, gatling guns had sufficient power and speed to entirely suppress charges from close range.

file no. 28 | *Cannon*

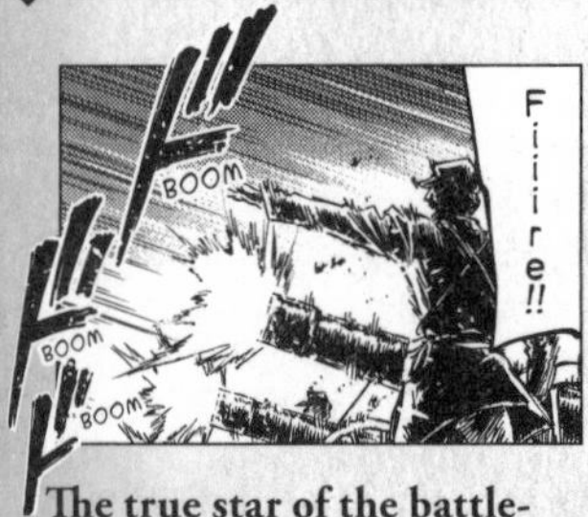
Fiiire!!
BOOM
BOOM
BOOM

The true star of the battlefield, claiming the greatest number of lives

The cannon has a long history. Through the centuries of use in the Old World, neither its shape nor purpose has varied much.

It employs the explosive power of gunpowder to propel a cannonball to smash the target. For this simple weapon, the most important thing is the strength of the barrel. With stronger barrels, one can shoot cannonballs farther and with more power. The prolonged Civil War led to advances in metalworking, resulting in two divergent evolutionary paths for the cannon—namely, lighter and heavier.

Light, sturdy small cannon were built with hilly or uneven terrain in mind, to be deployed in mountain ranges and badlands, and occasionally in surprise attacks where speed was of the essence. They could be operated by a small number of men, and also allowed for versatile strategies with larger numbers when assaulting a fortress.

Heavy, destructive, large cannon were used to defend forts and cities. While they had poor maneuverability, their range and power could prevent advances by the enemy, obliterate their ships, and crush the hearts of those who would face them. The range of explosion and the destructive power of shrapnel were far beyond that of guns; as a result, cannon claimed the lives of more soldiers than any other weapon. It is recorded in surveys that the Southern army had an Incarnate which used its enormous strength to wield cannon like rifles.

To the Abandoned Sacred Beasts

AFTERWORD PAGE

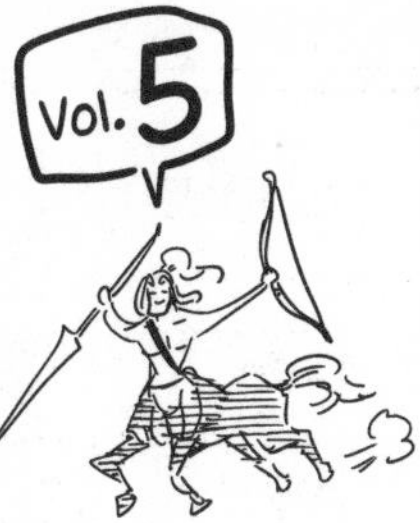

Vol. 5

So Volume 5 turned out to be nearly entirely an arc about Centaurus. We were hoping to move it along a bit more, but after all, war is the subject material we're dealing with, so we wanted to show some more of that... is what we were thinking when we produced this, with the result that the story doesn't advance much, and the ladies hardly got to do much. Well, the field of battle is a man's world... can't be helped... so, lots of men!

We've said what there is to say, and from now on we want to have more characters involved in the plot... we'll work hard to do just that.
See you in Volume 6!

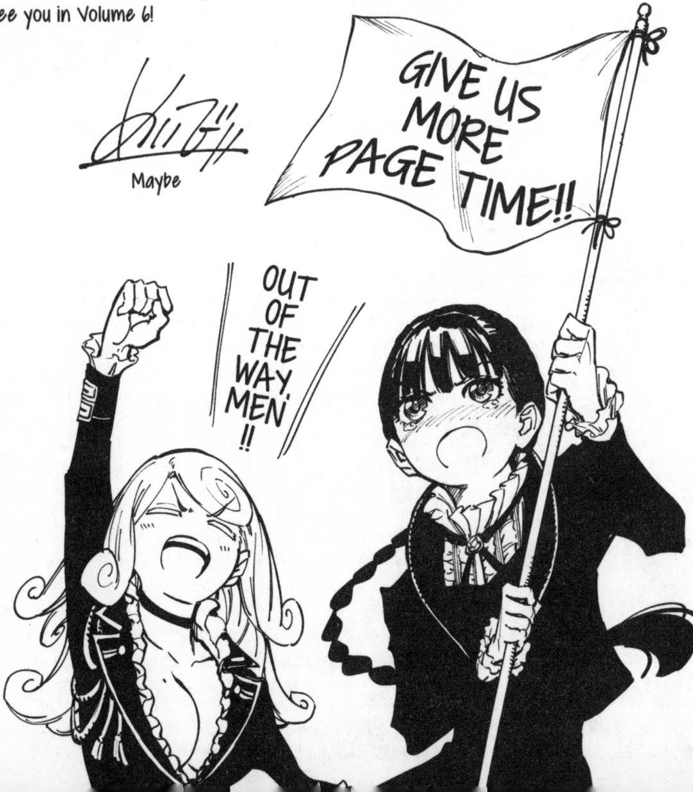

Maybe
GIVE US MORE PAGE TIME!!
OUT OF THE WAY, MEN!!

NEXT ISSUE

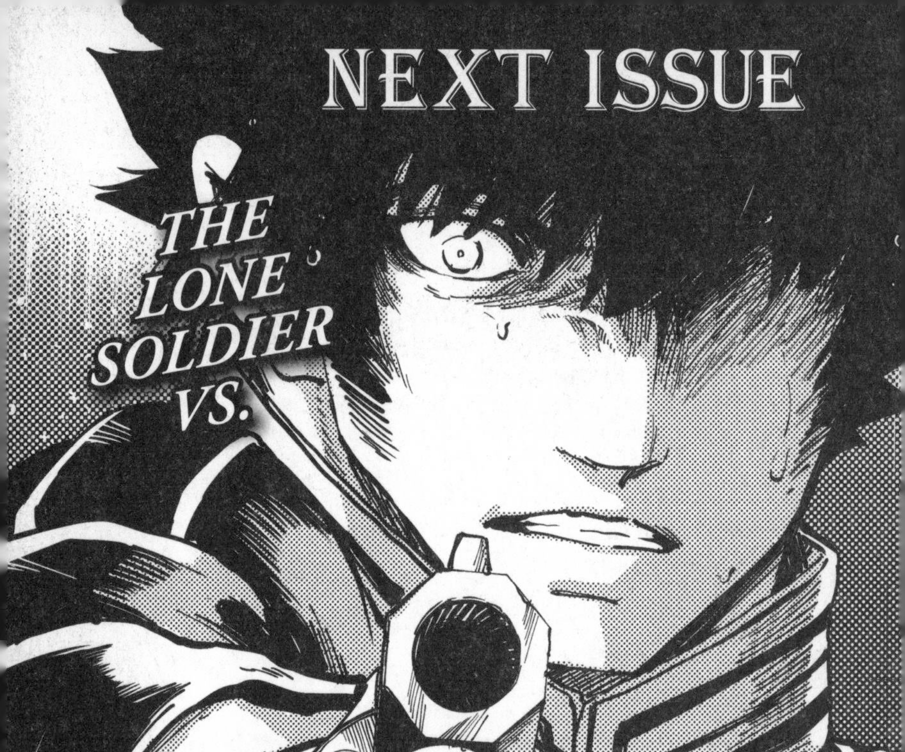
THE LONE SOLDIER VS.

The Incarnate Centaurus, the biggest obstacle in the battle to capture Bold Creek Fort, was felled by a poisoned weapon. The poison was developed by the Patrian government from the corpse of a fallen Incarnate, which means the government is treating Incarnates like so many guinea pigs. In the end, who can claim to be on the side of real justice—the government forces or the rebel army?! Once more, Hank faces off against Cain, the man he seems fated to encounter! How will Hank overthrow Cain, and will the fortress fall...?

COMING SPRING 2018

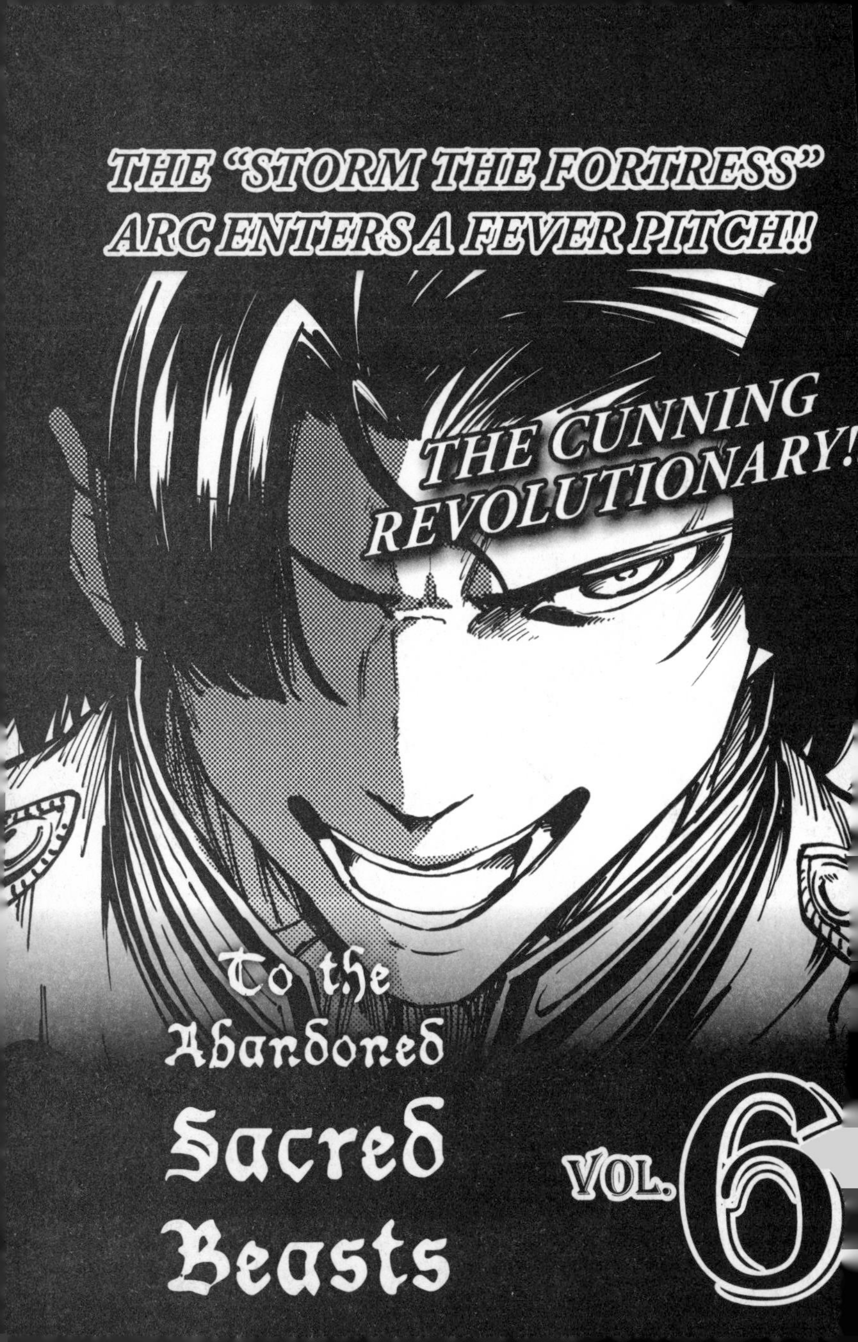
THE "STORM THE FORTRESS" ARC ENTERS A FEVER PITCH!!
THE CUNNING REVOLUTIONARY!
To the Abandoned Sacred Beasts
VOL. 6

To the Abandoned Sacred Beasts
Volume 5

Translation: Melissa Tanaka
Production: Grace Lu
            Anthony Quintessenza

Copyright © 2017 MAYBE. All rights reserved.
First published in Japan in 2017 by Kodansha, Ltd., Tokyo
Publication rights for this English edition arranged through Kodansha, Ltd., Tokyo
English language version produced by Vertical, Inc.

Translation provided by Vertical Comics, 2017
Published by Vertical Comics, an imprint of Vertical, Inc., New York

Originally published in Japanese as *Katsute Kami Datta Kemono-tachi e 5* by Kodansha, Ltd.
Katsute Kami Datta Kemono-tachi e first serialized in *Bessatsu Shonen Magazine*,
Kodansha, Ltd., 2014-

This is a work of fiction.

ISBN: 978-1-945054-20-4

Manufactured in Canada

First Edition

Vertical, Inc.
451 Park Avenue South
7th Floor
New York, NY 10016
www.vertical-comics.com

Vertical books are distributed through Penguin-Random House Publisher Services.